Identity by De

Identity by Design

Georgia Butina Watson and Ian Bentley

AMSTERDAM • BOSTON • HEIDELBERG • LONDON • NEW YORK • OXFORD • PARIS • SAN DIEGO
SAN FRANCISCO • SINGAPORE • SYDNEY • TOKYO
Butterworth-Heinemann is an imprint of Elsevier

Butterworth-Heinemann is an imprint of Elsevier
Linacre House, Jordan Hill, Oxford OX2 8DP, UK
30 Corporate Drive, Suite 400, Burlington, MA 01803, USA

First published 2007

Notice
No responsibility is assumed by the publisher for any injury and/or damage to
persons or property as a matter of products liability, negligence or otherwise,
or from any use or operation of any methods, products, instructions or ideas
contained in the material herein. Because of rapid advances in the medical
sciences, in particular, independent verification of diagnoses and drug
dosages should be made

British Library Cataloguing in Publication Data
Watson, Georgia Butina
 Identity by design
 1. City planning 2. Nationalism
 I. Title II. Bentley, Ian
 307.1'2

Library of Congress Number: 2006938782

ISBN-13: 978-0-75-064767-0
ISBN-10: 0-7506-4767-1

Typeset by Charon Tec Ltd (A Macmillan Company), Chennai, India
Website: http://www.charontec.com

Printed and bound in Italy
07 08 09 10 10 9 8 7 6 5 4 3 2 1

Contents

Acknowledgements

This book could never have been written without the generous assistance we have received from people across the globe. We owe debts of gratitude both to those who have provided information for specific case studies, and to others who have played key roles in pulling the whole project together.

Our understanding of specific case studies has been enriched by many local people, without whose insights we should never have penetrated beneath the tourist veneer. We wish to thank the following in particular: in Prague Michal Hexner and Jiři Štursa; in Ljubljana Richard Andrews, Stane Bernik, Peter Krečič, Vesna Grunčić-Vedlin and Braco Mušič; in relation to the Underground, Bob Langridge; in Mexico Diego Villaseñor, Ricardo Legorreta, Teodoro Gonzalez de Leon, Carlos and Lisa Tejeda, Cecilia Martinez de la Macorra, Ana Maldonado Villaseñor and Luis Gabriel Juarez; in Bologna Pier Luigi Cervallati, Gianfranco Caniggia and Nicola Belodi; in Perugia Lucia Vašak and Fabrizio Fiorini; in Malaysia Jimmy Lim, Mijan Dolbani and Bayo Bayudi; in Boston Eric Schmidt and Dick Gavers; and in relation to the Responsive Environments approach Paul Murrain, Ivor Samuels, Richard Hayward, Sue McGlynn, Graham Smith, Mariana Castaños, Dora Boatemah (who sadly died before the book was finished), Thomas Esterine and the residents of Brixton's Angell Town estate. We are very grateful to them all. The authors wish to thank the following for illustrations: Asia Publications, Concept Media, Boston Redevelopment Authority, Landscape Design Magazine, The MIT Press, the Trustees of the Public Library in Boston, Verso Publishing Company, Edizioni L'Inchiostroblu, Tachen, Electa, Arcadia, Institut Masyarakat, Escala, The Monacelli Press, Thames and Hudson, Birkauser Verlag AG, Studio Vista, Rotledge, Uiverza v Ljubljani and Foulis Press.

Producing a book, however, is not only a matter of intellectual debate. It also takes a great deal of practical hard work. Here too we have debts to acknowledge; in particular to Jane Handal, Jessica Keal, Catherine Smith, Maureen Millard, Linda New, Regina Mapua Lim, Anwar Punekar and Mario Reyes. Without them, we should never have got the book finished.

Finally, any long-running project needs constant challenge and encouragement to keep it going. *Identity by Design* is no exception; and we know how much we owe to David Watson, to Iva Bentley, to Christina Dorees, to all the students who pushed us to develop these ideas in the first place, and to the supportive climate of the Joint Centre for Urban Design.

Georgia Butina Watson
Ian Bentley

Introduction

Many people today, in many parts of the world, seem to feel that any place should have its own special character – "identity" is the word most commonly used – to distinguish it from other places. Once, so the story goes, special local and regional identities came into being without anyone necessarily trying to achieve them, because of the vernacular processes through which most buildings were produced. At least until the nineteenth century, everywhere in the world, transport limitations ensured that most buildings had to be constructed from locally sourced materials; whilst limited understandings of structural principles and constructional techniques restricted the range of building types in any particular place. Of course, we should not exaggerate the stability of all this. In many places, despite all these limitations, radical design changes sometimes took place. When suitable building timber had largely been used up in Britain's Cotswold Hills by the sixteenth century, for example, craftsmen began to build in a new way, creating the stone houses for which the region is now famous (Figure 0.1). Even when place-identity was radically affected by changes like these, however, the changes themselves came about not primarily by choice, but because the new constraints which builders faced were still mostly *local* in character.

With industrialisation, these local constraints were progressively loosened. By the middle of the nineteenth century, in the industrialising parts of the world, relatively cheap transportation by canal and rail meant that building materials, for example, could be drawn from ever-wider sources. Scientific advances, supporting an explosion of technological potentials, increased the range of ways in which these newly available materials could be used. New design ideas, taking advantage of these potentials, were spread by expanding numbers of design books and magazines, and by the growing number of designers who themselves now found it practicable to work across ever-wider geographical areas. New bye-laws and other regulations, introduced to try to control public health and safety in an era of rapid industrial urbanisation, also tended to erode local and regional vernacular differences through a search for common performance standards for predictable production. After more than a century of these changes, regionally distinctive built form no longer happens by default. This is clear to anyone who cares to think about it: as the architect Michael Hough points out, "the question of regional character has become a question of choice and, therefore, of design rather than of necessity".[1]

People from all walks of life now seem to have an interest in this particular question. Promoting one particular understanding of what place-identity might mean, for example, the Prince of Wales exhorts designers to "let where it is be what it's made of".[2] With very different values, but agreeing at least that place-identity *matters*, anti-establishment artist Lucy Lippard celebrates the "lure of the local", calling for an art "which would merge with and/or illuminate a place".[3] The widespread nature of such feelings gives them considerable political force amongst voters, so that issues of place-identity now engage mainstream politicians in many parts of the world. Singapore MP Hong Hai, for example, regrets the fact that "Singapore had sometimes cast aside buildings, places ... that collectively formed a people's roots and heritage".[4] Being now so widely valued, place-identity has also acquired economic salience. It has now become a sought-after sales commodity worldwide: the "unique selling proposition" through which localities are marketed as tourist destinations in what is now the world's largest industry. "Looking for what is distinctive and different is what tourism is all about", as Michael Hough reminds us.[5]

Faced with these increasingly powerful social, political and economic pressures, many designers

Figure 0.1
Cotswold vernacular buildings.

now wish to engage with issues of place-identity in their work. In Britain for example, research for the Department of Environment in 1996[6] showed the importance these issues had begun to take on for designers across a wide range of professions; and by 2002 Trevor Roberts, past president of the Royal Town Planning Institute, could suggest that identity was a "fundamental aim of planning".[7] This concern is not merely an aspect of the nostalgia which many see as a particular feature of British culture, for it has a far wider geographical spread. Practising in the very different – perhaps more future-orientated – cultural context of Malaysia, for example, Bob Giles remarks on the architectural significance of "the government's desire for national identity" there.[8]

It should be obvious, from some of these examples, that the widespread search for appropriate local and regional identities cannot be seen just as an unproblematic "good thing", and there is no shortage of design thinkers pointing out its negative aspects, two of which seem particularly important. First, the concept of place-identity has a long association with extreme right-wing political ideas: one thinks of the

roles of "the soil" and "the fatherland" in Nazi ideology, for example. Second, place-identity is in practice often reduced to a mere commodity to be bought and sold in the marketplace, as part of the Disneyfication of everyday life. These twin dangers are nicely summed up by Neil Leach when he suggests that "(w)e might therefore recognize within regionalism not only the potential dangers inherent in all such calls for a regional or national identity, but also the essential complicity of the concept within the cultural conditions of late capitalism".[9] These dangers certainly exist, but we do not see them as arguments for dismissing the relevance of place-identity in design. Indeed, the heady combination of widespread desire and inherent danger is precisely what makes place-identity so interesting, and precisely why it is essential to debate its implications for the practice of design if the dangers themselves are to be avoided. In this book, therefore, our purpose is to promote a practice-orientated debate about these issues within architecture, town planning and urban design.

"Identity" is a notoriously loose concept. As James Donald points out, "'Identity' is one of the

Figure 0.2
The Old Bridge, Mostar.

most overused but least considered terms in the lexicon of contemporary humanities and social sciences".[10] This looseness is not, in our view, a weakness: rather, it is a key reason why the term is valuable. As Paul Gilroy puts it,

> *(t)he sheer variety of ideas condensed into the concept of identity, and the wide range of issues to which it can be made to refer, foster creative links between themes and perspectives that are not conventionally associated.*[11]

Our own practical work in urban design confirms this: the concept of identity enables design issues to be debated in social and political terms, in ways which people seem to recognise as relevant to their own everyday lives. We have found that when we get beneath the surface of what users say when they talk about a place's identity, they usually have in

mind some sort of meaning the place has in terms of their *own* identity: how the place affects the way they conceive of themselves, or how they imagine it will affect the way other people will conceive of them. Two very different examples may help to clarify what we mean here.

The first concerns the town of Mostar, in Bosnia-Hercegovina, site of the world-famous Old Bridge across the Neretva River (Figure 0.2). The bridge was destroyed during civil war between Croats and Bosniak Muslims in 1993. The subsequent testimony of local Bosniaks[12] shows how the sudden destruction of the bridge highlighted the important role it had played in forming their own personal and social identities, to the extent that it had become seen literally as *part of themselves*: "I felt like any true Mostarian.... I felt like a part of my body had been torn off" said Bernaid,[13] a local man who had lived in Mostar all his life.

Bernaid's identification of himself as a "true Mostarian" is clearly linked to a positive evaluation of Mostar, and of the Old Bridge in particular, which he shared with other Mostarians: the bridge was "like a person with an exceptional soul with all the nice qualities a man should have", in the words of Enisa, a local woman.[14] From our own work in the very different context of run-down British social housing, however, we know that even places which are definitely *not* loved often exert powerful influences on the ways people feel about their own identities.

Since the late 1980s, for example, we have been involved, with residents, in the regeneration of the Angell Town housing estate which was built during the 1970s in Brixton, South London. During the 1990s, we worked with the residents to help create an urban design strategy to guide the place's future. As part of this strategy, we helped the residents define the place-identity they wanted to result from the regeneration work. To cut short a long and complex story,[15] intense discussions with a cross-section of residents about Angell Town's buildings, streets and green spaces led to the articulation of three key place-identity demands.

The first desire was to achieve the maximum spatial and perceptual linkage between Angell Town and its surroundings. The purpose here was to try to break down the perception, in residents' as well as outsiders' minds, of Angell Town as a ghetto, its "separateness" – and by association that of its residents – marked out by the fact that it differs in form from its surroundings. A sense of greater integration with a wider "Brixton identity", it was hoped, might have an empowering political impact; helping the residents break free from a social identity as ghetto people.

The second of the residents' demands was that the regeneration work should be designed so as to make the place more "homely". Discussions made it clear that "homely" was to be understood as the opposite of "institutional": the residents sought forms historically associated with non-institutional living, to support the (again empowering) development of a social identity as non-institutionalised people, able to take their own decisions about the transformation of the place in which they live.

The third and final desire expressed in the residents' "identity brief" was that the regenerated place should end up with a "modern" identity. The intention here was that forms associated with modernity – with an orientation towards the future, rather than being "stuck in the past" – would foster the empowering development of a social identity as forward-looking people with positive aspirations, rather than as no-hopers.

The point of this account is not to argue whether or not these demands were the best ones to serve the residents' interests, nor whether the actual designs of buildings, streets and green spaces which are resulting from these negotiations do or do not support the identity brief in practice (though the results on the ground seem so far well received) (Figure 0.3). The point is rather to show how closely these residents' place-identity demands were linked with concerns about their *own* current and desired identities.

To summarise, we can see close links between place-identity and people's personal and social identities in both Mostar and Angell Town, in relation both to a centuries-old engineering structure and to a modern council housing estate, the one loved and the other largely not, and in very different cultural contexts. The interweaving of place identity and human identity is clearly a broadly encountered phenomenon, which perhaps helps to explain why the term "identity" is used, in everyday speech, equally in relation both to places and to people.

Unfortunately, however, there is a distinct lack of useful theory about how architects, urban designers or town planners might work in relation to this interweaving process. Architectural theorist Neil Leach, for example, is surely right when he says that "the manner in which people actually identify with buildings has hardly been broached within architectural theory".[16] Before we can develop any useful ideas in "how to do it" mode, therefore, we have to develop some practice-orientated ideas about "how to think about it".

As Mostar and Angell Town both show, what matters in the construction of people's identities is not the hardware of buildings, streets and green spaces in themselves, so much as what these *mean* to people. This depends on what the events and

Figure 0.3
New Housing, *Angell Town*, Brixton.

artefacts concerned are seen as *representing*. In the case of English national identity, for example, Stuart Hall points out that:

> national identities are not things that we are born with but are formed and transformed within and in relation to representation. We only know what it is to be English because of the way "Englishness" has come to be represented, as a set of meanings, by English culture.[17]

The same necessarily holds true for imagined membership of *any* community. The importance of meaning here, however, should not be thought of *only* in terms of what a place represents to people, as the sociologist Scott Lash explains:

> The city signifies not as representations signify as we sit in the cinema, reading a book, listening to a concert or watching television. The city only signifies as we move through it, along its paths and thoroughfares, it is not a representation but total environment. In the city and the spatial field we are more active than the "active audience", more interactive than World Wide Web and CD-ROM users. Beyond and more interactive than interactivity is inhabiting. And we inhabit or "live" the fields of urban space.[18]

This process of inhabiting – Lash describes it as "beyond representation, or better well prior to representation"[19] – involves the whole body with all its senses, and generates meanings arising from patterns of human use as well as from the sensory associations of places themselves. The testimony of Mostar people is again relevant here. It demonstrates the importance of the experience of places through use in a particularly dramatic way, for the bridge was powerfully associated with particular patterns of human activity, linked to significant rites of passage in local people's lives, such as crossing the threshold to adulthood. For men, this threshold was crossed by being seen to summon up the courage to jump

5

off the bridge into the Neretva River: "when you've jumped off the bridge you know you're a man", as Lucy Blakstad reported.[20] For women, the significant event was different, as Zehra – a local woman now in her fifties – remembered: "In some ways the Old Bridge is the bridge of young lovers ... my first kiss was on the Old Bridge."[21] Jasna, another local woman, agreed: "there is no Mostarian who hasn't made love near the Old Bridge".[22]

The importance of meanings in relation to both use and form also comes across with cruel clarity if we consider *why* the bridge was a specific target for civil war destruction. At the level of use, it formed the only physical route for people to cross between the two halves of the town divided by the river: a link between people with different histories which had to be destroyed as part of the terrible identity-change strategy euphemistically known as "ethnic cleansing". The meanings associated with the form itself also mattered in this evil enterprise: the bridge's pointed Islamic arch stood for an Ottoman heritage, itself part of what was to be rooted out in the so-called "cleansing" process. "It is not enough to cleanse Mostar of the Muslims" said one of the attacking militiamen: "the relics must also be destroyed".[23]

To summarise, the multi-sensory process of inhabiting a place's structures and open spaces – those landscapes modified by human intervention which geographers call "cultural landscapes" – generates a complex of meanings in which patterns of use and form are both involved. If we want to understand why place-identity matters to so many people, then, we have to focus on the links between the meanings of cultural landscapes on the one hand, and human identities on the other. This is the overall perspective we take in this book, and it leads us to the particular definition of place-identity which underlies our thinking in the pages which follow. For us, place-identity is *the set of meanings associated with any particular cultural landscape which any particular person or group of people draws on in the construction of their own personal or social identities.*

From the Angell Town story, we can see that the residents wanted to be able to call on the place's cultural landscape in dynamic ways: they wanted to use the re-design of the estate partly as an aid to constructing renewed, more empowered identities.

The Angell Town residents are not alone here: the use of cultural landscapes as key sources of meaning in a *dynamic* identity-construction process seems to be a central issue in many people's lives today.

The dynamic nature of the identity-construction process is not the new phenomenon it is sometimes taken to be: there has always, at least to some extent, been a need to construct one's own identity rather than just passively accepting it as a given. Certainly the construction process took on a markedly fluid character long ago; for example wherever traditional religious conceptions of humankind as created in God's image were challenged by scientific evolutionary notions that humans had evolved from apes, at the same time as those same scientific ideas enabled the onset of a capitalist process of industrialisation which dynamited traditional certainties of all kinds. Themselves living through the exhilarations and fears of the early industrialisation process, Karl Marx and Friedrich Engels famously noted how "all fixed, fast-frozen relations ... are swept away.... All that is solid turns into air".[24] Writing slightly later, the German philosopher Friedrich Nietszche saw that cultural landscapes were involved in the process of identity-building in this new fluidity. Writing about the need for a new approach to design, he felt that people could no longer be satisfied with traditional buildings and outdoor spaces, because "we wish to see *ourselves* translated into stones and plants, we want to take walks *in ourselves* when we stroll around these buildings and gardens".[25]

During the twentieth century, ever-deepening levels of scientific exploration have still further undermined established sources of identification, based on previous certainties. For example, the identification of humankind as fundamentally distinct from nature has undergone a radical shift, as Adrian Franklin points out:

> *The idea of nature has shifted substantially in recent years from an independent reality external to and different from the human and the cultural to a domain that is increasingly dependent on and shaped by the operation of a global human society.*[26]

From a still wider perspective, humankind has also been conceptually uprooted from its former position at the centre of the universe. As John Gillott and Manjit Kumar see it,

> *Science has ... changed forever humanity's perception of its place in the cosmos. From being the inhabitants of a body at the centre of the universe, around which the rest of the universe revolved, we now see ourselves as the inhabitants of a tiny planet, we revolve around an ordinary star, on the fringes of a galaxy which is one amongst countless others.*[27]

In parallel with these shifts, the fluidity of the identity-construction process has increased still further because of changes in the core values governing many people's lives. Diverse thinkers from many fields of social theory agree that one of the most crucial of these value-changes involves the ever-growing importance of choice in everyday life. The sociologist Zygmunt Bauman, for example, tells us that choice is nowadays "the supreme value",[28] whilst Fred Inglis, writing from a cultural studies perspective, calls choice "the key moral act which fills the consumer with purpose and identity".[29] The key role played by choice is now even reflected in new approaches to defining poverty, as Violaine Courmont reports:

> *The World Bank 2000 report goes from the lack of goods – monetary or essential – to the lack of ability to choose, the possibility to choose being considered as the essential factor for well-being.*[30]

The key role which choice plays in so many people's lives has complex and contradictory implications for the identity-construction process. On the one hand, where choice is the supreme value, the ability to choose one's own identity – implying an extreme degree of fluidity in identity terms – is likely to be highly valued; at least by some people some of the time. The sense of exhilaration here comes over very strongly in this account by Allucquère Roseanne Stone:

> *I tend to see myself as an entity that has chosen to make its life career out of playing with identity. It sometimes seems as though everything in my past has been a kind of extended excuse for experiment with subject position and interaction. After all, what material is better to experiment with than one's self?*[31]

Some kinds of cultural landscapes support the desire to experiment with subject position and interaction better than others. The need here is for places which offer open potentials for the choice of a wide range of different patterns of activity and cultural interpretations: the kinds of places which are often called "responsive".[32] Responsiveness, however, is not all that matters: there is another side to this particular coin. Even someone as experimental as Roseanne Stone still feels the need for some deeper sense of stability in identity terms:

> *it's not exactly breaking new ground to say that any subject position is a mask. That's well and good, but still most people take some primary subject position for granted. When pressed, they may give lip service to the idea that perhaps even their current "root" persona is also a mask, but nobody really believes it. For all intents and purposes, your "root" persona is you. Take that one away, and there's nobody home.*[33]

In today's situation where choice is "the supreme value", "the key moral act" and "the essential factor for well-being", however, the construction of a stable "root" identity is no easy matter. People want to exercise choice in as many aspects of their lives as possible; including, necessarily, choosing the criteria according to which their choices are made. This potentially leads to an infinite regress of choice: a choice of ways of choosing how to choose, and so on *ad infinitum*. This situation offers no firm ground of foundational values as a basis for making sense of any particular choice, and yet sense has somehow to be made: feelings of senselessness, in relation to the "key moral act", can never be psychologically viable.

The pre-eminence of choice, then, generates fears as well as exhilarating freedoms so far as the identity-construction process is concerned. It creates the internal tensions which are so poetically expressed by Milan Kundera in the title of one of his best-known novels: *The Unbearable Lightness of Being*.[34] The construction of identity now depends in part on finding the right psychological weights to balance the pleasurable side of lightness, to prevent the self from drifting altogether into the void. With choice as the supreme value, these weights can only be found through a trial and error process of choosing and trying out, as Zygmunt Bauman explains:

> So there is a need for another trial, and another – and this can be attempted only by clinging desperately to things solid and tangible and their promising duration.[35]

Here, perhaps, we begin to see more clearly *why* cultural landscapes seem to have such particularly important impacts, both positive and negative, on the identity-construction process. Composed around long-lasting built and natural forms, they are redolent of a permanence uniquely suited to be "desperately clung to".

The Mostar example shows very clearly the sense of permanence which the Old Bridge had contributed to people's lives, made starkly apparent by the sense of loss at its destruction. Emir, a local man, felt that "the loss of the Old Bridge is the same as if you took some planet away from the Cosmos".[36] Enisa, a local woman who had lost close family members in the war, expressed her feelings on the same topic in still more remarkable terms:

> I could somehow accept that my mother and my husband had been killed in the war. People die. They disappear.... But not the Old Bridge which was built in 1566 and had been here for so many years.[37]

Cultural landscapes, then, are particularly well suited to supplying a sense of permanence, for anchoring the roots which are needed to counter the "unbearable" aspects of the sometimes exhilarating "lightness of being". But mere permanence, in itself, does not address a further issue which stems from the fluidity of today's identity-construction process. As Zygmunt Bauman explains:

> the necessity to choose comes without a foolproof recipe for proper choice.... Since the dividing lines between good and evil have not been drawn before they are drawn in the course of action, the outcomes of these efforts at drawing lines is akin to a string of footprints rather than a network of charted roads. And thus loneliness is as permanent and unevictable a resident of the house of responsibility as is ambivalence ... when unmitigated and unassuaged, that loneliness ... is excruciatingly painful to live with.[38]

One way of addressing this painful loneliness, at the same time as making sense of one's choices in the absence of foundational values, is by seeing oneself as part of a wider community of other people who make the same kinds of choices as oneself; so that one can validate one's own choices through the approval of other members of the community concerned. Cultural landscapes have important roles to play in fostering (or not) this perception of community membership. Before we can begin to explore these roles, however, we have to probe deeper into the concept of community itself in this context.

Faced with the threat of senselessness, the whole point of community membership is that it *will* validate one's choices. Since choice is the *supreme* value, however, this validation must not be achieved at the cost of *constraining* one's choices. Ideally, therefore, we desire membership of communities which we know will *always* approve *any* choice we make. In practice, of course, life is never that simple: these are communities which can exist only in the mind, as what the sociologist Benedict Anderson calls "imagined communities".[39] Speaking of nations, for example, Anderson points out that these are "*imagined* because the members of even the smallest nation will never know most of their fellow-members, meet them, or even hear of them, yet in the minds of each lives the image of their communion".[40] Because of their importance in a society where choice is the supreme value, membership of such imagined communities is central to most people's identities.

In complex modern societies, most people see themselves as members of several imagined communities. Some of these are relatively stable and long-lasting, like the nation-state which Anderson uses as his example above, or others linked with core dimensions of human life such as ethnicity, gender or one's stage in the human life-cycle. In contrast, at the other extreme, are relatively "shallow" and short-lived affairs; involving, for instance, fashion victims of all kinds. At all levels, even the shallowest, membership of any imagined community requires an element of *belief* in the community's "reality", as Zygmunt Bauman points out:

> belief in their presence is their only brick and mortar, and imputation of importance their only source of authority. An imagined community acquires the right to approve or disapprove in the consequence of the decision of the approval-seeking individual to invest it with the arbitrating power and to agree to be bound by the arbitration (through, of course, the reverse order must be believed to be the case to make the whole thing work).[41]

The element of belief here is central to the way in which membership of an imagined community can validate unfettered choice: the validation process cannot work if there is any element of pretence about it. This means that the existence of the community itself has to be "recognised" as real, as pre-existing one's own membership of it, rather than merely as *invented* to validate one's own choices.

The recognition of an imagined community as pre-existing one's own membership has to be based on convincing "evidence" of some kind. Pre-existing events and artefacts which surround us in the "real" world have to be interpreted as evidence which demonstrates that the imagined community "really" exists: that we haven't just "made it up". All aspects of our surroundings, from music and clothes to flags and urban form, can potentially be interpreted as confirming the prior existence of some imagined community or other; but particular aspects have particular significance at different "depths" within the range of imagined communities to which most of us typically belong nowadays.

Because of the ever more rapid fashion cycles associated with today's economic system, aspects of our surroundings such as clothing, music or surface décor are relatively disposable and short-lived. This implies that the meanings read into them are mostly suitable only for the construction of our most "shallow", dynamic and fleeting communities.

In contrast, the relative permanence of cultural landscapes – particularly public spaces to which all potential community members have the right to access – can be drawn on for constructing imagined communities of the most stable, "deepest" kind; to which some of the most stable, deepest aspects of our own identities relate.

People who are rightly concerned that overmuch focus on place might foster the development of dangerously nationalistic or exclusive communitarian identities sometimes argue that cultural landscapes are no longer appropriate material for identity-construction today. Neil Leach, for example, suggests that we are now in an age "that constitutes its identity less through notions of place – place of origin, birthplace, etc. – and increasingly through more transitory phenomena, such as jobs and possessions".[42] Unfortunately, however, not everyone is equally well-endowed in terms of their capacity to choose jobs or possessions, and many people – even in supposedly affluent societies – would find it hard to recognise that they live, as Leach suggests, "in a society that is constantly mobile, and whose archetypal space is the transport interchange or the airport lounge".[43]

In any case, we still have to face up to the issue which Talja Blokland raises when she reminds us that "we find that contemporary society instigates a constant search for the answer to the question: if we keep discovering new differences in our daily encounters with others, where do we belong?"[44] Perhaps the unavoidable need to address this question underlies the recent research finding that identity-formation still makes important use of cultural landscapes even in the case of truly nomadic people like New Age Travellers. Kevin Hetherington, for example, tells us that the landscapes which matter here are "places that symbolise uncertainty, ambivalence or marginality. As such, they will be taken as symbolic centres for out-groups on the margins of society".[45] "These places, such as Stonehenge", he tells us, "represent a symbolic field in which identities, alternative to the mainstream, are enacted and produced".[46]

On balance, therefore, it seems to us unrealistic for designers not to accept that identification through membership of imagined communities, constructed at least partly through reference to cultural landscapes beyond the transport interchange or the airport lounge, continues to be important for many people. And by the same token, it would be wise for designers to accept that they necessarily bear some responsibility for the identity implications of the changes they inevitably make to these wider cultural landscapes through their work.

To summarise, then, self-identification through membership of imagined communities is a powerful strategy for coping with the painful loneliness endemic to the infinite regress of choice, without losing out in terms of choice itself; and despite the importance of possessions and other belongings, imagined communities are likely to carry on being constructed at least partly in relation to notions of place. As Anne-Marie Fortier puts it,

> *Imagining a community is both that which is created as a common history, experience or culture of a group – a group's belongings – and about how the imagined community is attached to places – the location of culture.*[47]

And in any case, places are also themselves *part of* a group's "common history, experience, or culture": as Leach himself rather beautifully expresses it, "(m)emories of associated activities haunt architecture like a ghost".[48]

Commentators like Leach are surely right, however, when they point out that this haunting is potentially problematic, particularly because any place is nowadays likely to be home to people who see themselves as members of *different* imagined communities, with different values and histories. This situation, which becomes ever more complex in many parts of the world, faces designers with difficult issues. The key problem here is that any community is defined at least partly by distinguishing it from others: what makes us "us", at least in part, is that we are not "them". Distinctions of this kind can never be avoided, for they are inherently part of the identity-construction process itself: the conception of a "them" is central to the process through which we identify "us" in the first place. Even if we identify "us" as the whole of humankind, the distinction from *some* "other" – machines, "the wild" or whatever – cannot ultimately be avoided.

"Strangely", as Julia Kristeva says, "the foreigner lives within us: he is the hidden face of our identity".[49]

In some situations, it is clear that unbridled fostering of these us/them differences, through cultural landscapes or any other means, can have horribly negative consequences. Perceptions of difference can all too easily interact with other tensions to bring about the most terrible outcomes; such as we have seen in the "ethnic cleansing" of Mostar or, in the wider ecological sphere, in the destruction of entire species through the impacts of human development.

So far as the human sphere is concerned, the French sociologist Alain Touraine argues that a key pre-requisite for enabling people from different imagined communities to "live together" is the development of a mutual respect for what he calls "the Subject"[50]: the attempt, in which all humans are necessarily involved, to construct identities to make sense of life, no matter how different from one's own the identity-outcomes of others might be. This overriding respect for the value of the identity-construction process *for its own sake* calls for support from particular kinds of cultural landscapes. It reinforces the need for responsive places, which offer open potentials for the choice of a wide range of different patterns of activity, and which are also able to support cultural interpretations appropriate to a range of different imagined communities.

In today's multicultural societies, an important aspect of responsiveness is what the German philosopher Wolfgang Welsch calls "transculturality". Once we give importance to transculturality, this gives a particular emphasis to the way we think about places at all physical scales. As an example at the larger scale, we are led to agree with Talja Blokland's view that "the neighbourhood is not, never was and never can be a community. Instead, it serves a practical and symbolic purpose as a means to form and perpetuate many different communities".[51] At the smaller scale, we can follow Welsch in exemplifying transculturality by reference to Jean Nouvel's Institut du Monde Arabe in Paris (Figure 0.4):

> *Nouvel affects an encounter of European and Asian culture by operating with forms which can*

Figure 0.4
Institut du Monde Arabe, Paris (architect Jean Nouvel).

be read as high-tech documents and as Arabian ornamentation in one. The functional and ornamental are coupled in an amazing way; they are, so to speak, blended into one another.[52]

This transculturality is difficult for designers to address on a consistent basis, because it depends on an understanding of and feeling for a range of imagined communities different from the designer's own, which is not part of the usual stock-in-trade of current design cultures. Imagined communities, after all, are carried only in their members' minds: "in the minds of each lives the image of their communion", to quote Benedict Anderson again.[53] Specifically, this "image of communion" lives, like all social structures, in people's *memories:* in "the memory traces of knowledgeable individuals", as the sociologist Anthony Giddens puts it.[54] The social sharing (or not) of memories, however, is a

minefield for designers. The memory-associations of any particular pattern of forms or activities, which might support one imagined community, might as easily seem irrelevant or even hostile to another. To make matters more complex still, professional designers themselves – merely by virtue of *being* professional designers – usually feel part of their *own* "design community", with its own significant memories. As the architect Stanford Anderson (no relation to Benedict) points out, this is indeed a pre-requisite for the existence of autonomous architectural work; but it also carries with it the problem that the resulting "professional memory" may differ significantly from the "social memories" of *everyone* else.[55] In the face of this pervasive problem, it seems likely that the development of a thoroughgoing transculturality in design will require the development of new, more openly co-creative approaches to the design process itself, in which users will come to be regarded as collaborative experts in their own communities' values.[56]

Welsch contrasts the transculturality of the Institut du Monde Arabe with what he calls "turning the clock back in the direction of musty 'owness', which always stands at the threshold of intolerance".[57] This "turning the clock back", which is inherent in many well-intentioned but one-sided attempts to maintain existing place-identities by insisting on new development "keeping in keeping" with whatever already existed in the place concerned, encourages intolerance because it fosters the view that the past must be preferable to the future; which in turn encourages what Frank Furedi calls a "culture of fear", often hyped by the media, in which many people operate with a "morality of low expectations", and identify themselves as living in a "world of risky strangers",[58] where falling in love is dangerous, and even a friendly gesture such as shaking hands can constitute a health risk.

Recent urban transformations are themselves deeply implicated in the development of this culture of fear. John Rennie Short's explanation here stresses once again the key role which public space plays in the identity-formation process:

> The pervading sense of fear of the other in the USA can, in part, be attributed to the urban forms that mean people rarely meet people different from themselves in public and third spaces. As we become cordoned off into the separate spaces of life experiences, we meet others only through the stereotypes and fantasies of the media. When we lose the shared spaces that allow us to see the other in person, we lose an essential element of a truly civic society.[59]

When a generalised fear of "others" expresses itself in the economic sphere, it fosters tensions between imagined communities, even in relatively affluent societies, through what are sometimes called "zero-sum" conceptions of the economic resources available: conceptions which support the pessimistic view that if "they" improve their lot, then "we" necessarily get less; because there is only a finite, fixed sum of resources to go round. As the political thinker Ernst Gellner points out, any effective

approach to addressing such tensions requires, amongst other things, identities orientated towards a more optimistic, "non-zero-sum" view of the future: if "we" work *with* "them" then *all of us* might do better in the future.[60] If they are to help in developing these more optimistic, forward-looking identities, cultural landscapes will have to refer not only to the past, but also to an open sense of the future.

The desire for cultural landscapes to support the construction of personal and social identities which value an open sense of the future does not, however, imply that a sense of rootedness does not matter at all. Indeed, the logic of our argument so far suggests rather strongly that we need well-rooted identities if we are to break free from the "culture of fear", so as to develop the confidence to value open futures in the first place; and that cultural landscapes have a potential role to play in constructing these roots. From this perspective, the extreme disregard for established place-identities sometimes displayed in architectural culture, as exemplified by Rem Koolhaas's influential "fuck the context" position,[61] is just as one-sidedly negative as the "keeping in keeping" approach to which so many town planners adhere. Perhaps the best balance here is expressed by the non-professional residents of the Dorset village of West Bay, with whom we have recently been working, when they decided they wanted the place to be "rooted in the past but not stuck in the past".[62]

The need to break away from the "culture of fear", to support the development of rooted but optimistic "non-zero-sum" personal and social identities, also has important implications for the way in which humankind is identified in relation to "nature". If humans are to learn to live harmoniously with nature, we must stop thinking of nature as something external to ourselves, with fixed unalterable characteristics, and with which we have a zero-sum resource relationship. Here, recent shifts in conceptions of the human/nature distinction, which we have already seen as playing a part in increasing the fluidity of the identity-construction process, now also have a positive role to play in its reconstruction. As Adrian Franklin suggests, we would do well to follow thinkers like Bruno Latour[63] in "declaring the boundaries between humanity and nature to be a fiction",[64] reconceptualising nature itself as:

> *whatever happens to result from the interaction between species including the actions and designs of man; it is a result of history unfolding; it is the outcome of co-dwelling.*[65]

Personal and social identities which can be constructed free from the traditional human/nature dichotomy, and cultural landscapes which can support their construction, are essential to developing an optimistic, non-zero-sum, co-dwelling conception in which, as Moscovici puts it:

> *society will no longer be seen as functioning to shackle nature. Rather it will come into alliance with it, encouraging the beliefs and practices which will tend to enrich the possibilities of the species and increase the prospects for survival.*[66]

From the perspective of living together, both with the members of other human imagined communities and with nature, then, we have to develop rooted identities which are not *trapped* by their roots in a relationship which Kim Dovey calls "place bondage",[67] but are rather optimistically open to the future. Given the current pervasiveness of the "culture of fear", however, we need all the help we can get if we are to develop these open, optimistic identities. What is needed here is support for experimenting with new identities without having first to let go of our established roots. According to art theorist Arthur Danto, this support can be offered by some sorts of art, through the "not unfamiliar experience of *being taken out of oneself by art*".[68] Through this process of being taken out of oneself, people are enabled to take on "new art-relevant identities ... while somehow retaining their old ones", as the American philosopher David Goldblatt puts it.[69]

Any new identity supported through the influence of art might in principle be either positive or negative in terms of "living together". Goldblatt himself gives an example which is hard not to see in negative terms, when he talks about "the self transfigured by powerful buildings": "For example, it is easy to imagine the native Indian transfigured into a member of the British Empire."[70] But can art also help one try out new identities which might have *positive* co-dwelling implications? Certainly some writers on what has come to be called "New Public Art" suggest that it can. Nina Felshin, for example, sees the New Public Art as characterised by

> *the innovative use of public space to address issues of sociopolitical and cultural significance, and to encourage community or public participation as a means of effecting social change.*[71]

Potentially, therefore, it seems that there might be kinds of art with important roles to play in forming cultural landscapes in which people from different imagined communities might manage the difficult business of living together.

To summarise, our arguments so far suggest that there are four key issues currently at stake in the relationship between cultural landscapes and the construction of human identities. First, we need landscapes which will support the most open possible range of choices in people's everyday lives, and which will help us develop the sense of empowerment we need to take advantage of these opportunities in practice. Second, we need landscapes to support the construction of imagined communities, in order to dispel the inherent sense of lonely rootlessness which is the downside of the infinite regress of exhilarating choice. Third, we need landscapes to help us, as members of particular imagined communities, to get beyond the morality of low expectations, to develop the open, optimistic identities we need if we are to find transcultural ways of living together with others, in sustainable ways. And, fourth, we need landscapes which will encourage us to develop the capacity to live in harmony with the wider ecosystems we usually call "nature". But what does all this mean in practice? How can we get beyond a mere wish-list, towards practical ideas about how we should design?

First, a caveat: place-identity is not the be-all and end-all of design. Though important, it is only one amongst myriad issues which have to be addressed in practical design work. It would be merely myopic to focus on it exclusively, ignoring other factors which existing design cultures have been developed to address. Rather, we should seek to improve existing design cultures by identifying those aspects which should be developed because they seem valuable in place-identity terms, and those others such as knee-jerk "keeping in keeping" and macho "fuck the context" which we already know should be rejected.[72] As a starting point, then, how can we explore the pros and cons of existing design cultures, from the place-identity perspective?

Current mainstream design cultures have largely developed within a modernist tradition. Much of this tradition has evolved as part of the globalising form-production system which has so far seemed mostly to erase the local differences which are important for established place identities, rather than creating positive new ones. Not surprisingly, therefore, many mainstream modernist values and working practices make it hard for designers to engage creatively with the place-identity issues which today seem so important to so many people (including, of course, modernist designers themselves when they are "off duty").

Viewed in this light, the modernist tradition can all-too-easily be dismissed as part of the problem, in place-identity terms, rather than part of the solution. Nobody, however, should expect most designers to *abandon* the modernist tradition, as recent failed attempts to promote post-modern classicism show. Like everyone else, after all, designers feel the need to belong to an imagined community which can help them believe that the choices they make in their work are legitimate ones; and, for many, it is still membership of the modernist community which fulfils this need. Fortunately, however, the modernist community's emphasis on values of originality and innovation means that its members have never spoken with a single monolithic voice; and there have always been rebellious strands within the modernist tradition, some with positive value in place-identity terms.

The best way to develop a well-structured approach to the design issues involved in creating positive place-identities, therefore, is through in-depth case studies of creative design work which has addressed these issues in practice. We can find particularly interesting work throughout the period since the second half of the nineteenth century, when increasing industrialisation led on the one hand to an increasingly fluid process of identity construction, and on the other to the erosion of the distinctiveness of particular cultural landscapes which had previously helped to root that process. During this period, there have been a wide range of interesting design approaches, which have varied in response to all sorts of cultural differences in different places, and to changing design ideas over time. To get the benefit of exploring a full range of creative work, therefore, we have chosen to organise this book around case studies from a wide range of geographical locations, and from across the time-span of modernism itself. Overall, the studies are related together roughly in the chronological order in which they were initially designed; enabling us to explore the successive emergence of significant new approaches to achieving place-identity by design. The focus on historical continuity is important here: given the key role which modernism plays in many designers' lives, we want to demonstrate that what we are exploring is a genuine "alternative modernist tradition", developing within the modern movement since its inception, rather than just a series of isolated rebellions against it.

Each case study will focus primarily on the roles which architecture, urban design and town planning play in the identity-construction process. Because of the potential importance of the art-world as a whole in this process, however, it is important to explore the particular roles which built form can play, in distinction to other art media such as music, dance or painting, so that we do not mistakenly try to make the physical structures of cultural landscapes perform roles for which they are inherently unsuited. Where appropriate, therefore, each case study will situate built form interventions within a wider art-world, to help uncover their specific place-identity potentials.

In each of our cases, we shall explore how new design practice developed in complex interplay with new theory. As we shall see, new theoretical concepts arise through attempts to grapple with new practical problems. Practical problems, in turn, cannot be recognised *as* problems unless alternative ways of doing things – *solutions* – can be imagined; at least in their dimmest outlines. Theories, problems and solutions co-exist in complex interaction in particular cases. Each of the following chapters explores one such case in depth, and the book concludes by pulling together threads from all the various chapters, to map out the usefulness of different approaches in relation to different types and levels of imagined communities, at different physical scales of design.

Notes

1 Hough, 1990, 2.
2 Wales, 1989.
3 Lippard, 1997, 286.
4 Cited in Ko, 1999, 25.
5 Hough, 1990, 3.
6 Department of Environment, 1996.
7 Roberts, 2002, 3.
8 Giles, 1999, 41.
9 Leach, 2002a, 94.
10 Donald, in duGay et al., 2000, rear cover.
11 Gilroy, 1997, 305. For a negative response to this argument, see Brubaker and Cooper, 2000.
12 Reported in Blakstad, 2002.
13 Blakstad, 2002, 173.
14 Ibid., 158.
15 For more detail, see Bentley, 1993.
16 Leach, 2002b, 28.
17 Hall, 1992, 292.
18 Lash, 1999, 85–86 (emphasis in original).
19 Ibid., 86.
20 Blakstad, 2002, 156.
21 Cited in Blakstad, 2002, 159.
22 Ibid., 2002, 158.
23 Cited in Sells, 1998, 93.
24 Marx and Engels, 1848.
25 Nietszche, 1974, 226(280), cited in Welsch, 1997, 134.
26 Franklin, 2002, 19.
27 Gillcott and Kumar, 1995, 139.
28 Bauman, 1992, 170.
29 Inglis, 1993, 179.
30 Courmont, 2001, 4.
31 Stone, 1996, 1–2.
32 For theoretical exploration of responsiveness, see Bentley, 1999, and for design guidance, see Bentley et al., 1985.
33 Stone, 1996, 2.
34 Kundera, 1984.
35 Bauman, 2000, 83.
36 Cited in Blakstad, 2002, 174.
37 Ibid., 172.
38 Bauman, S., 1995, 2–3.
39 Anderson, S., 1983.
40 Anderson, 1983, 15 (emphasis in original).
41 Bauman, 1991, xix (emphases in original).
42 Leach, 2002a, 95.
43 Ibid., 96.
44 Blokland, 2003, 64.
45 Hetherington, 1996, 36.
46 Ibid., 47.
47 Fortier, 1999, 42.
48 Leach, 2002b, 292.
49 Kristeva, 1991, 1.
50 Touraine, 2000.
51 Blokland, 2003, 207.
52 Welsch, 1997, 144.
53 Anderson, B., 1983, 15.
54 Giddens, 1984.
55 Anderson, S., 1999.
56 For further discussion, see Bentley, 1999, Part 4.
57 Welsch, 1997, 143.
58 Furedi, 2002, 107–126, see also Sandercock, 2002; Beck, 1998; Park, 1967, Chapters 11 and 13.
59 Short, 2001, 271.
60 Gellner, 1988.
61 For discussion of this approach, and its influence on recent architectural culture, see Benedikt, 2002.
62 West Dorset District Council, 2002.
63 Latour, 1993.
64 Franklin, 2002, 255.
65 Ibid., 9.
66 Moscovici, 1990.
67 Dovey, 1992.
68 Danto, 1981, cited in Goldblatt, 2002, 163 (emphasis in original).
69 Goldblatt, 2002, 163.
70 Ibid., 164.
71 Felshin, 1995, 9.
72 For a fuller development of the logic of this line of argument, see Bentley, 1999.

1

Prague: The pursuit and perils of national identity

By the mid-nineteenth century, industrial capitalism had spread widely from its origins in eighteenth-century Britain, turning all that was solid into air in its wake, and creating ever more fluid conditions for the construction of human identities. In step with industrialisation, therefore, more and more people were attracted towards building imagined communities to belong to; transforming cultural landscapes to give these communities a sense of permanent roots.

The interweaving of imagined communities and cultural landscapes had important implications for the ways in which the territories of States were conceived, as lands and imagined communities were woven ever more tightly together to form nations in more and more people's minds. In turn, the shift towards the nation as a key focus for social identity had deep political implications, raising new kinds of questions about where "our" land ended and "theirs" began. In practice, there were often mismatches between any particular imagined community's sense of "natural" boundaries, and state borders already laid down, long before nations were imagined into being. Often enough, it came to seem, "we" don't have control of the land which is "naturally ours".

This mismatch was particularly problematic where "we" had *no* dedicated territory, but were rather treated as merely subsidiary to some larger unit controlled by some overlording "them". In Europe's industrialising areas, this situation existed most clearly in the long-established Hapsburg Empire; whose rulers held sway from Vienna over a wide spectrum of peoples with various languages and cultural traditions, each with potential for imagining into being new national communities, with aspirations to claim what were currently Imperial lands. All this posed fundamental challenges to vested Imperial interests, so the central power in Vienna had to seek ways of holding the Empire together. New national communities, therefore, were often constructed against Imperial opposition.

To achieve their territorial aspirations, subordinate communities had to find ways of building coherent cultural and political programmes to bind "us" together. As these came gradually into being, usually through messy trial and error, they began to provide increasingly powerful sources of meaning to support deeper and wider membership of the new imagined communities, even amongst rural populations still largely unaffected by capitalism's unsettling impacts. Gradually, therefore, the later nineteenth century saw nationalist cultural-political programmes growing ever stronger.

Nationalist pressures were first felt in areas where the most rapid industrialisation made the Imperial status quo most difficult to maintain. Within the Hapsburg Empire, industrialisation first took hold in lands long-settled by Slovaks, and in Bohemia, to the South and East of Vienna itself (Figure 1.1). Since Prague was this area's key cultural centre, designers there played a major role in developing nationalist cultural politics; exploring ways of reinterpreting and reconstructing cultural landscapes to support the creation of a new national community. With no established ways of achieving this, and working against the Imperial grain, Prague's

Figure 1.1
Central Europe in the mid-eleventh century (after Bideleux and Jeffries).

designers had to develop new approaches to creating national identity. Prague is therefore a birthplace of modernist thinking about place-identity, which is why our case-study explorations begin there.

The first conscious efforts to construct place-identity by design were made by artists and intellectuals, who were thin on the ground. If their programme was ever to gain enough power to achieve political independence, however, it would have to strike far wider cultural chords. This was difficult in Prague, because the city's population had great cultural complexity. Differences of spoken and written language, through which so much cultural meaning is expressed, were overlaid by distinct rural and urban ways of life, each with its own internal divide between aristocrat and peasant, or businessman and worker, as well as religious differences between Christians and Jews. To help national identity develop, the meanings of cultural landscapes had to bridge across these cultural barriers to support a powerful sense of "us".

Early attempts to construct these landscapes, against official culture, had to operate in marginal ways; either gaining resources by subverting official initiatives meant to promote other causes such as public health or historic conservation, or by building new myths and interpretations: landscapes in the mind, rather than on the ground. Working at these margins, intellectuals and artists had to build bridges outwards from their own elite cultures, to connect with others who might potentially share the same national identity, but were otherwise different from themselves and from each other. The difficulties were compounded by censorship, which forbade the clear expression of anti-Hapsburg nationalist sentiments, but in practice mostly affected the written word.[1] Since non-verbal culture also bridged language barriers, many early attempts to re-interpret existing cultural landscapes were developed through music and the visual arts.

In music, for example, Bedřich Smetana provided a new, modern take on "our" national landscape in his tone poem cycle *Ma Vlast* (my country), reinterpreting the countryside to urban sophisticates as a priceless national heritage. Reaching across other social barriers in his opera *Libušine*, Smetana also celebrated Prague's mythical foundation by the legendary queen Libušine and her ploughman husband. The mythic themes here – the "golden age" of self-determination in ancient times, and the role of the "united people", aristocrat and peasant united to create it – were common building blocks for many emerging nations. Later, more direct links across barriers between elite and popular cultures were explored by Antonin Dvořák, himself of humble rural origins: his *Slavonic Dances* founded high-art music on folk culture; involving the whole body in building national identity through dance, promoting the native polka over the Viennese waltz.

Linking elite and popular cultures, however, was always a contentious project. Many cultural movers and shakers felt that overmuch emphasis on folk culture would limit the development of the future-orientated national identity which would be needed to break free from established Imperial cultural and political structures. In painting, for example, the search for national modernity took artists away from folk art inspiration. It also took them away from Viennese art, despite Vienna's standing as a centre of artistic modernity, because of its obvious Imperial connotations. It equally pulled them away

from other key centres such as Berlin or Munich, linked to Austrian culture through the German language. Ultimately, it drew them towards Paris: a world-class centre of modern painting, seeming "other" to Germanic culture, particularly after the 1870 Franco-Prussian war. In Paris, it was rebellious Impressionism which caught the nationalist imagination of the painter Antonin Chittossi: the modern images which he and his later followers created helped reinforce music's earlier representation of the Bohemian landscape as a cultural bridge across the urban/rural divide.

Creative developments in music, dance and painting, then, supported new structures of feeling which eventually fostered new interpretations and transformations of the cultural landscapes of Prague itself. Since Prague is an ancient city, we have briefly to trace its earlier development before we can understand how these new interventions worked.

From the beginning, Prague's development was underpinned by topography. It lies on the river Vltava; a major tributary of the Elbe, and a strategic trade route long before passable roads. In the ninth century, this trading advantage was reinforced by building two castles on high bluffs on both sides of the river. With trade taxes amongst the lowest in Europe, Prague had wide renown by the tenth century: Ibrahim ibn Yacoub, one of many foreign visitors, could term it "a busy trading centre" by 965.[2]

Growing trade required a large market, which developed on flat land opposite Hradcany Castle. Around the market developed the settlement of Stare Mesto (Old Town), which grew in importance after it was linked to the castle, in 1170, by the first stone bridge across the Vltava. Under the protective walls of the castle itself there developed a second settlement, Mala Strana (Small Town) which was eventually expanded by the planned extension of Nove Mesto (New Town) during the fourteenth century. By that time, Prague was already a major city, with 50,000 people and Central Europe's first university. The right to build a town hall, symbolising the city's autonomy, was granted by royal decree in 1338, but the autonomy of Prague, and of Bohemia as a whole, was not to last. Political turmoil, religious rebellion and confused struggles between feudal

Figure 1.2
Prague: the spatial sequence we shall follow.

lords led to declining trade, and by 1526 Bohemia was taken over by the Hapsburg dynasty.

To nineteenth-century nationalist designers this Hapsburg takeover seemed a historical disaster, whilst by contrast the pre-1526 city core represented a golden age of pre-Hapsburg freedom. Nation-building intellectuals did not want to *re-create* the Golden Age, however. They wanted rather to develop a new modernity from its roots. How could this be done? And how could the resulting cultural landscapes also be made to bridge across the various barriers fragmenting "us" into separate cultural compartments?

Prague's most creative designers explored approaches to these issues at all scales of the cultural landscape, from the overall structure of public space, through buildings and public art works down to street furniture details. These cultural landscapes are experienced through inhabitation, not passive contemplation. They are moved through rather than looked at; so they are unavoidably experienced sequentially, rather than bit by separate bit. To learn useful lessons from them, therefore, we must analyse them sequentially too. Let us now work our way along one particularly significant sequence, developed to organise the rapid growth of the city during the nineteenth century's later years.

Much of the city's expansion was planned to the north, across the river from the town centre: a practical concept for making best use of the city's central facilities, by developing equally around them. Crucial to this expansion concept was a spatial sequence linking Wenceslas Square through Old Town Square, and across the Vltava to the cliffs and parks of Letna beyond. This was intended as a key link to tie the expanding city together: both functionally and symbolically, a fundamental expression of the "one people" theme. Because of the rich set of ways in which a range of designers sought to achieve this expression in practice, we shall explore this sequence in detail (Figure 1.2).

The Southern end of the sequence begins in Wenceslas Square, now the main shopping, cultural and social centre of the city. This is an ancient public space, with "Golden Age" connotations, founded by the Bohemian King Charles IV in 1348 as a horse market. The square's large dimensions − it is 750 metres long and 60 metres wide − give it great memorability as a key element of Prague's overall urban structure. As part of the gradual development of the nineteenth century nation-building programme, it was slowly changed in character from a low-status, utilitarian market to a key ceremonial and cultural space, and given the name it currently enjoys.

The timing of the name-change, and the name itself, are both significant in terms of building a national identity. The re-naming took place precisely when limited administrative freedom was first won from the Hapsburg Empire, in 1848. And the name refers to Saint Wenceslas, a Bohemian King canonised after his assassination in 929: a truly "golden age" figure, whose martyr's death gave rise to a tradition ranking him as the chief patron saint of Bohemia.

The square's importance was enhanced, related to the "golden age" theme and re-interpreted for modern life by two more recent interventions. The first was the building of the National Museum by Josef Schulz, completed in 1890, which encloses the southern end of the square (Figure 1.3). The museum is built on rising ground so it has to be "looked up to", emphasising its importance as a showcase for constructing Czech history. The level change from front to back is taken up by a monumental plinth on which sits Queen Libušine, surveying the city she mythically founded, and forming the symbolic foundation from which the body of the museum springs (Figure 1.4a). The building's central focus, forming a landmark directly on the long axis of the square, is a tall pantheon, painted inside with significant events from Czech history, and housing bronze sculptures of famous Czechs from both the arts and the forward-looking world of the sciences. The pantheon's dome forms a glass lantern through which, symbolically, Czech cultural achievements shine out, illuminating the city's public realm.

The second intervention in the square's design − smaller, but still with great visual impact − is Josef Myslbek's 1912 equestrian statue of Saint Wenceslas, reinforcing the national and religious symbolism of the square's name. The dramatic mass and silhouette of the sculpture, dominated by the King-Saint's helmet, clearly echoes the lantern of the museum against which it is seen; pulling the museum's influence right into the public space, riding out from the museum's space of memory into the future-orientated space of the rapidly-expanding city itself (Figure 1.4b).

The sculpture's message links across some social barriers − but perhaps emphasises others − by reference to the Christian religious sentiments then so important to all but the non-Christian minorities which it excluded. Wenceslas, a saint as well as symbolising the Golden Age of Bohemian self-government, is flanked by four more Bohemian saints: in front, Ludmilla and Procopius; behind, Agnes and Vojtech.

Riding forward along the square, Wenceslas also dramatises the space's role in linking onwards to the Old Town's "Golden Age" mediaeval core. Along this axis, at a slight angle, the tower of the Old Town Hall stands out as a key "golden age" symbol restating the long tradition of pre-Hapsburg self-government. Moving downhill towards it, past new streets opened to focus attention on further golden age landmarks (Figure 1.5a), the square is terminated by the mass of the Czech National Bank, shouldering into the public space as a monument to Czech financial power, becoming ever less dependent on Vienna (Figure 1.5b).

Past the bank, the golden age symbolism of the entire Old Town area is marked by an abrupt change in spatial character. The street narrows and bends right, in a way which would be disorientating except that the new alignment directs attention towards the Old Town Hall tower itself. The decision to accept the pre-existing form of the curved street, rather than straightening it to make the linkage more

Figure 1.3
National Museum at the head of Wenceslas Square.

direct, has a powerful effect in dramatising the impact of the Town Hall and its tower, for the bend ensures that the building is not seen until one is at close quarters with it. The extra impact this provides is important in nationalist terms, given the symbolic value of the Town Hall's long association with the self-government of the region: "*Praga caput regni*" (Prague, head of the Kingdom), as it says on the facade (Figure 1.6a). The design decisions about what to leave alone, in this situation, are as significant as those about when to intervene, back in Wenceslas Square.

The visual importance of the fairly small Town Hall building is further enhanced by ensuring that its small-scale facade can only be experienced from close-to, from a small annex space leading into the main Old Town Square. These close views are made extremely memorable, despite the building's small size, by focusing attention on a large puppet clock from the Golden Age (Figure 1.6b). Dating from 1410, this had its visual impact increased in 1866, with painted decorations by Josef Manes.

The angled approach past the Town Hall leads one naturally into the main space of Old Town Square, past the base of the Town Hall tower, which forms a powerful landmark at the next direction-change of the spatial sequence as a whole. The immense space of the Square itself is mostly left alone, as a splendid symbol of the Golden Age, save for conservation work to enhance its grandeur, and a sculpture placed within it. Erected in 1915, this is a massive monument to Jan Hus, another key historical politico-religious figure from the Bohemian golden age: Czech preacher and reformer, early

Figure 1.4
(a) Queen Libušine, surveying her city. (b) The Wenceslas sculpture.

champion of Czech national and cultural independence, burned at the stake as a heretic in 1415 (Figure 1.7). As in the case of Wenceslas's statue, the monument to Hus links nationalist values to the Christian ones which, at the time, would have struck responsive chords in the minds of all but members of religious minorities; reaching across other barriers of language, class and ways of life, so increasing the effect of the nationalist message itself.

The statue's huge size, its dark stone, and the verticality of Hus's figure all echo the nearly Gothic church of Our Lady of Týn, in which Hus preached many famously inflammatory sermons. The church itself, though dramatically visible from the Old Town Square, is physically separated by lower secular buildings: as with Wenceslas and the National Museum, Hus symbolically draws the church, and its associations with his own historical role, into the square itself; whilst the sheer scale of the figure, and the huge mass of its base, its jagged outcrops and stepped terraces spreading into the square beyond,

give Ladislav Saloun's design the visual impact to strengthen its message still further.

The sculpture also shifts the axis of attention towards Pařizka (Paris) Street, the next stage of our spatial sequence, opened in 1906 to link Old Town Square across the river Vltava to the public open spaces of the Letna heights beyond (Figure 1.8). It is easy to understand why this new street is called after Europe's pre-eminent non-German cultural centre, whose role in the development of Czech national culture we have already begun to explore. The logic of its alignment, however, is less immediately obvious.

When Pařizka Street was opened, it destroyed a large swathe of the old urban structure in its path. This is quite different from the design approach which we saw elsewhere in the ancient city core, where most of today's streets were formed through mere widenings and minor adjustments to the older structure. This conservation-oriented approach is obviously in tune with the nationalist design approach

Figure 1.5
(a) The gothic Powder Tower from Wenceslas Square. (b) The Czech National Bank at the foot of Wenceslas Square.

we have outlined, for the ground-plan of the Pre-Hapsburg city heart is itself a Golden Age artefact of fundamental historic and symbolic significance. Why, then, is Pařizka Street an exception to this rule?

There is a sinister explanation for this apparent aberration. Pařizka Street was cut through an area long associated with Jewish culture, which did not seem a worthy part of the city's heritage from an ethnic nationalist perspective. Drawing heavily on Christian symbolism to bridge across other social barriers, and conceiving the cultural landscape as a homeland for the national community thus formed, this could all too easily imply the exclusion of Jews as rootless "wanderers" responsible for the death of Christ himself.

Partly, perhaps, the area was demolished for genuine public health reasons: it had dark, narrow streets, and would have been difficult to bring up to modern standards of hygiene. Franz Kafka, Prague's most famous Jewish writer, himself born in Josefov, another Jewish area of Prague, had this to say of his memories:

Today we walk through the broad streets of the rebuilt city, but our feet and eyes are unsure. Still we tremble inwardly as if we were in the wretched old streets. Our hearts have not yet registered any of the improvements. The old unhealthy Jewish district within us is more real than the new hygienic city around us.[3]

The relative "unreality", to Kafka, of the new hygienic district partly arose, no doubt, from the way in which the new buildings and public spaces "reject" earlier Jewish public buildings – synagogues, school, town hall – of great age and architectural importance. Following the logic we have encountered so far, we should expect these to be celebrated through the city's new spatial structure.

Figure 1.6
(a) The Old Town Hall facade. (b) A Golden Age artefact: the puppet clock Orlož.

Instead, Pařizka Street ignores them altogether. It runs physically close to two major synagogues, but passes at the backs of these ancient monuments to Prague's Jewish culture, at an accidental-seeming angle, so that they can only be entered from minor back streets (Figure 1.9). The Jewish cemetery and the rest of the monumental buildings are also given "back street addresses", in a backwater altogether bypassed by the new public space structure: a symbolic expulsion of Jewry from the city's cultural landscape, which is otherwise so carefully manipulated as an expression of the "national unity" theme.

Continuing along the line of Pařizka Street, we find that this theme is further expressed through a symbolic linkage of town and country, by directing the street's axis across the Vltava River to focus on the wooded cliffs of Letna beyond, where our spatial sequence ends. The strongest potential barrier to this final linkage is the river itself, though its effect is minimised because it is here at its narrowest. The detailed form of the new Svatopluk Cech bridge – designed in 1906 as a modern, forward-looking iron structure by Jan Koula – further reduces the river's disruptive impact on the spatial sequence as a whole; for the tall art-nouveau street lamps which line it on either side, and a pair of monumental columns at the far end, give the space sufficient enclosure to carry across the river without too much of a perceptual break (Figure 1.10).

The emphasis on modernity expressed in the iron structure of Koula's bridge also played an important role when designers explored ways of constructing national identity through the design of individual buildings. The designers involved in these explorations were influenced in part by the rational

Figure 1.7
The Jan Hus monument.

approach to function, structure and construction promoted by the Viennese architect Otto Wagner, who had taught many of Prague's key architects at the Empire's central Academy of Architecture in Vienna, and influenced others by example through his work as *de facto* city architect of Vienna itself (Figure 1.11a).[4] To young designers throughout the Empire, including many from Prague, Wagner was important primarily because of his search for a *Moderne Architektur*: the significant title of his most influential book. This emphasis on modernity seemed essential for constructing imagined national communities able to break free from established cultural and political structures, but Wagner's *particular* conception of modernity, in principle applicable anywhere because its rationality was "above" local cultural differences, seemed inimical to building the

imagined communities they sought. Even his favourite pupil and one-time close colleague, the Slovene architect Jože Plečnik, whose own work we shall see in the next chapter, saw aspects of Wagner's work as "without race, not distinct".[5] New design ideas, different from those of Wagner, were needed to help imagine a new national identity into being in Prague. To follow through their development, we shall have to consider these new ideas in a wider context.

For the architect Pavel Janák, another of Wagner's former pupils, radically new conceptions of form were most likely to be found by emphasising the art dimension of architecture, rather than through Wagner's own emphasis on materials and construction: indeed, Janák called for "their subordination to artistic intention".[6] This subordination did not,

Figure 1.8
Pařizka Street towards Letna.

however, imply abandoning rationality altogether, for an unfettered art of self-expression: "we need a new theory", Janák felt.[7]

The architect Jan Kotěra, from 1898 professor of Architecture at the Prague School of Industrial Arts, saw one way of developing this new theory:

> *Reasoning on the foundation of our popular art, I shall learn what is our own construction, what are our own materials, in order to create a form which will therefore be our own.*[8]

A delicate balancing act was called for to follow this line in practice. To maintain a sense of modernity, the new architecture had to find a way to make strong, clear links between Kotěra's interest in the local rootedness of "our popular art", and radically new conceptions of form.

Ways of making such connections were available within the Paris art-world, linked with the development of Czech nationalist culture since the Impressionists' days. Perhaps the most rebellious movement in Parisian studios around 1909 was Cubism; originally a term of derision, but soon a hot property promoted through Daniel Kahnweiler's influential gallery. Cubist works were well-known to Prague artists almost from their inception. The 1910 exhibition of Cubists' works at the Paris *Salon des Independents* was reviewed by the Czech magazine *Mánes*, and Cubist paintings were also present in Prague in the flesh: Dr Vincenc Kramar began buying works by Braque and Picasso in 1911 and,

Figure 1.9
The Old New Synagogue from Pařizka Street.

building direct contacts with Kahnweiler, had by 1914 accumulated one of the most important collections of Cubist paintings outside France. Prague also hosted Cubist shows organised by the *Skupina Vytvarnych Umelcu* (Group of Art Craftsmen): Picasso, Braque and Gris exhibited in 1912 and 1913, confirming the movement's credibility amongst Prague's intelligentsia, including her architects: Prague was small as major cultural centres go, and architects and painters often frequented the same cafés (Figure 1.11b).

Cubism signified modernity, but that was not its only potential relevance to those seeking a modern *national* identity. In France itself, Cubism was linked to debates about French national identity,[9] and these links were theorised, for example, by Jean Metzinger in his influential *Cubisme et Tradition* of 1911. Extolling the "indispensable mixture of certain conventional signs with new signs",[10] his ideas suggested how

Cubism might offer a way of linking popular culture ("certain conventional signs") with the latest avant-garde significations of modernity.

Links of this kind could easily be imagined between Cubist forms and a particular tradition of "Baroque gothic" architecture found only in Bohemia and Moravia (Figures 1.11c and 1.11d). The Czech architectural historian Vladimir Šlapeta sees this link as a key to understanding the Czech adoption of Cubist forms in architecture:

> *a major inspiration was found in Czech historical architecture: the late-Gothic diamond vaults of Southern Bohemia and Southern Moravia which anticipated the Cubistic morphology, and the sporadic early-eighteenth century work of Giovanni Santini-Aichel, conceived in the spirit of the Baroque Gothic.*[11]

According to François Burckhardt, diamond vaults were still being built until the 1880s,[12] so they offered an almost unbroken tradition of distinctive local precedent to draw on. Certainly this architectural tradition was known amongst Czech avant-garde architects: as Šlapeta points out, "Zdeněk Wirth, an art historian and friend of the *Mánes* Group of Architects, wrote his dissertation on the Czech Baroque Gothic in 1908".[13] Cubism, then, could be imagined as rootedly Czech as well as signifying modernity, but it had yet a further attraction for those trying to transcend the domination of Austrian culture: its forms were strikingly different from the flat, patterned surfaces typical of the Austrian avant-garde of the Viennese Sezession. This difference was clearly valued: as Janák put it, "Olbrich and Hofmann used ornament, where we feel there should have been a plastic form".[14]

All in all then, there were multiple affinities between Cubist forms and the search for a modern Czech identity. There could have been, no doubt, many other potential sources of artistic inspiration available. Some of these might have had powerful connotations of modernity. Others, even, might have had associations with previous Czech architecture, whilst others again might have been suitably *unlike* the latest Austrian forms. But Cubism uniquely lay at the intersection of modernity, Czech history and a rejection of Viennese artistic influences. It was in no

Figure 1.10
Spatial definition across *Svatopluk Cech Bridge*.

sense inevitable, but we can see why Cubism happened in Prague.

In architecture, unlike painting, Czech Cubism was not so much influenced by French experiments as created in parallel with them, and to a far higher level of sophistication. The earliest fully-fledged Cubist building in Prague, Josef Gočár's *House of the Black Madonna* in Celetna Street, was designed in 1911–1912, at about the same time as Raymond Duchamp-Villon's *Maison Cubiste* in Paris.[15] Unlike the Maison Cubiste, which was merely a mock-up exhibited at the *Salon d'Automne*, and which proved a dead-end in the development of French architecture, the House of the Black Madonna – originally a department store – was a major city-centre building, and the precursor of an important line of Czech architectural work (Figure 1.12).

The building follows the lead of French Cubist theory by incorporating Metzinger's "conventional signs"; not only in the Cubist vocabulary's basic reference to the faceted forms of the Gothic Baroque tradition, but also in the way Gočár relates Cubist forms to the precedents set by the earlier buildings which form the Black Madonna's physical context. The building sits at the junction of two streets of different character, and links visual themes from both (Figures 1.13a and 1.13b). Eaves and string courses, at approximately the same levels in both streets, are continued round the corner between them to link them together. The design of the new facade also incorporates pilasters echoing those in the adjoining building on Na Prikope Street, but combines these with large, modern areas of glazing. Potentially these larger windows might have created

29

Figure 1.11
(a) Majolikahaus, Vienna: Otto Wagner. (b) Portrait of Ambroise Vollard: Pablo Picasso, 1909–10. (c) Baroque Gothic vault. (d) Portico of Baroque Gothic inspiration.

a ratio of void to solid alien to neighbouring precedents. This is overcome by moulding the glazed areas into angled, projecting bays which, though made of glass, have enough apparent solidity through their form to match that of the surrounding buildings. Additionally, these faceted forms themselves call on adjacent precedent, echoing the shape of a prominent balcony a little further along Celetna Street; and this restatement of contextual themes continues in the main entrance, hall and stairwell. The entrance portal itself, with its dramatic columns and decorated doors (Figures 1.13c and 1.13d), and the sculptural

stair-hall to which it leads, both come from the same family of forms as certain Baroque entrances nearby (Figure 1.11d).

This way of designing – suggesting a high degree of transculturality by bridging between the traditional roots of popular culture, and the high-art, future-orientated Cubist vocabulary – is used more radically in the work of Josef Chochol; particularly in his apartment block on Neklanova Street, in the suburb of Vyšehrad. Typologically, the Neklanova Street building is a traditional apartment block. Indeed, at a certain level, this building departs from its traditional

Figure 1.12
House of the Black Madonna: general view.

type even less than does the Black Madonna; since the ratio of solid to void in its facades, and the vertical proportions of its windows all follow traditional precedent. The firm use of precedent underlying the design contrasts with vigorous Cubist forms at a more detailed level. The modelling of the external walls is far more dynamic than in the Black Madonna, with the corner carved entirely away to form balconies (Figure 1.14). This use of dramatic angular forms is carried consistently through to details such as windows, doors, and even hardware, so that Cubist modernity is physically felt through the hand each time the door is opened.

It is also felt in the private spaces within, for the cubist movement engaged with the design of all kinds of furnishings, from chairs to ashtrays, in the Wagnerschule tradition of the "total art work".

When taken to extremes, this could have negative implications for the identity-construction process, with expressions of imagined community steam-rollering over any scope for individual choice. The dangers here were noted in 1900 by the architect Adolf Loos; when he satirised the "poor rich man", effectively imprisoned in a home designed in every detail as a total work of art, with no scope left for individual expression.[16]

Despite all the bravura in its details, the Neklanova Street building and its neighbours form a remarkably homogenous district. This is certainly not the result of any attempt on Chochol's part to "keep in keeping" with pre-existing buildings, since his own was constructed before its neighbours on either side. Rather it appears to arise from the fact that all these buildings, Chochol's included, use the same pre-existing type as

Figure 1.13
(a) *Black Madonna* details in context. (b) Rooted but forward-looking details. (c) Entrance to House of the *Black Madonna*. (d) *Black Madonna* stair well.

Figure 1.14
Neklanova Street apartments.

the starting point for their various designs. Indeed, it appears that Chochol's very tight adherence to the type in terms of overall building mass, and of the placing and proportion of the major external elements such as doors and windows, allows him to interpret other more minor elements extremely freely – to a far greater extent than is the case with the Black Madonna – without causing the building to stand out unduly from its surroundings. Stand out it does, but only to the modest extent appropriate to its minor-landmark position at the crossing of two streets and a railway line.

The Neklanova Street building was designed in 1913, just before the outbreak of the First World War. With the dismantling of the Hapsburg Empire at the post-war Treaty of Versailles, the imagined community of the Czechs gained its political

independence. The Czech Republic was formed in 1918 – significantly, independence was declared at the foot of King Wenceslas's statue in Wenceslas Square – and joined by the Slovaks to form Czechoslovakia in 1920. With the Czechoslovak nation state now representing the established status quo, in a context where the manifest horrors of a World War fought in its name had made many progressive people feel that nationalism was utterly bankrupt as a basis for constructing a new post-war identity, the situation now called for new kinds of imagined communities, with new kinds of roots.

The new Czechoslovakia, however, still had its complexly mixed cultural inheritance, with people speaking Czech, Slovak, German, Polish and Yiddish, and with continuing conflicts of economic interest between industrialised and agrarian areas. This complex situation generated serious tensions, expressed politically through disagreement between the ruling Social Democrats and the right-wing Agrarian Party. Tensions worsened during the later 1930s, as Nazi Germany exerted further pressures from outside; claiming to support the interests of Czechoslovakia's sizeable German-speaking minority. Faced with this conflictual situation, progressive designers and their middle-class social democrat clients sought cultural landscapes to support the construction of identities "above" cultural particularism: for obvious reasons, this was a position which attracted support from many of the most progressive Jewish designers. In Prague, the most influential search for these new cultural landscapes took place through the Devĕtsil movement.

In the field of built form, Devĕtsil can be understood as Czech cubism transformed from a nationalist to an internationalist impetus, and therefore shorn of its specifically Czech form-vocabulary. The sharply faceted "Czech" forms which designers like Gočár had earlier used, for example, gave way to a more abstractly geometric vocabulary, shared with progressive designers in many other countries, which was later aptly termed the International Style. This design culture was clearly universalist and internationalist, rather than locally regionalist in its orientation.[17] It sought design principles "beyond" any particular locality, and as part of an international movement developed a vocabulary of forms with no *intentional* reference to any particular local or ethnic tradition, again at all scales from the city to the ashtray in continuation of the "total art work" tradition.

Devětsil was a broadly-based cultural project. During the 1920s, František Šmejkal tells us, it attracted "most progressive writers, painters, architects, photographers, composers, theatre managers, critics and journalists of the young generation".[18] Its values also had an obvious appeal to social-democratic politicians; so that a major part of the great exhibition held at Brno to mark the 10th anniversary of Czechoslovakia's foundation, and to celebrate its new identity, took the form of a small Devětsil housing scheme.

Within Devětsil's broad overall field Karel Teige, the movement's key theorist, tried to reconcile two completely contradictory tendencies. As he himself put it, "Constructivism is a method with rigorous rules, it is the art of usefulness. Poetism, its living accessory, is the atmosphere of life, ... the art of pleasure."[19] Within Devětsil, Constructivism and Poetism related to different cultural fields: built form was to be rigorously Constructivist, whilst the Poetic dimension related to such arts as painting, music and writing.

Constructivism, then, emphasised the importance of issues such as physical health, which mattered equally for all humankind, across *all* imagined communities, rather than more obviously cultural issues such as spirituality or aesthetics, which were seen as Poetism's realms.[20] Teige, writing in 1924 as editor of the architectural magazine *Stavba* (Building), put it like this:

> We refuse, therefore, to allow any aesthetic considerations to predetermine construction, because they hamper the progress of architecture. New architecture must be hygienic. The achievements of medical science should determine layout, construction methods, and town-planning principles. This is all [of] the utmost importance for the health of mankind.[21]

Cut free from any concern for developing roots in the existing cultural structures of real living people, the Constructivist tendency was open to all sorts of

utopian fantasies. Many of these were drawn from the USSR[22] via magazines, through the personal friendships which many Devětsil members formed with the Soviet Press Attaché Roman Jakobson, and through visits to the USSR itself: Teige, for example, went there in 1925. Prominent amongst these utopian ideas was the rejection of contemporary distinctions between public and private; both in the social realm and in its underpinnng spatial structures. Teige himself suggested that

> The smallest apartment in a collective house shall be a cubicle for living in, a room for an adult person. These cubicles shall be arranged in the fashion of a large beehive. The way of leading one's life necessitates abolishment of the traditional family household and socialization of children's upbringing and education. In these cubicles there is no dining room, no living room and no children's room. It is a place for sleeping, for resting alone, for studying and for cultural work, for the intellectual and personal life of each individual.[23]

Such ideas seem to have been roundly rejected, even by convinced Communists. Stephan Templ tells us that when the Communist workers' cooperative Včela held a housing competition in 1931, it rejected such ideas in favour of "traditional 'petty bourgeois' living arrangements and designs".[24]

In terms of getting built forms on the ground, then, a more culturally-rooted line had to be taken, in which Constructivism and Poetism come together. This accommodation can most clearly be seen in Prague's Baba housing area, built under the auspices of the Czech Werkbund from 1932 to 1936.[25] Like Cubist designs before it, Baba was built on foundations of popular culture. First, the overall master plan by Pavel Janák maintained the format of positive public space, in which the fronts of buildings faced the public streets, with the private backs behind them. Second, the importance of historical roots is exemplified by the fact that when pre-Christian archaeology was discovered during preparations for building, the site of these remains was left unbuilt. Third, the planning of the individual dwellings, though often spatially innovative, showed no desire to

Figure 1.15
Baba Master Plan.

promote the radical change of existing family structures. Finally, unlike the various Werkbund estates outside Czechoslovakia, Baba was privately funded in the manner traditional for family houses. In addition, Baba's layout was firmly rooted in its particular landscape: Janák's chequerboard master plan (Figure 1.15) was designed to link all houses to views of the Vltava river landscape below.

Overall, then, Baba's cultural landscape was firmly rooted in culture and place, but its radically "modern", future-orientated detailed appearance (Figures 1.16a and 1.16b) saved it from being merely *stuck* in the past. This particular balance between roots and open futures seems to have been positively received across a wide social spectrum. Certainly the residents themselves, though all relatively well-off, came from a wide range of occupations; from artists through civil servants to the military. Politically too they varied widely, including both a Socialist People's Party representative in the Czechoslovak National Assembly, and an active fascist. Though rejected as "bourgeois" by radicals like Teige, contemporary newspaper accounts suggest that Baba was widely acclaimed. Twelve thousand people visited the estate during its public opening, and Stephan Templ tells us that "even the conservative German-language 'Prager Tagblatt' has something positive to say about the buildings with the flat roofs. Similar critiques can be read in 'Národni Večernik' ". [26]

Its accessible balance between roots and open futures saved Baba from Devětsil's debilitating split between Constructivism and Poetism, which all-too-often meant that Constructivism's attempts to create new, potentially more inclusive cultural landscapes by merely ignoring negative cultural traditions, rather than engaging with them, was in practice doomed to failure. The meanings *intended* by progressive designers were one thing, but the meanings which users actually read into these new forms depended on users' *own* social identities; and in many cases these

Figure 1.16
(a) Baba: general view. (b) Baba: a forward-looking image.

were still structured around imagined communities in which religion and perceived ethnicity continued to play foundational roles. Whatever their designers' intentions, the new "Constructivist" landscapes took on unintended meanings when viewed from some ethnic and religious perspectives. To many, they seemed "foreign", and it was easy for unscrupulous demagogues, noting the major role which Jewish architects played in the functionalist movement, to exacerbate anti-Semitic feelings by interpreting the new architecture as itself "Asiatic" or "Jewish". Baba, by contrast, did not lend itself to manipulations of the kind demonstrated by the Nazi postcard of Stuttgart's Weissenhof housing project, with added palm trees to suggest its similarities to Jewish Haifa or Tel Aviv.

With the ascendancy of anti-Semitism under the Nazis, who occupied Czechoslovakia in 1939, most of Prague's Jewish people were murdered. In parallel with exterminating the people themselves, however, the Nazis built up Prague's Jewish Museum, formerly a very small affair, until it contained some 200,000 items, looted from synagogues all over Czechoslovakia and beyond. Unlike the National Museum in Wenceslas Square, which had been founded to construct an awareness of the historical roots of contemporary achievements, as a foundation for building a national future, the new Jewish Museum sought to portray the Jews as an extinct, exotic people, irrelevant to modern life and with no future at all.

After the Nazis were overthrown in 1945, there were few opportunities to change the cultural landscapes of Prague before Czechoslovakia was taken over as a Russian satellite under Stalin's rule in 1948. Stalin had much earlier rejected and banned constructivism in the USSR, because it merely ignored existing cultures rather than seeking to marshal them in the Communist cause. Stalin supported a "Realist" art, linked to popular culture, which he hoped would be easily understood by the masses, and therefore might act as a good vehicle for state propaganda.[27] Under Stalin, therefore, the "functionalist" architecture of the inter-war avant-garde was emphatically rejected by the state, in favour of a "socialist realist" approach to design. In pursuing the socialist realist project, according to the Russian philosopher Boris Groys, Stalin (like Hitler) was continuing the project of the

total art work, now with immense political power to implement it in reality, rather than as a dream:

> in Stalinist Russia (as well as in Nazi Germany) the project of the avant-garde passed into its final phase: political power refused the favours of the avant-garde artist and itself started the artistic transformation of the world according to its own notions.[28]

True to the total artwork tradition, Socialist Realism was to hold sway over the entire cultural landscape. As theorist G. Nedushivin saw it in 1938, "each railing of a new bridge" was to be thought of as "a link in the chain of the organic ensemble of the city"[29]: a complete submergence of the part in the whole, mirroring and promoting the subservience of the individual to the socio-political system.

As well as bridge railings, the total artwork of socialist realism needed monuments. Since 1948 was the heyday of what Soviet historians have come to call "the cult of the individual" – the individual being Stalin himself – images of the Russian leader were reproduced endlessly across the cultural landscapes of Central and Eastern Europe. The American novelist John Steinbeck, who visited the Soviet Union in 1947, made this note in his diary:

> Everything in the Soviet Union takes place under the fixed stare of the plaster, bronze, drawn or embroidered eye of Stalin … without a doubt, one of the greatest industries in the Soviet Union is the drawing and casting, embroidering and forging of images of Stalin. He is everywhere, he sees everything.[30]

Prague was no exception. In 1949, a monument to Stalin was commissioned as a landmark to complete the vista along Pařizka Street, in what the Czech artist Pavel Büchler was later to see as a symbolic takeover of the spatial sequence we earlier followed from Wenceslas Square:

> At any moment, Stalin would step off the plinth and follow the axis of his gaze on the city plan, across the bridge . . . to the John Huss monument in the Old Town Square. He would extend his hand to the late-fourteenth-century reformist preacher

Figure 1.17
(a) The Stalin monument. (b) Stalin's nemesis: an inflatable Michael Jackson.

and embrace him in the sportsman-like manner in which a champion shows his respect for the loser.[31]

There seems no doubt that the impact of Stalin's socialist realist art really did play a powerful identity-building role for many Central and Eastern European people, even when they despised it *as* art; as the Russian academician Aleksandr Sidorov makes clear:

It was permeated by a feeling for a common cause useful to all and by the immutable, optimistic, triumphant basis on which it operated. Right up to the present day, [he was writing in 1991] this has had an almost irresistible effect upon us Soviets, the contemporaries of another era, and this is so despite our critical attitude towards the 'masterpieces' of Stalinism.[32]

That Prague's particular Stalin had a similar impact, particularly on young people, is confirmed by Pavel Büchler, who recalls having his photo taken next to the Stalin monument as one of his earliest memories: "(it) was a proud moment in which my 5-year-old self enlisted Stalin as the great wonder of the world, and which continued to resonate years later"[33] (Figure 1.17a).

By 1956, however, the cult of Stalin – and with it the Socialist Realist approach to design[34] – had been denounced by a new Russian leadership; and all over Central and Eastern Europe officials were busily organising the removal of his myriad images. Prague's Stalin, however, was immense: 30 metres high, it weighed 14,000 tons – the very hillside beneath it had to be reinforced with concrete – and it had taken 600 men to build it.[35] It was not to be easily demolished. As a stopgap, it was shrouded in scaffolding to block Stalin's gaze, while plans were laid for its destruction. Perhaps not surprisingly, given the resources which had gone into building Stalin in the first place, negotiations to remove him were protracted. In 1990 Jiři Štursa, one of the monument's original designers, recounted the efforts he had made to get official agreement to transform the symbolism of the statue rather than simply destroying it: "it was, after all, part of our history".[36] His suggestions included removing Stalin himself but leaving his supporting cast of workers, or adding new elements to turn the work into a monument to Communist womanhood. "Good advice from Moscow", as Štursa sadly put it, eventually prevailed: Stalin was dynamited in 1962.

Though few regretted the passing of Stalinism as a totalitarian regime, Jiři Štursa was not the only person in Prague to feel ambivalent about the sanitisation of history which the monument's removal entailed. The Czech novelist Milan Kundera, for example, saw it as part of a dangerous process with deep roots in Prague's history, through which that history itself has been continually and systematically erased:

> The street Tamina was born on was called Schwerinova Street. That was during the war, when Prague was occupied by the Germans. Her father was born on Cernokostelecka Avenue. That was under Austria Hungary. When her mother married her father and moved in there, it was Marshal Foch Avenue. That was after the 1914–1918 war. Tamina spent her childhood on Stalin Avenue and it was on Vinohrady Avenue that her husband picked her up to take her to her new home. And yet it was always the same street, they just kept changing its name, brainwashing it into a half-wit.[37]

Not only the names were changed to remove guilty traces:

> Wandering the streets that do not know their names are the ghosts of monuments torn down. Torn down by the Czech Reformation, torn down by the Austrian Counter-Reformation, torn down by the Czechoslovak Republic, torn down by the Communists; even the statues of Stalin have been torn down.[38]

However, the ghosts of the monuments torn down *do* still wander Prague's cultural landscapes. Given the identity impacts of Socialist realism generally, and the Stalin monument in particular, the mere destruction of Stalin as *artefact* was not enough to erase Stalin as *memory*. As Pavel Büchler puts it:

> like many other sites, buildings or institutions which remain known under their original

> denomination long after their function or purpose has changed, "Stalin" is "Stalin" with neither affection nor aversion … "Stalin" is not just a physical location or structure, but an aspect of Prague's genius loci and a state of the city's collective mind.[39]

The process through which Czechoslovakia eventually broke free from Soviet domination, initially with little political power, called once more for the development of new social identities; supported by new tactics to change Prague's cultural landscapes yet again. With no power to initiate changes from above, landscapes were once again transformed from the margins. The landscape of Wenceslas Square, for example, was changed for ever in many people's minds[40] when philosophy student Jan Palach publicly burned himself to death there as a protest in 1968.

The broader idea of developing a "Second Culture" in opposition to the totalitarian First Culture, particularly amongst younger people, was first articulated by the art historian and cultural theorist Ivan Jirous, member of the subversive rock group *Plastic People of the Universe* in 1974.[41] The Plastic People snapped at the heels of the so-called Communist regime with titles like *Egon Bondy's Happy Hearts Club Banned*, with satirical lyrics by the poet Egon Bondy. The violent police repression to which the *Plastic People* and their fans were subjected, catalysed an increasingly widespread sympathy, amongst others from the avant-garde playwright Vaclav Havel, which led directly to the formation of the broader-based Charter 77 human rights movement.

A tactic of *incorporating* the actions of repressive regimes to subvert them, rather than trying to erase them from history, early hinted at in the Plastic People's "Banned" title, became a fundamental principle of later Velvet Revolution works of public art such as *Pink Tank*, where local politicians and art students painted and repainted pink a World War Two Soviet tank used as a war memorial, against continual official counter-paintings. Later, the Stalin monument's indestructible substructure was transformed into *The Bunker* nightclub: again, using the body in "western" dance to express a "free" social identity amongst the relics of repression, and thereby change their meanings in the landscapes of the mind.

What many of these Velvet Revolution tactics had in common was *humour*: an approach whose liberating potential has perhaps been most powerfully expressed from within Soviet totalitarianism itself, by Mikhael Bakhtin:

laughter demolishes fear and piety before an object, before a world, making of it an object of familiar contact and thus clearing the ground for an absolutely free interpretation of it.[42]

After the success of the Velvet Revolution in regaining Czech sovereignty, there are heartening indications that more complex, inclusive but open notions of imagined community might find themselves on Prague's political agenda. Vaclav Havel, now elevated from *Plastic People* supporter to President of the Republic, had this to say when he received a peace prize in 1989:

We are now better equipped than ever before to see the human world as it really is: a complex community of thousands of millions of unique, individual human beings. . . . They must never be lumped together into homogenous masses . . . and then en bloc — as 'classes', 'nations' or 'political forces' — extolled or denounced, loved or hated, maligned or glorified.[43]

The latest step in the Stalin saga seems to reflect this approach very well. During September 1996, Stalin's massive substructure, designed to hold up 14,000 tons, was used to support the unbearable lightness of a huge inflatable figure of Michael Jackson: now, one might hope, indelibly in dialogue with Stalin's ghost in the minds of those who saw it (Figure 1.17b). A monumental example of the liberating power of humour in the cultural landscape, it would be hard to imagine a more suitable figure than Michael Jackson's to infect Stalin's ghost with a spirit of open choice, for as Jean Baudrillard points out, "(he) is . . . an embryo of all the forms of mutation we have imagined to deliver us from race and sex".[44] Clearly, however, this is not just a simple matter of substituting one hero for another, akin to writing a political slogan on a wall. To many, the Jackson image also speaks eloquently of the ascendancy of a vapid consumerism in

Central Europe: no simple-minded extolling or denouncing, loving or hating, maligning or glorification here.

To conclude, our analysis overall brings out a range of useful lessons for designing cultural landscapes from the place-identity perspective, particularly at the level of cultural meanings. In terms of designing to support users in constructing a rooted sense of imagined community, we saw the importance of particular aspects of the pre-existing cultural landscape which can help this "rooting" process. In Prague, the ones thought valuable varied in scale from the whole "golden age" core of the city, through particular spaces such as the Old Town Square or buildings such as churches or the Town Hall, down to small-scale artefacts such as the Orloz clock, and even the naming and re-naming of spaces. In terms of using them in design, we saw ways both of highlighting these aspects of the cultural landscape, and of linking them perceptually together so that the whole is made more than the sum of the parts. We saw highlighting strategies at all scales: streets focused on particular significant buildings; mythically, historically and spiritually significant figures such as Libušine, Wenceslas and Hus dramatised in monuments; these monuments themselves designed to draw further significance through their spatial and visual relationships with the National Museum and the Týn church; and the showcasing of historical events and artefacts within the National Museum itself. And we saw how all these particular highlights were linked together into larger wholes through sequences of public space such as the one we explored from Wenceslas Square to Letna.

Investigating all this, we also learned an important negative lesson: we saw how all these same strategies were used in reverse to downgrade significant Jewish places and buildings, thereby devaluing the role of the Jewish community itself. This tragically negative experience itself suggests a positive lesson: at the outset of the design process we should try to map out as many as possible of the social groups to which members of a place's existing population imagine they belong. In Prague, we found no systematic way of doing this, so this is a topic we shall have to explore further in later chapters. Given the problems we saw in Prague, it seems likely that the better we carry out this preliminary mapping, the better our chances of developing cultural landscapes within which all might live together.

We also found useful lessons – albeit many of them also negative ones – in terms of designing to support users in developing a sense of empowerment *vis a vis* their own particular imagined communities. We saw problems with both utopian Constructivist and Socialist Realist attempts to foster the creation of new progressive, empowered identities. On the one hand Constructivism ignored real, existing communities' cultures, trying to promote the construction of new identities from a cultural blank sheet which can never in reality exist. On the other hand, Stalin's Socialist Realism did try to engage with real existing cultures, but was ultimately unable to do so because its totalitarian lack of choice ignored the increasingly widespread importance of choice itself as a key cultural value.

We also found both negative and positive lessons in relation to the design of cultural landscapes to subvert the meanings associated with disempowering regimes. In Prague, we found a number of approaches to this issue. We suggested that attempts to sanitise history, by tearing down statues or renaming streets, merely sweep transcultural problems under the carpet rather than helping work them through. More positively, we saw the Velvet Revolution's creative strategies for subverting the meanings of negative landscapes, through changes of use such as *The Bunker* nightclub or events where art and humour elide, such as the *Pink Tank* repainting, and the inflatable Michael Jackson. Interestingly, in Prague none of these positive subversive strategies involved architecture, urban design or town planning as usually conceived. They all involved elements of shock or surprise, in which people are "taken out of themselves by art", to recall Arthur Danto's phrase. It seems difficult for relatively permanent buildings or public spaces to have this kind of impact: not only does their expense require support from the very agencies currently in economic or political power, but also their permanence itself leads to habituation; so that shock wears off and humour wears thin. At least in terms of the strategies used in Prague, the more permanent components of cultural landscapes do not themselves seem to be

media for protest, so much as media through which the impact of protest might be stabilised and reinforced.

Finally, we can learn a great deal from the Prague story in terms of designing to support the members of each imagined community in living harmoniously with other communities. Particularly at the detailed scale of design, we saw how Czech Cubism sought an architecture rooted but not stuck in the past, developing a form-vocabulary which linked the sense of local roots offered by the uniquely Bohemian baroque-gothic, with the (non-Hapsburg) modernity of Parisian cubist art. We saw how this vocabulary was creatively adapted to its urban context to support a sense of continuity in the city's public realm, where all communities meet; and we saw how a sense of open futures was still further supported by those aspects of inter-war modernism which avoided Devětsil's later split between Poetism in art and Constructivism in design.

That enervating split was mostly avoided in the design ideas which were developed, largely from origins within the Prague cultural milieu, in the nearby new state of Yugoslavia during the interwar years. We might therefore hope to learn fruitful new lessons there; and it is these which the next chapter seeks.

Notes

1 For discussion of nineteenth-century censorship, see Goldstein, 1989.
2 For early cultural influences from foreign visitors, see Charvat and Prosecky (eds), 1996.
3 Cited in Institute of Contemporary Arts, 1983.
4 For insights into the links between Wagner's teaching and Central European architecture in general, see Pozzetto, 1979.
5 Plečnik, 1908, 115–116, cited in Šlapeta, 1986, 85.
6 Cited in Margolius, 1979, 35.
7 Ibid.
8 Kotera, 1900, 92, cited in Kubová and Ballangé, 1986, 97.
9 For discussion of these links, see Antliff, 1992.

10 Cited in Antliff and Leighten, 2001, 115.
11 Šlapeta, 1992, 37.
12 Burckhardt, 1992, 9B.
13 Šlapeta, 1992.
14 Cited in Margolius, 1979, 35.
15 For discussion of the Maison Cubiste, see Cottington, 1997.
16 Loos, 1966 (1900), 223–225.
17 This is not to say that this was a totally homogenous movement: for an interesting discussion of subcurrents within it, see Šlapeta, 1996.
18 Šmejkal, 1990, 9.
19 Cited in Šmejkal, op. cit., 18.
20 For an exploration of the genesis of this particular design culture, see Gartman, 2000.
21 Cited in Lešnikowski, 1996, 15.
22 For discussions of Soviet influences, see Šmejkal, op. cit., 13.
23 Teige, 1932, cited in Templ, 1999, 19.
24 For discussion, see Templ, 19.
25 For an excellent account of Baba, on which this section draws, see Templ, 1999.
26 Templ, op. cit., 36.

27 For discussion, see Bown, 1991, 92.
28 Groys, 1993.
29 Nedushivin, 1938, 22 cited in Bown, 1991, 76.
30 Cited in Bown, 1991, 175.
31 Büchler, 1997, 26.
32 Sidorov, 1991, 17.
33 Büchler, 1997, 26.
34 For discussion of the demise of Socialist Realism in Czechoslovakia, see Åman, 1992.
35 Büchler, op. cit., 27.
36 Discussion between the authors and Jiři Štursa, December 1990.
37 Kundera, 1996 (1978), 216–217.
38 Ibid., 217.
39 Büchler, 1997, 32.
40 For discussion of the potential power of short-lived interventions, see Freshman, 1993, 20–21.
41 For an account of the *Plastic People*, see Yanosik, 1996 and Riedel, 1999.
42 Bakhtin, 1990 (1981), 23.
43 Havel, 1989, cited in Sayer, 1991, viii–ix.
44 Baudrillard, 1990, 147.

2

Plečnik's Ljubljana: The social relevance of a personal vision

In the last chapter, we saw that Czech Cubism offered valuable ideas about identity by design. These ideas were developed more richly, and with wider relevance, in Ljubljana, in the nearby new State of Yugoslavia; particularly by the architect Jože Plečnik from 1920 until his death in 1957. In this chapter, we shall explore Plečnik's work.

Plečnik was involved in the early development of Czech Cubism in Prague. As we saw, Czech Cubism was developed into functionalism during the period after the First World War; in the process largely losing touch with the rootedness of popular culture. In Ljubljana, however, the situation was different. Here, Plečnik continued to develop the positive place-identity potentials which Cubism had embodied, to a far higher level of sophistication. To understand these developments, we first have to understand something of Plečnik's own early background.

Plečnik is usually thought of above all as an *artist* architect: Pavel Janák, whose work we also encountered in the last chapter, once referred to him as "an artist who simply builds".[1] Though Plečnik certainly did see architecture as an art form, he did not take a simplistic "art for art's sake" approach. His personal conception of art was intimately linked to social values and to religion. Born into a deeply Catholic family, he was exposed to a particular, socially concerned approach to religious values from his earliest years: the family subscribed, for example, to the very liberal newspaper *Slovenski Narod* (Slovene People).[2] Later, the links he saw between religious and social values attracted him to the teachings of the Benedictine Beuron Congregation, whose members

sought to develop the active participation of the people in the church's official worship. To bring this about, they had to find ways of bridging between popular culture and the church's official institutions; for example by reading out the litany in the local vernacular language in the body of the church, at the same time as the priest celebrated in Latin. The Beuron Congregation also saw art as an important bridge between official worship and people's everyday experience, and founded a school of religious art with this in mind. Influenced by this kind of thinking, much of Plečnik's mature design work is shot through with similarly motivated – but increasingly sophisticated – approaches to integrating the voices of popular "low" and official "high" cultures, in a search for cultural landscapes with a broad social relevance.

Plečnik was drawn to this transcultural approach to design at least partly because he spanned between popular and elite cultures through his own life trajectory. At the level of language, one of culture's foundations, Plečnik was born a Slovene speaker in a context where German was the dominant Imperial tongue. To carve out a career in architecture, he had to become fluent in German: the need to build bridges between popular and elite cultures was necessary for his very survival in his chosen *métier*.

Plečnik also had to build bridges between social class positions. Born into an artisan family, and not performing well in his basic schooling, he entered his father's joinery workshop as an apprentice in 1886, at the age of 14 years. His apprenticeship gave him a lasting feeling and respect for the craftsman's role in the production of architecture, but his outstanding design ability gained him a scholarship to the Technical School in Graz in 1888. Graduating in 1891, he joined the Viennese furniture firm of Müller but soon became frustrated with the restricted field of furniture design. In 1894 he showed a portfolio of drawings to Otto Wagner, then professor of architecture at the Vienna Academy, who was sufficiently impressed to offer him a place in the first year of his course; but shortcomings in his formal education soon forced Plečnik to withdraw. By 1895, however, he had returned to the Academy and was working in Wagner's office as well. Talent and diligence won him a Rome Scholarship in 1898, and this gave him the opportunity to study Italian architecture first hand. After graduating in 1898, Plečnik became a member of the Vienna Secession. By 1905 he had become its secretary, and had achieved an eminent position in the Viennese *avant-garde*. His acceptance into the design elite seemed complete.

On his own retirement in 1911, Wagner proposed that Plečnik should take over his professor's chair at the Academy of Building Art; but Archduke Franz Ferdinand, the Empire's heir apparent, was firmly against him: his candidature was three times rejected. Plečnik himself always believed he was rejected on ethnic grounds, and this strengthened his consciousness of his own Slav origins. Meanwhile his friend Jan Kotěra, with whom Plečnik had studied at the *Wagnerschule*, had for some time been trying to persuade him to leave Vienna for Prague, the pre-eminent Slav cultural centre. In 1912, disillusioned with his situation in Vienna, Plečnik took up the post of Professor of architecture at Prague's school of decorative arts, where he stayed until the breakup of the Austro-Hungarian Empire after the First World War; playing an integral role in the development of the nationalist architecture we discussed in the last chapter.

With the post-war formation of a new Kingdom of the Serbs, Croats and Slovenes, later to be called Yugoslavia, a new University was set up in Ljubljana, the Slovene capital, with a school of architecture organised by Ivan Vurnik, another fellow student of Plečnik's in Vienna. Offered a Chair in this new school, Plečnik left for Ljubljana in 1920, though he continued to work on projects in Prague for many years.

From this time until Yugoslavia was occupied during the Second World War – a period of more than 20 years – Plečnik had great architectural authority in Ljubljana; holding the posts of Professor of Architecture and (de facto) City Architect; just as his mentor Otto Wagner had earlier done in Vienna. Close friendships with Matko Prelovšek, the City Engineer, and with France Stelè, art historian and city councillor, helped with public commissions; whilst both his nationalism and the intensity of his religious beliefs now stood him in good stead: the former, such a disadvantage in the days of the Austro-Hungarian Empire, now seemed highly attractive in official circles; whilst his religious stance found favour amongst the influential Catholic intelligentsia grouped around the journal *Dom in Svet* (Home and Faith).

When Plečnik returned to Ljubljana in 1920 he was nearly 50 years old, and already had a considerable reputation as a mature and accomplished designer of buildings, interiors and furniture. The search for an environment possessing great variety and richness within a powerful overall order runs through Plečnik's work at all physical scales. At each scale, Plečnik sought to support the new sense of national identity; but even an architect as creative and experienced as he could not conjure a new architecture, appropriate to the new spirit of independence, from thin air. It could not be "made-up", as it were, by one man or even by one group of people: that would probably render it strange, incomprehensible and alienating to others, at least until years of familiarisation had passed. In terms of supporting a sense of national identity, that alienating quality would have been counter-productive indeed; so the new architecture had to be designed around common elements of experience – traditions – appropriate to as many social groups as possible. But since these groups ranged from illiterate peasants to a highly educated cosmopolitan elite, there was no widely shared design tradition. It was necessary to explore ways in which several different traditions could co-exist in one architecture; reinforcing one another so that a single building could carry associations appropriate to all social groups. The associations themselves had to be of two kinds: it was necessary to promote both a sense of Sloveneness and a sense of democracy, to replace the overtones of foreign autocracy which were implicit in much of the existing environment.

These overtones arose because major commercial and public building before 1918 had been commissioned by the dominant (mostly Austrian) institutions of the time. They were mostly designed within the *Wagnerschule* tradition, and had therefore acquired strong associations with colonial rule. Plečnik himself could hardly be expected to escape the influence of the *Wagnerschule*. As Wagner's designated successor, this tradition formed one natural basis of Plečnik's own designs.

On the other hand, the *Wagnerschule* clearly also represented the Austrian presence. In Ljubljana its clearest expression was in Slovene Square. Here each building's façade has a taut unity, within which the individual architectural elements are firmly subordinated to the overall concept (Figure 2.1). The same is true of the square as a whole; within which each building is no more than a mere incident. Equal bay widths, consistent building height and corners emphasised by symmetrically placed towers, are all devices which make the unity of the whole square

prevail over the expression of its individual buildings. It is not only the buildings' style which speaks of Austria: the whole concept of the square, a concept of limited individual freedom within a strong externally imposed framework of rules, is an analogue of Teutonic order; quite inappropriate as an expression of the new Yugoslav society.

To counter this aspect of the *Wagnerschule*, Plečnik could call upon a second tradition: that of the craftsman within which he had spent his first creative years; but this had evolved for building farmhouses, barns and the like (Figure 2.2), which restricted its usefulness as a direct model for a public architecture. This was a serious limitation, since it was above all urban public buildings which had previously carried the colonial stamp, and which therefore stood in particular need of a new architectural expression. Certain decorative details, and a penchant for designing with large exposed sections of stone and timber, were the craft vernacular's only direct contributions to the detailed vocabulary of a new national architecture.

Finally, there was a third design tradition on which Plečnik could draw. Through centuries old trade links

Figure 2.1
Wagnerschule buildings in Slovene Square.

Figure 2.2
A vernacular barn near Ljubljana.

with Venice, Ljubljana had a fine stock of buildings in a somewhat homespun version of the Italian Baroque; strongly Mediterranean, rather than Teutonic in character. These constituted a design tradition free from Austrian associations, and well adapted for public buildings. But the Slovenes had no more wish to be Italian than they had to be Austrian, so the Italian Baroque could not be taken literally. For most people its elements – columns, pediments and so forth – had appropriate associations of "public building", but the Baroque had to be transformed to enable it to take on associations of "*Slovene* public building". Early in his career Plečnik had been interested in the transformations to which established architectural systems could be subjected: amongst the photographs which he sent home to his family from his 1899 Italian tour were, significantly enough, two illustrations of Michelangelo's Laurentian Library (Figure 2.3). Michelangelo's mannerist reversals of the usual relationships between the elements of classical architecture foreshadow much in Plečnik's own work.

Plečnik used his own home as a test bed for developing his design ideas, so it is instructive to explore his house in more detail. All three-design traditions – the craft vernacular, the Mediterranean

Figure 2.3
Michelangelo's mannerism: Laurentian Library.

classical and the *Wagnerschule* – were called upon in this, his first design after his return from Prague. The house seems, at first glance, to be a vernacular building (Figure 2.4a). It was formed by converting and extending an old house, in a quiet street which to this day retains the village flavour it had in the 1920s, when the area was an outlying suburb. Vernacular associations are contradicted, however, by the design of the walls around the entrance. Here the house's original rendered walls are cased in a precise, patterned skin, as a *Wagnerschule* building might have been.

Any potentially Viennese overtones of this skin, however, are contradicted by its construction as a collage of as-found fragments (Figure 2.4b). Bricks, blocks, limestone, marble and granite are all used; but even when the fragments are irregular they are assembled with great precision into a very smooth skin. Projecting from this, placed high to emphasise their precious nature, are various carved stone capitals and mouldings salvaged from old buildings. An attitude of respect for other people's work, implied by the re-incorporation of these elements, is reinforced by the appearance through the new skin, like a fossil in the face of a quarry, of one of the house's original vernacular windows. The new skin is carried over the old window by a massive (but broken) stone lintel, simultaneously raising and dispelling questions about whether the skin is structural or decorative.

The imagery here carries participatory associations in at least five ways. First, it refers to all three local traditions – the tiled roof and rolled eaves of the craft vernacular, the smooth patterned skin of the *Wagnerschule*, with a craftsmanly expression of its constituent parts denying its Austrian associations, and the carved stone fragments of the classical tradition. This multiple reference gives it broad appeal, across narrow social boundaries.

Second, the complex collage skin could not have been designed on paper: even measuring all the fragments would have been a stupendous task. Since it is unlikely that Plečnik would have had time to direct every step of the masons' work, there must have been some worker participation in designing this aesthetically critical element.

Third, the house re-uses parts of other buildings – capitals and mouldings, fragments of polished stone

and the original window. An attitude of respect for the work of their anonymous builders is made explicit in the new design.

Fourth, the wall is a riddle. In its design it constantly contradicts the usual connotations of architectural elements: the peasant building with a sophisticated skin, the mouldings and capitals wrenched out of context, the non-structural skin which yet has a lintel to carry it over a window, and the use of a *broken* lintel to show that it is *not* structural after all: there is plenty here to fascinate people interested in unravelling riddles. This is not a matter of mere *divertimenti*, for riddles like these encourage a participatory relationship between user and building by promoting a creative approach to perception. All perception has *some* creative element, but the creativity involved in solving a riddle is much greater than that required in ordinary perception. The exhilarating "Eureka!", which is the reward for solving a riddle, is the common ground of all creative endeavour: the "environment as riddle" provokes a creative, participatory response from those who use it. Others – probably many – do not find the built environment a congenial creative medium, and are therefore not interested in such participatory games. For them, Plečnik's wall has enough conventionally "beautiful" elements to be consumable, passively, with pleasure.

Lastly, there is an "open-ended" quality about the wall which suggests that it is legitimate to extend or alter it. For instance, many of the collage fragments are of red brick or clay block whose appearance, even today, implies "incompleteness" in a city where by tradition virtually all buildings are rendered. This open-ended quality is reinforced by the adjoining veranda with its "temporary" corrugated roof on flimsy steel supports, and is also carried through in the house's additive massing (Figure 2.5), which suggests the possibility of making a wide range of equally "sympathetic" additions.

The concepts developed at a small scale in his own house were selectively employed in larger-scale urban interventions. The importance of the part in relation to the whole implied a mistrust of "top down" design approaches of the "total art work" kind, and therefore of town planning as a design field: Plečnik had not previously worked at the town planning scale, and we are told that he himself felt that he had no

Figure 2.4
(a) Plečnik's house: street view. (b) Plečnik's house: walling detail.

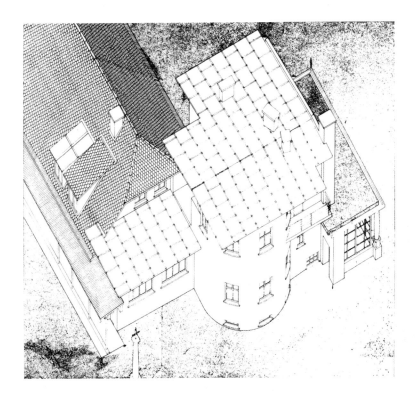

Figure 2.5
Plečnik's house: additive massing.

particular talent for such work.[3] That is not to say that he was not interested in how individual projects contributed to larger urban wholes: rather, he rejected the idea that the large-scale plan should *determine* the constituent parts. Instead, he favoured an approach in which individual projects, addressing particular problems and opportunities as they arose, were each designed in relation to the pre-existing context; to build up to an ever-evolving whole: the overall plan as result rather than generator.

This "bottom up" attitude to urban design had much in common with the craft approach to design which Plečnik had learned in his father's workshop. Because of the limitations of materials, tools and workmen's capabilities, most large craft objects are built up from component parts. Though the craftsman knows perfectly well that in the end the parts gain their significance by being parts of a larger whole, it is nevertheless the *part* on which he works, and which is in the forefront of his mind for much of the time. Parts have an inherent importance for the craftsman, which they often lack

for more academically trained designers: hence the vigorous way in which parts are expressed in many design traditions where the craftsman is himself the designer. If a *Wagnerschule* environment speaks of limited individual freedom within a strong framework of rules, then the craft tradition can be seen as its converse. If the one is an analogue of an imposed Teutonic order, then the other suggests an order made up from accommodations between individual elements; expressing a more democratic spirit appropriate to the new national space, and liberating Plečnik from the potentially totalitarian grip of the "total art work" tradition, leaving him free to generate an overall spatial structure in which each part had its own clear autonomy, as well as contributing to a coherent larger whole which was greater than the mere sum of the constituent parts.

Pursuing this approach, it is not surprising that Plečnik's first Ljubljana interventions took place without him developing any plan for the city as a whole. Central government, however, demanded that all major Yugoslav cities develop master plans, so Plečnik was called on to produce one for Ljubljana. His approach to this new scale of work drew creatively on the ideas we have already explored in his own house. In particular, both his respect for the work of others and his consequent willingness to incorporate "as-found" elements in his own work are carried through to the larger urban scale. His desire to give importance to the smaller scale, local "part" leads him to seek ways of bringing out the different potentials of different types of urban situations within a nonetheless coherent whole. To do this, he makes creative use of "as found" plans by a variety of other designers.

A rich source of such ideas was provided by plans which had been developed after a catastrophic earthquake in 1895 had damaged or destroyed many buildings, leaving many areas in urgent need of repair. On the initiative of the Town Council, under the leadership of Ivan Hribar, the city's first Slovene mayor, a number of eminent architects, both Slovene and foreign, had been invited to prepare plans in a competition to address some of the city's immediate post-earthquake problems, and also to regulate future urban growth. A number of competition entries had been prepared, of which the most significant for Plečnik's own later plan were those of Camillo Sitte and Max Fabiani; and later work by Ciril Metod Koch which showed how ideas from both might be synthesised.

Sitte's plan offered ideas in relation to the older parts of the city, of which Plečnik was particularly fond. It followed the aesthetic ideas set out in his influential book *Planning According to Artistic Principles*,[4] a copy of which had formed part of his competition submission. The design created major vistas oriented towards the Castle, and also respected and reinforced the different characteristics of the historic parts of the city remaining at this period: at the time of the earthquake, the city contained morphologically distinct elements from various periods of urban development. Firstly, there persisted remnants of the layout of the Roman settlement of Emona. Secondly there were three medieval units – Mesto, Old Market (Stari Trg) and New Market (Novi Trg). Thirdly, eighteenth- and nineteenth-century residential development spread along the major regional roads.

Sitte's plan took the logic of these existing patterns as the basis for his new proposals. For example, new development on the left bank of the Ljubljanica river was intended to continue and reinforce the pattern of the Mesto area, below the Castle hill on the opposite bank, whilst the land subdivision pattern proposed for the Old Market (Stari Trg) followed the lead of earlier medieval layouts.

In considering how to expand the city into previously undeveloped areas of countryside, Plečnik tied "nature" into the heart of Ljubljana's overall cultural landscape through a green wedge formed by Tivoli Park; linking the city centre outwards into the relatively undeveloped countryside through an avenue of large trees, whose significance is reinforced by an "axis of light" tying together "human" and "natural" realms (Figure 2.6). Functional considerations of infrastructure were also of fundamental importance. Here Plečnik was strongly influenced by Fabiani's plan, which established functional linkages between the various parts of the city. In Plečnik's design, however, the street layout is used to far greater "artistic" effect; achieving a great variety of spatial experience through a combination of straight and curved streets, whilst at the same time giving the city a strong spatial structure with major avenues reinforced by large-scale tree planting, and marked by public buildings located at key points. The overall impression is of a fan-like form, achieved by a combination of axial avenues and curved residential roads (Figure 2.7).

The radial streets extending from the city centre were further linked by a new peripheral ring road of a far more rural character, placed amongst "*fields and trees through which extended a major curvilinear road surrounded by at least half a thousand vegetable gardens providing the greenery which is always needed in a modern city*".[5] Here we see the influence of a third strand of town planning theory: the "Garden City" ideas of Ebenezer Howard,[6] to which Plečnik was attracted because of his interest in the role of nature in human life, and which he called on in forming the basic tissues of the areas between his functional radial avenues, with relatively low densities and with terraced or detached family houses placed amongst gardens and parks.

From this synthesis of the functional, artistic and Garden City approaches to planning, Plečnik developed three key themes which were to underlie his subsequent work. First, there is the search for a

Figure 2.6
Axis of light through *Tivoli Park.*

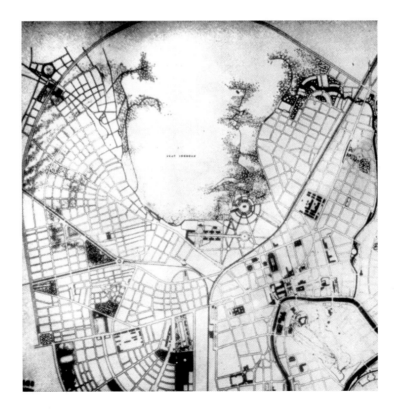

Figure 2.7
Ljubljana Master Plan.

powerful spatial structure to serve as a general framework for development, and regulating the location, scale and types of the smaller elements of the city. Second, there is a parallel search for a diversity and variety of individual spaces and buildings, freely expressed within this general structure. Third, there is the idea that out of the juxtaposition of overall (public) order and detailed (private) variety would arise an environment appropriate in social terms, validly expressing both communal and individual interests.

His artisan interest in the practicalities of how things are made is carried creatively through in considering how these concepts might be realised in practice, rather than merely being drawn on paper. For example, the plan itself proposed a number of changes in the land ownership pattern and the system of local government. These involved, for example, proposing that the City Council should have powers of compulsory land purchase, together with measures to prevent land speculation. They were never accepted by the powers that be, which in part explains why Plečnik's plan proved largely impotent in the face of political and economic pressures beyond any designer's control: a fact which reinforced his innate mistrust of town planning work, and his preference for working towards larger wholes through smaller-scale interventions. Many of these interventions were inspired through direct experience, in the course of Plečnik's own walks through the city;[7] so let us explore a selection of them through one such walk from his house through the city centre and back.

Next door to Plečnik's house is the nineteenth-century church of Janez Krstnik, built next to the small river Gradaščica, with very little space between its front and the riverbank. Here, in 1932, Plečnik built a new bridge; at one level merely a functional link, but also designed with sufficient width to create in effect a parish square in front of the church itself, to form a gathering place for "us" to replace the river's former separation between "us" and "them".

A spirit of co-dwelling with nature is also created here, both by positioning a human-use place directly above the natural system of the river itself, and also by enclosing the bridge–square with birch trees planted on the bridge itself, giving natural elements a central role in the creation of the human space, in a way which is dramatised through the almost surreal unfamiliarity of a forest on a bridge (Figure 2.8a).

The rows of trees, which continue from the church along Emonska Street into the heart of the city, echo in the public space the rows of the columns inside the sacred space of the church itself. Together with stone pyramids on the bridge balustrade, which exactly echo the angles of the gables and spires of the church itself (Figure 2.8b), the trees suggest an interpenetration of the sacred and secular realms, infusing the public space with ethical meaning, and reminding the religious of their social responsibilities.

If we follow the Gradaščica river downstream, we find ourselves walking through a narrow but lush linear park, defined by a mixture of chestnut and weeping willow trees. The chestnuts pre-date Plečnik's intervention: with their high crowns allowing clear views under their branches, they define the space but provide little intimacy. Plečnik therefore interspersed them with informally spaced weeping willows, whose low branches create a far greater sense of a green urban oasis, within which one can have the choice to feel private in the city's public space (Figure 2.9). At intervals, steps and paths give access from the upper banks to the water itself – in summer a mere trickle running in a narrow channel in the smoothly paved river bed – along which one can walk below the level of the surrounding housing, with only the sound of water for company (Figure 2.8b). Again, a sense of co-dwelling with nature within the urban environment is powerfully promoted in a very small space.

Walking further along this green space, we come to the confluence with the wider river Ljubljanica: here we have our first view of the city's castle on its high bluff. To make the most of this symbol of historical roots, Plečnik treats this as a key location. On the south side of the confluence, he formed a series of stone picnic terraces so that people could linger down at water level, in spaces again made intimate by weeping willow foliage (Figure 2.10a). To the north, he proposed a small square with a view of the castle, defined by the rivers on two sides, with the remaining edges formed by an unexecuted project for Houses under a Common Roof. Here local

Figure 2.8
(a) Janez Krstnik Bridge: general view. (b) Janez Krstnik Bridge: view of the river below.

Figure 2.9
The green oasis of Gradaščica's banks.

(a)

HIŠE
POD
OBČINSKO STREHO

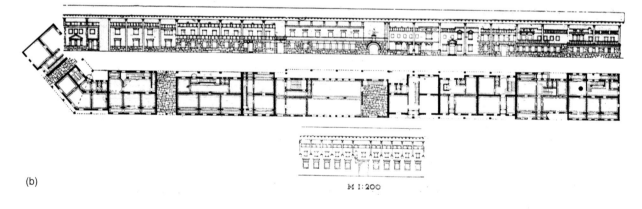

(b)

M 1:200

Figure 2.10
(a) Ljubljanica terraces in winter. (b) Houses under a common roof.

Figure 2.11
(a) *Shoemakers' Bridge*: dovetailed into the earlier urban fabric. (b) *Shoemakers' Bridge*: site of a summer open-air café.

government was to have provided basic supports of roof and services, opening up the potential for individual and family involvement in particular house designs, to create an overall image which supports the sense of individuals as able to influence the larger collective in significant ways (Figure 2.10b).

Turning north along the Ljubljanica's west bank, crossing the line of the old city wall into the historic core, the character of the riverbanks changes from rural to become increasingly formal. Plečnik modifies the utilitarian quality of the pre-existing banks, created by the engineer Keller in 1913, by adding an intermediate planted ledge between the bankside streets and the level of the water; with occasional steps down to water level, and small projecting viewing platforms providing a choice of waterside experiences.

Where benches are provided, they too contribute to the sense that one is approaching the city centre. At the rural edge near the Gradaščica, benches are simple and utilitarian, of unmoulded concrete with timber seats and with logs as backrests. As the city centre is approached, the benches – still of the same generic type to reinforce the overall unity of the public realm – take on an increasingly detailed formality. This increases the legibility of the urban structure as a whole through its details; thereby strengthening the overall expression of "us", whilst expressing the importance of the part in relation to the whole.

Plečnik planned a series of bridges, to zip the two sides of the river together to form a more unified overall structure, but as yet only two have been built. The first we encounter on our walk – Shoemakers' bridge – again takes the form of a small public square; its axis focused on the castle above, and its platform carefully dovetailed into the public spaces to which it links on either bank (Figures 2.11a and 2.11b). The space of this square – more urban in character than that at Trnovo – is this time defined not by trees but by freestanding columns. Despite the lack of greenery here, however, the sense of co-dwelling with nature comes over very strongly from the positioning of the human-use space – the site of an open-air café in summer – directly over the natural system of the river itself (Figure 2.11b).

The columns which define the space of the bridge create a continuity with the pilasters of the pre-existing buildings at either end of the bridge, linking old and new into a single composition. The sense of roots created by these historical links, however, is counterpointed by the non-traditional nature of the bridge/square type itself, and also by constructing it in modern reinforced concrete, with precast details, rather than in traditional materials. This is no simple exercise in "keeping in keeping": it is very much "rooted but not stuck in the past".

Crossing Shoemakers' Bridge we enter Mesto, the oldest part of the city. This was traditionally the site of many Jewish businesses, but rather than wanting a Prague-style demolition, this was an area which Plečnik especially loved: *If one . . . walks along the beautiful curve of the main street, which softly follows the natural line of the foothill, one will certainly feel an intuitive love for the beautiful gables of the old houses.*[8] Following the curve of the river along the east bank, we come to the next of Plečnik's bridge interventions, carried out to relieve congestion on Francisco Camolo's 1841 bridge to St Mary's Square. Plečnik's original idea was to widen the bridge to form a new civic square spanning the river, as he had done at Trnovo and Shoemakers' bridges. In the end, however, his interest in historical continuity – he was in principle opposed to the removal of old buildings[9] – led him to retain the existing bridge; supplementing it with new pedestrian ones on either side.

The design of the new concrete bridges retains the sight of the older stone structure from both directions along the river (Figure 2.12a), maintaining familiar views of the historical crossing place; but the whole ensemble is unified by replacing the older concrete bridge's iron balustrades with new concrete ones, and by tall concrete lamp standards. Together, the balustrades and lamps give a strong visual definition to the space of the Three Bridges as a single unit; again emphasising the unity of the public space structure against the river's potentially sundering impact (Figure 2.12b).

A sense of co-dwelling with nature is also rein-forced by the integration of trees into the spatial structure of the bridge ensemble. Planted in the gaps between the bridges on the banks below, these trees grow up through the bridge level, so that the unusual experience of walking at crown rather than trunk

Figure 2.12
(a) The old bridge glimpsed through the new. (b) The three bridges as a single unit.

level foregrounds their importance in the minds of passers by.

Other values too are supported through the spatial structure here. In one direction, the geometry of the whole ensemble is focused on the historic symbol of the Castle. In the other, the most intensively used of the pedestrian bridges focuses in the foreground on a statue of the national poet France Prešern and his muse, seen against the more distant landmark of the tower of the Franciscan church: the same synthesis of national and religious values we encountered so many times in Prague (Figure 2.13a).

Once across the Three Bridges, and turning back along the opposite bank in the direction we came from, Plečnik's ability to see larger-scale potentials even in the smallest interventions comes over very strongly in his design for one of the quayside lamp standards. Here the form of the lamp itself operates

as a riddle – why on *earth* is it this weird shape? – and then suggests an answer: its family resemblance to the distant silhouette of the Ursuline church brings the church itself into a far stronger perceptual relationship with the major structuring element of the river sequence itself (Figure 2.13b).

Continuing along the bank, we come to the square Novi Trg and the National University Library (NUK). When Plečnik began designing NUK in 1931, Yugoslav independence was a mere 13 years old. As the scheme progressed, the growth of Fascism in nearby Italy followed by the German takeover of neighbouring Austria in 1938, gave warning that this hard-won independence might not last much longer. When the building was finished in 1941, Ljubljana was already occupied by Italian troops.

Against this background, there was clearly a role for architecture in reinforcing the national image, as

Figure 2.13
(a) Superimposing Prešern and the church tower. (b) A lamp links to the Ursuline church.

literature had traditionally done. Nineteenth-century Slovene romantic writers, keeping alive the Slovene language and a spirit of national unity during the Austrian occupation, were popularly acclaimed as national heroes: early anti-fascist Partisan battle units, formed around the time NUK was finished, named themselves after the authors France Prešern and Ivan Cankar. NUK, as the repository of a literature so emotionally charged, was a building of the highest symbolic importance.

The attempt to realise this potential as a symbol of national unity governs much of NUK's design, but this interacts with an equally intense desire for the building to reinforce the image of its urban context. This strong contextual concern is shown by the form of presentation chosen for early publicity material for NUK: in both plan and section, the urban context is shown as being equal in importance to the new building itself (Figure 2.14a).

This contextual concern has various design implications. First of all, three sides of the building can be seen, at long range, from several different points in the streets and squares around. For the building to work as an identifiable landmark from all directions, these views must share a strong resemblance; so that the building needs three similarly designed facades. This idea is reinforced by the expectation – probably shared by virtually everyone at that time and place – that any important public building should be symmetrical.

The distant image of the building is strengthened by the design of its exterior which, as a strident pattern of red brick and white stone, stands out clearly from its surroundings. Closer to, NUK reinforces its immediate context in several ways. First, its bulk gives strong enclosure to the corner of Novi Trg (Figure 2.14b). On the other side, it defines Vegova Street, which is very wide, by a high mass which rises above the adjoining buildings to add to the enclosure of Trg Francoske Revolucije.

The massive, highly patterned block which fits these general requirements is modified to make special design responses to the varied urban spaces which surround it. The enclosure of Trg Francoske Revolucije is strengthened by increasing the building's scale at the corner with a giant column four storeys high, displayed against a setback of dark glass (Figure 2.15a).

Gosposka Street poses the opposite problem: how to reduce the block to a smaller scale in this relatively narrow space. First, the device of setting back and glazing the end of the block, which increased the scale of the opposite façade, is used again both to satisfy the requirements of symmetry in the internal spaces and, paradoxically, to *reduce* the effective scale along Gosposka Street. In this narrow space one is not aware of the upper levels of the building, except in sharp perspective; and its mass dissolves into a shimmering play of projecting stones and bay windows, with a complex skyline. Close to, the setback glazing above first floor level reduces the height of the street wall to a single storey (Figure 2.15b). In addition, small-scale incident is provided at low level on this side of the building by the projecting side entrance and sculpture.

These design concepts could have been realised with the aid of many architectural vocabularies. In fact, Plečnik used forms familiar across a wide range of social groups. There are "craft vernacular" references in the random use of local limestone and in the prominent display, in urns over the entrance, of the ubiquitous Slovene geraniums. Transformed Mediterranean classical imagery is seen in the design of the urns themselves and in the giant columns, cornice and balustrades. The prismatic block form, patterned walls and regular windows of the *Wagnerschule* are also there; but contradicted by massive stones which disrupt the wall plane, removing all associations with Teutonic order. Finally, NUK incorporates clear references to modernist forms in the reading room's tall expanses of glass walling in precast concrete frames: despite Plečnik's own increasing antipathy to the "rootless" aspects of such forms – forms which he himself had done so much to develop in his own early Viennese work – the modernist vocabulary had clearly now become familiar to many people, since Stane Bernik tells us that "as the 1920s gave way to the 1930s, functionalist architecture already dominated Slovenia".[10]

In the design of NUK, all the references to established forms have themselves begun to coalesce into a new tradition: to anyone familiar with Plečnik's other works – and this would have included most of NUK's "audience" in 1941 – this is unmistakably a Plečnik building, a contemporary Slovene building

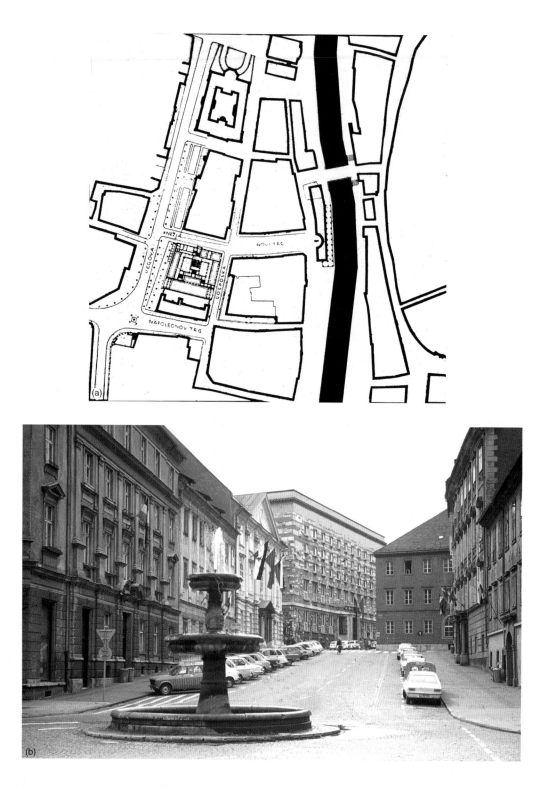

Figure 2.14
(a) NUK in context. (b) The bulk of NUK from Novi Trg.

Figure 2.15
(a) A giant landmark column. (b) Reducing the scale of *Gosposka Street.*

in its own right. Integral to this new tradition are the participatory design ideas developed in Plečnik's earlier buildings. Here, for example, are the suggestions of incompleteness then associated with the use of brick as an exposed building material. Here too are hints of worker participation in the design: one senses the difficulty of designing, on paper, walls of randomly sized, differently tooled blocks of stone with three colours of brick. Here too is the architecture of collage: the inclusion on a prominent corner of what looks like an old cornice stone suggests that other elements may also be as-found objects. One – the expressionist sculpture by Lojze Dolinar in Gosposka Street – certainly is: even though the sculpture was chosen fairly early in the design process, its "as-found" character is emphasised by giving it

an undersized base which does not match its own scale (Figure 2.16).

This "as-found" theme also generates a series of riddles. The "old" cornice stone already mentioned is strangely formed, with a curiously neat slice missing from its corner. Is this really an old stone? Or is it a new one inserted to suggest, and also counter-suggest, the presence of old elements? Looking elsewhere in the building to resolve this question merely compounds the riddle. The capitals of the giant columns, for example: they have been given bronze volutes. Is this because they are re-used capitals from an earlier building of too small a scale? This hypothesis is supported by the exaggerated weathering of both the capitals and the upper parts of the columns. But this weathering is all at the back, which is relatively

Figure 2.16
As-found sculpture.

well protected from the weather. Can the weathering have been artificially induced to make the columns *look* old? Or have they genuinely been taken from somewhere else, and turned round to conceal the weathering?

Both inside and out, the building abounds in other riddles, contradictions and surrealist inversions of normal expectations. For example, a broad expansive entrance is contradicted by the undersized, claustrophobic lobby to which it leads. This, in turn, opens into a black marble stair hall which is extremely dark and violently dynamic in character; much of it taken up by a great staircase directly along the entrance axis. The darkness and directionality of this space are radically contradicted – with no preparation other than three enigmatic pairs of doors – by the reading room to which it leads. This is very tall, flooded with light high up on all four

sides, with a powerful axis at right angles to that of the stair hall itself, extending out from the building through totally glazed end walls. Two spaces more violently different, brought together more brutally, would be hard to imagine. However one moves through the building, the expectations raised by one space are directly violated by another (Figure 2.17).

A surreal inversion of convention carries through even to minor details. The base for a sculpture grows up through a pedestal to *become* the sculpture itself, eroding the normal distinctions between building elements, whilst the conventional use of building materials is subverted in the doors to a first floor exhibition room, whose marble panels are set in a hardwood frame.

All these games are played against a background of fulfilled expectations. These are satisfied by the wide accessibility of the architectural vocabulary itself,

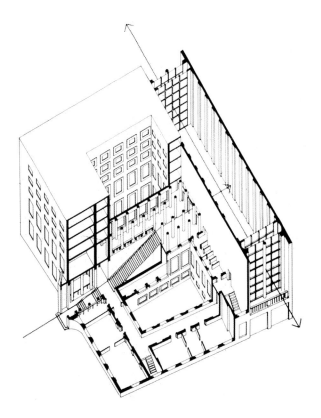

Figure 2.17
NUK: internal spatial relations.

satisfied by the enhanced legibility of the urban context and satisfied by the conventionally "valuable" and "beautiful" character of many of the elements from which the riddles are composed. The riddles of NUK, therefore, add up to a building which is involving and absorbing rather than confusing or alienating.

The incorporation of modernist forms into NUK's design, despite Plečnik's own antipathy to them, was doubtless reinforced by the collaboration of Plečnik's former pupil Edvard Ravnikar in working up the library's construction drawings. Ravnikar was far more sympathetic to the modernist *avant-garde* than was Plečnik himself, and went from NUK to work in Le Corbusier's office in Paris: one of a number of Plečnik's students to be welcomed by Le Corbusier for the excellent drawing skills developed in Plečnik's studio.

Potentially, at least, these former students might have broken free from Plečnik's own antipathy to modernism, to link his ideas to those of the modernist avant-garde; thereby carrying Plečnik's own transcultural rootedness forward to new open futures. Though the 1939 outbreak of World War Two restricted design opportunities, one powerful example of wartime transcultural design can be seen in Ravnikar's 1941 symbol for the Slovene Liberation Front, linking together Communism and nationalism – which potentially split the Front's members – by using the national symbol of the three-peaked silhouette of Mount Triglav to evoke the rising of the Communist morning star (Figure 2.18).

Unlike the situation elsewhere in Central and Eastern Europe, the liberation of Yugoslavia during 1944–1945 was carried out largely by the communist-dominated Yugoslav partisans themselves, with only limited Red Army help. This led to a power-balance very different to the Czech situation which we explored in the last chapter: Yugoslavia was very much independent, rather than a mere Russian satellite. Though Russia's revolutionary prestige led to some initial influence from a nationally orientated Socialist Realism,[11] this was largely ignored in practice because of the government's desire to unify Yugoslavia's disparate constituent nationalities, torn by conflicts exacerbated through war. This push for transnational unification had two main impacts on Yugoslav cultural landscapes. First, it led to a proscription of all potentially divisive religious symbols; from the banning of the Moslem headscarf to the silencing of Christian church bells: in Ljubljana, Ravnikar's sister remembered,

> the church bells, which rang boisterously through my youth until 1945, were silenced with the arrival of socialism . . . . They used to be a musical background to us children.[12]

Second, it generated a desire for rapid industrialisation – against the wishes of the USSR, which wanted Yugoslavia to remain merely a source of cheap raw materials for Russia's own development – which was meant rapidly to reduce regional economic disparities and thereby, according to Marxist theory, erode the foundations of former national and religious antagonisms. This emphasis on industrialisation had impacts both inside and outside professional design culture.

Figure 2.18
The Liberation Front symbol.

Inside it, the drive towards industrialisation favoured the functionalist strand of design culture so hated by Plečnik, based on conceptions of buildings as objects in space, and of urban areas as functional zones or as subject to overall master plans with parts subservient to wholes. Outside professional design culture, by contrast, the desire to industrialise the production of buildings in a context where, for example, homes were still often produced by families for their own use, led Plečnik's former student Edvard Ravnikar to produce in 1945 a *Do it Yourself Concreting* manual for the Ministry of Construction, which "was considered to be of the utmost importance for the countryside, according to the higher officials in the Ministry".[13] This in turn supported a rapid growth of peripheral urban development, with no sense of any larger "whole" spatial structure more than the mere sum of the individual parts. Both inside and outside professional design culture, Plečnik's balance of part and whole was lost, supplanted by a polarisation of professional "all whole" or popular "all part" urban structures.

From 1948, an acrimonious political split between Yugoslavia and the USSR[14] led to a renewed search for internal stability, and a consequent rapprochement with local national and religious institutions, which had been affronted by earlier proscriptions.[15] This opened up a new cultural space which, in principle at least, was more sympathetic to ideas like Plečnik's.

In Sarajevo, for example, Plečnik's former pupil Dušan Grabrijan, together with the Croat architect Juraj Neidhardt, who had earlier spent 3 years with Le Corbusier, developed transcultural ideas for the future of the Baščaršija area. Their proposal created perceptual, spatial links between existing buildings of the Orthodox, Catholic, Muslim and Jewish faiths, to promote a reading of Baščaršija as a place where all cultures were united, with a new "modern" urban tissue rooted in those aspects of the Ottoman, Muslim design tradition which Le Corbusier had found so inspirationally "modern" through his work in Algiers, in which Neidhardt had been closely involved.[16] Whether this new cultural landscape might in practice have helped in developing a more future orientated but still rooted transcommunal identity we shall never know, for the project was soon abandoned in favour of straight conservation, as part of a large-scale programme intended to promote the tourist industry and thereby gain much-needed foreign exchange.

As part of this new programme, Plečnik was given his own last commission, for the conservation of the monastery of the Teutonic Knights (Križanke) in Ljubljana, as a venue for international arts festivals. Partly a conversion of existing monastery buildings, and partly new-built additions, this final work – designed during the mid-1950s and completed in 1957 – brings together all the strands of Plečnik's

Figure 2.19
Križanke's complex language.

complex nationalist vocabulary: the "national antique", vernacular and transmuted classical (Figure 2.19). In addition, it displays a franker use of purely modernist elements, in the dramatic tension structure supporting the roof over the major auditorium space. Even here, though, cultural continuity is stressed: this structure – so advanced, in engineering terms, for its date – is used to construct a velarium roof obviously based on an ancient Roman type.

From Križanke, it is only a short walk along the avenue of Vegova Street to its termination on the bridge/square at Trnovo, adjoining Plečnik's own house, where our sequence began and where he died in 1957. As he lay on his deathbed, so Damjan Prelovšek tells us, "his house was visited by a continual stream of devotees, and ordinary folk who simply wanted to pay their respects".[17]

In contrast, however, his ideas had come to seem irrelevant to many design professionals. In many people's minds, both nationalism and religion were associated with hideous wartime atrocities. With the communist government in power, Plečnik had lost most of his work opportunities. His friend and ally Prelovšek had retired from his post as City engineer, whilst churches were no longer built, and Plečnik's well-known religious background counted against him so far as other large-scale commissions were concerned. His days as a major design influence were past.

This was also partly because Plečnik himself never articulated a coherent theory: he greatly mistrusted those who theorised and wrote about design. "His conviction was that an architect should express himself only through drawing and building", as the architect France Ivanšek remembered.[18] Second, his teaching methods never stressed *principles* of design. Remembering Plečnik's earliest teaching experience in Prague, Otakar Novotný wrote that:

Plečnik helps his students with direct interventions in their work; as a result, they grow lazy in their ideas. Therefore this teaching and method does not leave permanent traces, and as the time goes his students abandon even the little of Plečnik's greatness that they were able to understand.[19]

Third, Plečnik never managed (or even tried) to build a broader cultural movement with other designers. Edvard Ravnikar, who knew him for many years, tells us that "In all those years, I never heard him say about one thing that a contemporary architect designed, that he thought was good".[20]

Not surprisingly, this negative approach had made Plečnik unpopular with many of his professional and academic colleagues, who were therefore unwilling to make the effort to understand the increasingly anti-modernist stance which he developed in his later years. This antipathy also affected the reception accorded to those of his former students who *were* able to articulate the ideas they had developed from Plečnik's teaching. When Grabrijan and Niedhardt, for example, drew on their Sarajevo work to write their *Bosnian Architecture and the Way Forward* in 1957, articulating a potentially powerful approach to generating "rooted but not stuck" places, their message fell largely on deaf ears.

Plečnik's own work, however, still seemed relevant to *popular* culture during the 1960s and 1970s, judging by the frequency with which it was illustrated in the picture books produced in great numbers to foster the tourist industry.[21] By the late 70s, his work also began to be rehabilitated in Slovene and international professional circles, as modernist tenets began to be questioned. As art historian Peter Krečič saw it, "the architecture of Jože Plečnik ... is probably one of the greatest architectural discoveries of the 1980s on the world level".[22]

Plečnik's work, however, was not consigned to renewed obscurity as the "world level" interest in post-modern classicism waned. Without the charismatic unifying influence of Marshal Tito, Yugoslavia's communist leader since the Second World War who died in 1989, economic and political rivalries amongst the country's constituent republics were rapidly intensified; and Plečnik's work once again seemed relevant to an increasingly nationalist culture; offering a sense of roots in an increasingly turbulent world. With a new national government seeking a rooted

sense of "being Slovene", we find Plečnik's own image, and that of his buildings, used as icons on social and economic linkage systems such as postage stamps and banknotes.

In a post-communist Slovenia, however, Plečnik's work clearly also had its dangers in identity-construction terms, associated as it was with nationalist and fervently religious meanings which had been used to legitimate terrible events during the Second World War, but which the official communist culture had largely papered over. In one of Central Europe's most interesting cultural movements, the psychological denial of such events was addressed head on from 1980 onwards; first by the post-punk industrial music group *Laibach*, and later by the wider group of artists collectively known as Neue Slowenische Kunst (NSK).[23] Rather than attempting to destabilise particular images of totalitarianism, as we saw with Stalin/Michael Jackson or the Pink Tank in Prague, NSK seek to address a deeper level of the identity-construction process: the denial of responsibility for terrible historical events which enables people to construct identities which can all-too-easily allow those events to recur in the future. As we already saw, neither architecture nor urban design can ever be suitable media for this kind of endeavour: they require too much implementation support from the official power-structures of the status quo, and their impacts are endemically subject to habituation. More ephemeral art forms such as musical performance, however, do not suffer from these constraints: the sociologist Stanley Cohen, for example, sees rock music in this context as "a symbolic vehicle to bypass conventional structures".[24]

Laibach's performances seek to help audiences become aware of the ways in which a longing for community can potentially be manipulated to draw "us" towards totalitarian forms of national identification. Performances begin by getting the audience into a suggestive state: making them wait for long periods, subjecting them to loud repetitive noise and shining searchlights on them as though they themselves were the performers. The performance itself is replete with totalitarian symbolism; involving uniforms, classical imagery such as Plečnik sometimes used, symbols of Nazi domination (Laibach itself is German for Ljubljana), and with references to fundamentalist Christianity and militaristic music. As Winifred Griffin recalls:

> *While the spectator can feel drawn to the performance ... he or she may also feel an uneasy sense of guilt in observing what Laibach puts forward ...While s/he is caught up in the music the experience is exhilarating. After the music stops, a sense of awkwardness spreads over the audience. The awkwardness results from the spectator's realisation that s/he has been deceived through a manipulation of his or her desire. This deception has resulted in an identification with an "undesirable" form of nationalism to which s/he had previously considered him/herself immune.*

Denial, in other words, is undone; through what Alexei Monroe calls a "homeopathic principle of beating poison with poison".[25] It is interesting, he goes on to say "to note the lack of overt (rather than covert) nationalism in Slovenia", suggesting that by "mapping out and occupying such an extreme frontier Laibach may have, to some extent, set the limits on potential radicalism in Slovenia".[26] And in relation to Plečnik's work, Laibach's conscious appropriation of his buildings in their shows helps those who have attended their performances to be wary of reading Plečnik in negatively nationalistic ways.

To conclude, then, what can we learn from our analysis of Plečnik's work and its subsequent reception and appropriation? It is clear that the Ljubljana case study has many lessons to offer in terms of identity by design; albeit mostly at the level of meaning rather than use. Let us now draw these out in relation to the key dimensions of the identity-construction process.

First, we can glean many new ideas about helping users to construct a rooted sense of imagined community. Particularly in Plečnik's work, for example, we saw a range of initiatives for making public space more legible. Often these made creative use of low key, cheap elements such as trees, columns and street lights to enhance spatial definition, but also designing these to help users locate themselves within the public space network as a whole; as in

the "family" of benches whose members become progressively more formal as the centre of the city is approached.

We also saw great scope for incorporating "rooted" elements into new designs at all scales. At the largest scale of the landscape itself, we saw Edvard Ravnikar's synthesis of the form of mount Triglav with the communist rising star; to create a national symbol whose initial public resonance was so strong that the symbol endures to this day, despite a series of radical changes in political regime. We saw also the re-use of historically important buildings for radically new uses, as in the Križanke monastery become cultural centre. We saw the recycling of historically important building *sites*, as in the construction of the NUK library on the site of the former Ducal Palace, in a place with even earlier Roman links. And, at the smallest scale, we saw the re-use of historically significant building *elements*, from whole porticoes down to individual stones.

There are also lessons to be drawn from Ljubljana to help us design places to support positive co-dwelling with the wider ecosystem, at least at the meaning level: ideas for making positive human use of natural systems, to make these socially valued parts of the city's spatial structure. At the largest scale, we saw how the urban plan attempts to break down perceptual barriers between "city" and "nature", both by enfolding the Tivoli park into the overall city form, and by penetrating it with "city-ness" through Plečnik's symbolic axis of light. We saw, too, the ways in which the Ljubljanica and Gradaščica rivers have been designed to encourage a variety of social experiences of the city's water system. And at the smallest scale, we saw the development of the "inhabited bridge"; where nodal activity is concentrated over water, to emphasise the water's importance in the city's social life.

At a third level, what can Ljubljana teach us about ways of designing to help members of different imagined communities live harmoniously with others? Here too, we can see both positive and negative lessons at all scales.

On the positive side, we saw Plečnik draw on the inner resources offered by his own life-trajectory, to build creative, transcultural bridges between the formal vocabularies and compositional strategies associated with different social groups; particularly in the overall city plan and in major public buildings like NUK. To some of these groups Plečnik's work seemed "new", supporting the sense of open futures essential to fostering transculturality. To others – notably the ever more influential modernist wing of the architectural profession – it seemed merely nostalgic. We should learn a negative lesson from the way in which Plečnik himself constantly failed to build bridges with his modernist critics, for this meant that his transcultural ideas were largely rejected by design professionals once his own personal power base was eroded after the Second World War. As we saw, this had wider repercussions; for the cultural climate thus created proved impervious even to belated efforts to build such bridges, such as Niedhardt's and Grabrijan's attempts to draw out connections between Corbusian design ideas and the Bosnian vernacular.

In terms of the fourth plank in our identity-construction programme, the need to design so as to help users develop a sense of their own empowerment, the Ljubljana case again has much to offer. The "small things matter" message has come through strongly, particularly through Plečnik's additive approach to design, in which it is made clear that each "whole" is made up of parts which matter in their own rights; at all levels from urban design down to the smallest scales of buildings and street furniture. The social relevance of this additive approach comes over most strongly when Plečnik tries to bring out the creative efforts of the makers and users of places, expressed most powerfully in the project "Houses under a Common Roof". Further, Plečnik's frequently *ambiguous* use of elements and relationships within his highly rooted design vocabulary produced design "riddles", whose solution requires users' capacities for making sense of places to be brought into play at the conscious level: one knows that one has oneself *made* the meanings of such places, because one knows that the meaning could have been otherwise. The sense of empowerment here runs deep.

As in Prague, however, none of this support for empowerment through architecture or urban design promotes subversive meanings to challenge the political status quo. Once again we see how the design

of major built form requires resources which are usually controlled by the current power bloc, so that subversion is difficult to achieve. Even Ravnikar's once-subversive People's Front symbol first took root in the "minor" field of graffiti. It seems clear that other arts, which require fewer resources – arts such as Laibach's music and performance – can have far greater subversive impact. Again, this reinforces the message that physical design should be seen, from the empowerment perspective, as part of a broader strategy for forming cultural landscapes in the widest, cross-disciplinary sense. All this strengthens the importance of building bridges with mainstream institutional cultures, if we want to get beyond mere rhetoric to make significant impacts on the ground.

So far, we have only explored these issues within the "old world" of European cultures. But place-identity concerns arise across a wide cultural range, and we shall not serve the cause of transculturality unless we open ourselves to ideas from wider sources. In our next chapter, we shall move to the "new world" setting of Mexico; where approaches akin to Plečnik's were developed in a cultural context far more sympathetic to mainstream modernist ideas.

Notes

1 Cited in Šlapeta, 1986, 91.
2 Stelè, 1967, 241.
3 Cited in Prelovšek, 1997, 267.
4 Sitte, 1889.
5 Plečnik, 1929.
6 Howard, 1898.
7 Grabrijan, 1957, 80–82, cited in Krečič, 1993.
8 Mušić, 1981, 101.
9 Prelovšek, 1997, 229.
10 Bernik, 1990, 49.
11 Djilas, 1985, 197.
12 Ivanšek, 1995, 188.
13 Cited in Ivanšek, 1995, 179.
14 For a first-hand account, see Djilas, 1985.
15 For discussion of Yugoslavia's changing political ideologies during this period, see Burks, 1972.
16 For in-depth discussion of the Baščaršija project, see Alić and Gusheh, 1999.
17 Krečič, 1993, 191.

18 Ivanšek, 1995, 178.
19 Cited in Šlapeta, 1996, 48.
20 Interview in Vuga, 1995, 426.
21 For example, see Krečič, Murko and Zavašnik, 1975.
22 Krečič, 1990, 28.

23 For discussion of Laibach and NSK, see Griffin, 2002 and Monroe, 2000.
24 Cohen, 2001, 291. For further discussion of rock music in this context, see also Westley, 1991.
25 Monroe, 2000, 4.
26 Ibid., 6–7.

3

Mexico: Complexities of culture and landscape

The "inclusive" approach to constructing place-identity explored by Plečnik, which we discussed in the last chapter, was further developed in Mexico from the 1920s onwards; when Mexican people began to come to terms with their varied cultural origins, their turbulent colonial past, and their many imagined communities. Closer links with North America and Europe were important factors here, and were linked to a programme of modernisation, economic growth and educational reform. Other developments in literature, music, art and architecture also contributed to the social, political and cultural redefinition of a pluralist Mexican society and its search for *Mexicanidad*. A wide range of cultural material was employed by Mexican designers, ranging through natural landscapes, the physical and spatial structures of cities, and building types from popular and vernacular sources, high art, music, dance, myths and legends.

Most fundamentally, the contexts within which ideas and interpretations of Mexican identity took place are *geographically* determined. The country's location – between the USA to the North, and the Latin American countries of Guatemala and Belize to the south – creates certain tensions in terms of cultural direction. Mexico's vast territory is defined by arid, dry, desert landscapes to the north; by lush, tropical forests to the south and east; and by the Pacific coastline to the west, with a volcanic range in the centre. Equally varied is the country's fauna and flora, ranging from many desert cacti to lush, tropical forests and colourful trees such as *tricolores*, *jacarandas* and *bougainvilleas*.

Second, it is important to understand how Mexico's political, social and cultural circumstances supported a search for new, united imagined communities. Over centuries, different tribes – Zapotecs, Olmecs, Mayas and Aztecs – contributed to the area's cultural development, and to the formation of magnificent settlements such as Palenque, Chichen Itza, Monte Alban and Teotihuacan (Figure 3.1). The gradual decline or destruction of these early civilisations is attributed to issues such as tribal invasions, diseases and overexploitation of natural resources; but the most dramatic factor was the Spanish conquest of 1521, which turned a huge and powerful ancient empire into a colonial state named *Nueva Espana* (New Spain). Colonial rule introduced a new legal system, Catholicism and new settlements constructed after the Spanish building tradition.[1]

Between 1876 and 1911 the Mexican political scene was bedevilled by the dictatorship of Porfirio Diaz and war. The 10-year long Mexican civil war (1910–1920), known as the Revolution, produced heroes such as Pancho Villa and Emiliano Zapata who symbolised a different kind of Mexico: a different cultural tradition, rooted in peasant and traditional values rather than in an upper and middle class colonial inheritance.

During the first post-Revolution decades of the 1920s and 1930s, the new government of Alvaro Obregon began to work on reforms aimed at creating better living conditions through modernisation, as part of a broader agenda linked to a spirit of "building the new world".[2] Similar movements and

Figure 3.1
The Pyramid of the Sun in ancient settlement of Teotihuacan, Mexico.

ideas were also explored in Venezuela and Brazil; countries which, according to Valerie Fraser "sought to promote an image of themselves as modern".[3] Especially important in Mexico were educational reform policies, introduced by Education Minister José Vasconcelos from 1921 to 1924, in line with the new constitution of 1917 that "had included resolutions concerning the universal right to a state education, healthcare and affordable housing".[4] Vasconcelos, a well known philosopher and humanist, "perceived art as a way of awakening the illiterate masses";[5] and an already-established Mexican muralist painting tradition, rooted in popular folk art, was the most obvious route for attempting to bring this awakening about. Vasconcelos therefore commissioned mural paintings to decorate new ministerial buildings, with

the purpose both of educating the masses and of promoting a New Mexican identity. In 1921, he took Diego Rivera and other Mexican painters to Yucatan, to familiarise themselves with the ancient and traditional artistic heritage of Mexico "since this would form the basis of their future work".[6]

Between the 1920s and 1950s a whole new generation of muralists appeared. According to Mariana Yampolsky their work "reflected the search for a Mexican identity and espoused the cause of public art".[7] Diego Rivera – the best known member of this group – travelled the country studying murals in pre-Hispanic sites, colonial monasteries and *pulquerias* (local pubs where *pulque*, a local drink made of blue agave cactus, is

Figure 3.2
Diego Rivera's mural painting known as *The Carnival of Mexican Life* (1936).

drunk) which had been decorated by local Indian artists. Other key muralists who shared similar beliefs and painting practices were Carlos Mérida, Amando de la Cueva, Xavier Guerrero, Fernando Leal, José Clemente Orozco and Juan O'Gorman.[8]

Both the style and the content of these murals were devoted to expressing a complex Mexican history. Diego Rivera, leader of the new muralist group, immersed himself in the production of big epic scenes such as *The Political Vision of the Mexican People* (1923–1928), painted for the newly established Ministry of Education. Equally important are his murals in the *Palacio National*, telling the complex story of the Mexican people through heroic scenes such as *Epic of the Mexican People* (1929–1935), *Pre-Hispanic Mexico – The Early Indian World* (1929), *The Carnival of Mexican Life* (1936) and many others (Figure 3.2). In addition to heroic historic scenes, Rivera, Orozco and other muralists also portrayed

ordinary, everyday events; using Mexican women and children, and local and Indian groups to illustrate the rich and varied traditions of Mexican life. Through this work, the muralists and other painters also expressed the bridging of two different art-worlds and two imagined communities – Indian and Spanish – intimately linked through inter-marriages between Spanish soldiers and local Indian women, producing mixed-race descendants known as *mestizos*.

Although many of the murals had Mexican themes, they were painted in modern techniques, learnt in contemporary studios in Paris and other European art centres; creating a fusion of the modern and the traditional in Mexican art. This attempt by painters to search for a new *Mexicanidad* was also helped by writers and literary critics such as Octavio Paz, who in a similar way celebrated the multiple cultural traditions of the Mexican people, and their varied imagined communities. According to Paz "the art of mural painting has provoked debate about the future of the nation. It has become a model of cultural identification".[9]

Similar ideas were explored through the medium of the natural and built environment. As in Prague and Ljubljana, Mexican designers inherited spatial structures and built form elements from previous generations of city builders. This spatial and built form inheritance formed a third source of ideas for constructing a new Mexican place-identity. We shall explore this in the context of Mexico City, where the ideas of *Mexicanidad* were most fervent because of the importance of the city as the national capital.

The spatial structure of the city as inherited by early 20th century designers was a complex one, resulting from many radical transformation processes linked to historical, political and cultural events. The basic morphological structure of the city's historic zones was established during the formation of the ancient city of *Tenochtitlan* (Figure 3.3), founded as the capital of the Aztec empire in 1325. *Tenochtitlan* was the last urban centre to emerge in pre-conquest Mexico, and Aztec city builders drew on the knowledge and traditions of earlier civilisations such as *Teotihuacan* and the Toltec capital of *Tula*.[10]

The city was sited near the western shores of the swampy lake *Texcoco*, accommodating some 200,000 people (400,000 in the greater region). The overall urban plan followed a gridiron system of canals and mud platforms – *chinampas* – whose layout was based upon cosmological interpretations of the movements of the stars and planets. The whole system was connected to the mainland by three causeways. *Chinampas* were artificially built from canal silt and marsh weeds, and were very sustainable as they could easily revert to their swampy status (the remains of this ancient ecological system can still be seen in the area of Xochimilco). The great Aztec respect for nature is symbolised by their Goddess of Nature, represented as a woman's head with plants growing out of her hair.

The city was organised into five districts called *campan*, each defined by four main avenues facing the four cardinal points, with a gateway at the end of each avenue. A large square occupied the centre of the settlement, and this was defined by pyramids used for public, administrative and religious purposes; again aligned with the orbits of the Sun, Moon, Venus and other planets. By 1502 when Moctezuma II ascended the throne, the Aztec empire had become the most powerful force in the region, rich in agricultural and other products, crafts and political superiority.

Tenochtitlan, like so many other pre-conquest Mexican cities, was a "city-state". Urban planning was co-ordinated by a planner termed *Calmimilocatl*, who allocated, aligned and supervised sites for new *chinampas*, canals and footpaths.[11] There were many public and social institutions such as schools, other educational establishments and markets; and aqueducts were constructed to bring fresh water from the nearby mountains into the city. The remaining urban areas were organised into neighbourhoods or *calpulli*, laid out on a gridiron system, with plots allocated to individual families. Various *calpulli* were designated for particular types of craft or food production, but there were also areas of mixed activities.

Within the overall grid plan there were several different building types. The most prominent were the pyramids, *Tlaloc* and *Huitzilopochtli* being the most important as they served as temples for Aztec gods. Pyramids and other important buildings located in the main square were built of stone, with pebbles and mortar binding each stone together, a method still sometimes used today (Figure 3.4).

The hierarchical social structure of *Tenochtitlan* was evident through the housing typology. Buildings closer to the city centre housed military and other socially important families. Houses were compact or courtyard types, two-storey structures, flat roofed and built of stone on platforms to avoid flooding. Dwellings occupied by less well-off families were generally single-storey types, either flat roofed or thatched, "beautifully worked, some being pyramidal, some square, some round and some of other forms", as Fray Juan de Torquemada noted in 1521.[12] Walls were built of mud, leaves and other local materials; whitewashed or painted in bright colours with dyes extracted from local plants, soil and mineral pigments. Some houses were faced with stucco; which was burnished until it gleamed like silver and the houses seemed as "made of jewels". Many of

Figure 3.3
The ancient city of Tenochtitlan, the capital city if the Aztec Empire, Mexico.

Figure 3.4
A model of the central part of Tenochtitlan, Mexico.

these house types continued to be built by local Indian builders for centuries, and can still be found in some rural villages. They have become an important source of ideas for developing Mexican architectural identity today.

When Hernan Cortés and his troops arrived in *Technochtitlan* on the 13th of August 1521, they thought that they had arrived in heaven: what they saw was a city built on lakes, surrounded by snow covered, volcanic mountains enveloped in purple haze. On that occasion, the Spanish soldier Bernal Diaz del Castillo wrote that it "was like the enchantments in the book of Amadis, on account of the great towers and temples and buildings rising from the water, and all built of masonry".[13] But this beauty did not stop the Spanish troops from destroying the city of *Tenochtitlan*, in order to build a new European settlement that would reflect and support their own imagined community.

The new city plan was entrusted by Cortés to Alonso Garcia Bravo, a soldier who was also an excellent surveyor. Garcia Bravo could see the value of the old Aztec master plan, and decided to retain its overall spatial structure. However, he replaced the pyramids and other buildings with Spanish architectural types, and transformed the canals into paved streets. Even the old Aztec plaza remained, but in a Spanish version as a Plaza Mayor (or Zocalo), paved with stones collected from the Aztec buildings that were demolished. The new Plaza Mayor was enclosed by new civic and religious buildings, and with arcades designated for traders (Figure 3.5).

These morphological overlays and urban transformations, through which the Aztec pattern was adopted but modified by a new Spanish layer, have produced double coded meanings of identity. Even today, for example in the South of the La Alameda neighbourhood, local residents attach meanings to both cities – *Tenochtitlan* and the colonial Spanish. Miller[14] and other interpreters of Mexican urbanism claim that the Aztec legacy of city building processes produced morphological and spatial layers that reflect a sense of permanence and what some critics call a deep sense of rootedness.[15]

In addition to Aztec built-form sources, 20th century ideas for constructing a new Mexican identity came also from new building typologies that the Spanish conquistadores introduced. The early colonial house-types were courtyard structures, made of thick walls, serving as defences in case of Indian

Figure 3.5
Mexico City, Plaza Mayor or Zocalo; built by the Spanish after the conquest in 1521.

attack. Towards the end of the 16th century, a greater variety of house-types was introduced, based on a more open types that originated in Andalucia and Castilla, and had therefore been influenced by Islamic prototypes. These courtyard and other house-types, imported from Spain, adjusted well to the Mexican context due to similar climatic conditions.[16] Over time, the two house-building traditions – local Indian vernacular and the Spanish courtyard – were merged into mutation types known as *tequitqui*,[17] because most house builders were local Indians who continued with their own house patterns and building techniques. Different variations of the Spanish courtyard house-type resulted in a variety of these mutation types, such as *casas de taza y plato*, *tiendas de tejada* or *casas de entresuelo*,[18] ranging from small houses to bigger

buildings with commercial activities on the ground floor and apartments above.

Mexico City underwent rapid change and expansion during the seventeenth and eighteenth centuries. New residential and mixed-use districts were built following the pre-established grid structure. Buildings were of two main types. First, there was a large apartment block dwelling-type with mixed uses on the ground floor, heavily decorated with Spanish Baroque motifs. The second type was the residential villa, a large single family dwelling based on the *hacienda*. The San Angel and Coyoacan areas have good examples of these types.

Turbulent political events, and the independence from Spanish rule gained in 1821, brought about many changes in political and socio-economic structure. The country was renamed Mexico, after the ancient Aztec name *Mexica*, and its capital city was named *Mexico City*. By 1850, a new programme of infrastructure improvement was launched, opening up many possibilities for the expansion of residential, industrial and commercial districts. A gradual weakening of Spanish architectural influences was manifested through the introduction of new building types imported from California and France, exemplified in many Neo-Colonial and Art Nouveau buildings.

By the 1920s, in the years following the Revolution of 1910–1920, "the memory of colonial rule was overlaid with feelings of national pride and self-confidence".[19] Mexican people were ready to engage in new development opportunities, linked to the process of modernisation and to political, socio-economic and cultural reforms. Such circumstances created fertile ground for Mexican architects and urban designers to express their interpretations of a new *Mexicanidad*, a new united version of imagined community.

The architectural and urban design vocabulary available to Mexican designers during the early years of the 20th century was multifaceted. We have already seen how the urban grid of Mexico City was double-coded in urban design and spatial terms. It had a deep-rooted meaning for the descendants of the ancient Aztec tribes as well as for the Spanish colonisers and their descendants. Mexican town planners and urbanists therefore continued expanding the city with the urban grid as a basic morphological pattern (Figure 3.6). Each new addition, however, was designed to reflect local topographic potential; resulting today in a collage of grids, stretching in length and width to some 25 miles in each direction and housing some 22 million people. Within the urban grid structure in place, Mexican architects and urban designers focused their attention on developing a range of architectural types, drawing ideas from a rich tapestry of vernacular and high art sources. They also explored the wealth of landscapes, saturated with rich and varied natural elements as well as symbolic meanings linked to turbulent Mexican historic events.

The search for and construction of a new Mexican identity, expressed in built form patterns, is first of all evident in the building of major educational, art, archaeology and other public institutions, influenced by the educational and cultural reforms we have already discussed. Building a major national university, for example, had as much significance for Mexican people as Plečnik's National University Library had for the Slovenes.

The *Ciudad Universitaria* or the University City of the *Universidad Nacional Autonoma de Mexico (UNAM)* stands out as one of the largest government projects and, according to Valerie Fraser, as "a showpiece of the Mexican government's achievements in modernizing the country since the Revolution".[20] The driving force behind the project was the country's President Miguel Alemán, who wanted to create a monument to his political achievements whilst in office. The first idea of building the National University began to germinate in 1928, but it was not until the 1940s and 1950s that these ideas were realised. In 1943 the University authorities bought the so-called *terrenos ejidales* in the area known as *El Pedregal*, which was common land with grazing rights on the outskirts of the city. Many design proposals were explored by some 150 architects and many architecture students. The final masterplan, based on the ideas of Teodoro González de León,[21] was executed by Enrique Del Moral and Mario Pani. The main part of the university was built between 1950 and 1955 under the supervision of Carlos Lazo (Figure 3.7).

The overall spatial plan was based on the ancient settlement of *Teotihuacan*, located 37 miles northeast of Mexico City, and famous for its political, economic and military supremacy between 300 BC and 100 AD. The central University plaza (campus) is a re-interpretation of the ancient Teotihuacan main space known as *The Street of the Dead*; whilst individual faculty buildings represent various ancient pyramids. The main pedestrian plaza is planted with *jacaranda* trees and local shrubs, symbolising an important link with nature. The plaza is connected to other sections of the university by pathways constructed from the dark lava rock found on the site itself.

We can identify two main design directions here: on the one hand, there is reference to Mexico's past, tradition, topography and landscape; on the

ESCALA GRAFICA

KM

Figure 3.6
Carlos Contreras's plan for the expansion of Mexico City, 1935–1985.

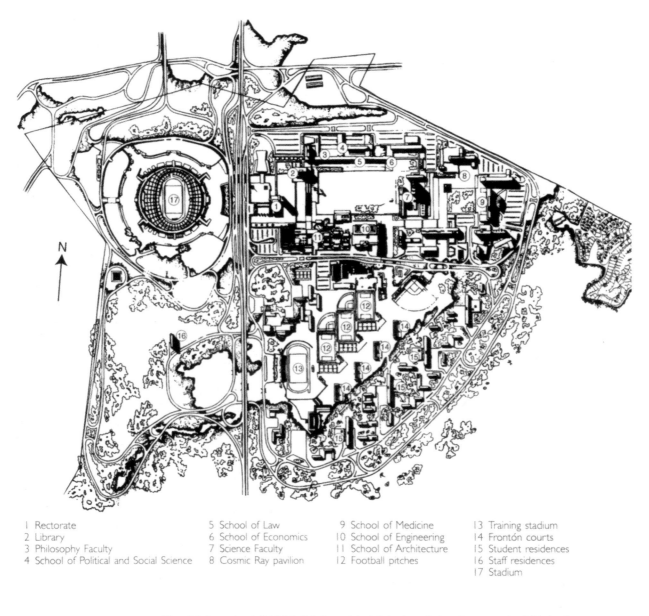

1 Rectorate
2 Library
3 Philosophy Faculty
4 School of Political and Social Science

5 School of Law
6 School of Economics
7 Science Faculty
8 Cosmic Ray pavilion

9 School of Medicine
10 School of Engineering
11 School of Architecture
12 Football pitches

13 Training stadium
14 Frontón courts
15 Student residences
16 Staff residences
17 Stadium

City University, UNAM (Universidad Nacional Autónoma de México),
Mexico City, 1950–52, plan.

Figure 3.7
The Plan of the University City (Universidad Nacional Autonoma de Mexico – UNAM, 1950–1955).

other hand, we can see how Mexican designers used modernist concepts from the Bauhaus and Le Corbusier to create a truly monumental complex.[22] Two key buildings stand out: the Chancellery (The Rectorate) and the main Library.

The Chancellery was designed by Mario Pani, Enrique del Moral and Salvador Ortega Flores. The 15-storey tower block is decorated by a bas-relief titled *The People for the University, the University for the People* (1952–1956): an amalgam of painting, sculpture and glass mosaic designed by David Alfaro Siqueiros (Figure 3.8). The Library adjoins the Chancellery, and was designed by Gustavo Saavedra, Juan O'Gorman and Juan Martinez de Velasco. It is famous worldwide for Juan O'Gorman's mosaics, which represent a vision of Mexico's past and future. The entire surface of this simple cube structure is covered by murals and mosaics comprised of coloured rocks from different parts of Mexico. The scenes represent the history and cosmology of Mexico, both past and contemporary. From a distance, the mosaic resembles *Tlatloc*, the "Goggle-eyed" Aztec Rain God. Here again we can see the fusion of pre-colonial art and architecture with modern ideas; expressed both in the building design and in the techniques of collage developed by the European cubist artists. Being a National University complex it also benefited from the ideas of many other architects, designers and artists, some from the popular sector, to help in the construction of a project imbued with strong feelings of Mexican identity (Figure 3.9).

According to Hans Haufe, "the integration of art into the campus became a hallmark of UNAM".[23] With its hundred buildings, educating some three hundred thousand students, UNAM has become "a city within a city" and a cradle of important social and political movements and ideas. This large complex is also an important link in the development of Mexican identity expressed through urban design, architectural and art projects. On the one hand, there is also a continuation of the muralist ideas initially developed by Rivera, Orozco and others through José Vasconcelos's educational projects: in a way, this also resonates with the ideas of the "united arts" that were the focus of Bauhaus teaching and practice during the 1920s and 1930s in Germany. On the other hand there is also what David Craven[24] calls a distinctive set of historical convergences, whereby both traditional and modern ideas are united to project an evolving concept of Mexican identity. Today, UNAM is still a cradle of key political movements and liberal ideas. It is also an important link between the muralist projects of the 1920s and new art, urban design and architecture directions linked to the country's urbanisation processes and intellectual maturations.

A key figure in the evolution and formation of what is commonly understood as Mexican critical regionalism[25] is Luis Barragán Morfin. Barragán's early architectural works and ideas were strongly influenced by his aristocratic, agrarian, politically conservative and religious background. Later he began to question these roots. In a similar way to Plečnik's personal journey of discovering his own identity, Barragán's quest for his roots, his own identity as well as identities of the Mexican people, was also important for the formation of his design ideas.

The first key factor in Barragán's personal development was the ideological and cultural milieu of Guadalajara, where he was born and raised. Whilst he was studying engineering in the early 1920s, the city was "a cultural environment that lived the process of modernisation of the Mexican nation with an intensity inspired by the desire to defend both its political and intellectual identity with respect to the centripetal power of Mexico City".[26] Second, Barragán's friendship with muralist painters, particularly Diego Rivera and Clemente Orozco, drew his attention to the Mexican past and to the interpretation of Mexican landscapes, as well as to a deep-rooted attachment to ordinary Mexican people and their way of life. Third, artistic and architectural developments promoted by European avant-garde groups enriched Barragán's understanding of modernisation.

Fresh from his undergraduate studies in engineering, and imbued with the cultural and intellectual climate of Guadalajara, Barragán embarked on his first European trip in 1925; seeking to discover the roots of civilisation and also some of the roots of Mexican identity. He studied Andalucian architecture, which in turn guided him to the North African citadels, known as *casbah,* of Morocco. There he

Figure 3.8
The Chancellery, designed by Mario Pani, Enrique del Moral and Salvador Ortega Flores (1952–1956), UNAM, Mexico City.

Figure 3.9
UNAM: The Library, designed by Gustavo Saavedra, Juan O'Gorman and Juan Martinez de Velasco (1952–1956), Mexico City.

learnt the principles of spatial sequencing and the art of building courtyard houses that, as he saw it, provide perfect integration of man, society and environment. Barragán's trip to Paris in the same year introduced him to two influential figures: Le Corbusier and Ferdinand Bac. Le Corbusier gave Barragán the knowledge of modern city planning and architectural design principles that he was to employ so skilfully upon his return to Guadalajara and later in Mexico City. Ferdinand Bac, theorist and landscape designer, showed Barragán that designers can fuse traditional and new sources, and create powerful re-interpretations of old and new themes. Bac's *Les Colombières* exhibition on the theme of the Mediterranean Garden was a rich source of ideas for Barragán to use in developing his own garden designs in Mexico. During his stay in Paris, Barragán also attended a performance of the Russian ballet; interpreting scenes from Russian history with dancers dressed in vibrant colours, which reminded him of traditional Mexican costumes and the similarly intense colours of some of the vernacular Mexican building traditions.

Upon his return to Guadalajara, Barragán was inspired by what he had seen and learnt in Europe. He started to develop a new Mexican style of architecture, which was modern but inspired by traditional shapes, forms and colours, reflecting the deep-rooted meanings of the rich history of Mexico and its people. He achieved this by studying the towns, villages and houses of the region of Jalisco, and by working with local builders and craftsmen, who brought their own experiences to the modern interpretations of Jaliscan houses. This phase of Barragán's work fitted well into the political, intellectual and cultural spirit of Guadalajara, whose key protagonists believed that out of the fusion of different traditional cultures, with modern ideas and forms, a new expression of Mexican identity would emerge.

When Barragán finally accepted the challenge of Mexico City, and settled there in 1935, the ground was already prepared for his ideas. His first attempts to construct modern Mexican identity were expressed through a series of modern functionalist buildings. Especially important are his houses for rent (*Casas para renta*), which bear a typological

similarity to ancient Aztec dwellings, but use modern construction techniques and materials.

As a result of the country's modernisation processes, a rapid urban expansion of Mexico City took place during the 1930s and 1940s, with many new areas developed to accommodate housing and other needs. By 1940 the city had reached two million inhabitants. With such a rapid urbanisation process, Barragán could not resist challenges at a larger scale of design. It was Barragán's painter friends Clemente Orozco, Diego Rivera and Gerardo Murillo, a landscape painter known as Dr Atl, who drew the architect's attention to a large area of volcanic landscape in the Pedregal area of the district of *San Angel*, an old part of the south-west area of the city, which they used as a source of inspiration for their work. Whilst Dr Atl introduced Barragán to the locality's beauty and mythology, Orozco praised its landscape qualities where past, present and future are "mixed in the current of time".[27] For Rivera, Pedregal represented potential business opportunities and wealth. Barragán was attracted to the site for its dramatic landscape qualities which satisfied his deep metaphysical desire for solitude. According to Martinez "like Faust, Barragán put to the test all his tools of knowledge, all of his weapons from science to ideology to religion that allowed him to study the world of the past and make sense of contemporary chaos".[28]

Barragán worked on the *Jardines del Pedregal de San Angel* between 1945 and 1953, in collaboration with the German émigré and modernist architect Max Cetto. Prior to the volcanic eruption that gave it its name, "the gardens of the stony place", the region was home to *Copilco* and *Cuicuilco*, two of Mexico's earliest cities, whose remains were unearthed in the late 19th century. Its enigmatic ruins, the rugged scenery, distinctive landscape and vegetation, its myths and legends contributed to Pedregal's scientific, historic and cultural significance (Figure 3.10a).

According to Keith Eggener, the Pedregal "was a dramatic, desolate and venerable place, a visual mixture of violence and serenity, like a turbulent body of water suddenly frozen".[29] The site was home to native flora such as *palos bobos* ("crazy trees"), and its rugged and dramatic ruins gave it a reputation as a

Figure 3.10
(a) Luis Barragán: The rocky terrain of the Pedregal Gardens, San Angel, Mexico City (1945–1953). (b) Aerial view of the site plan for the Gardens, drawn by Luis Barragán and Carlos Contreras (1945).

dangerous and mysterious place. A historical publication of 1913 reported that "according to the Indians, the Pedregal is full of monstrous spirits and terrible witches, so much so that rare is the Indian who will walk through the place at night . . .".[30] They call the Pedregal de San Angel "the primary school of witchcraft".[31]

In 1945, Barragán bought 865 acres of land in the area, and started to work on his housing design and also on his advertising campaign. Carlos Contreras, Colombia University trained city planner and author of the master plan of Mexico's Federal District, assisted Barragán with the overall street layout; whilst Max Cetto participated in the design of the model houses and Mathias Goeritz contributed with sculptural elements. By 1952 some 100 houses had been completed, of which only 10 have been definitely credited to Barragán. By 1958 there were 900 houses built; stretching to 1,250 acres the land which Barragán acquired during the course of the project. So what were the design principles that Barragán employed in this major project? The first, according to Barragán, was "to preserve the harmony of the architectural development and the landscape" or to "humanise the landscape".[32] By "harmony" he meant integrating landscape and architecture to form a unified scheme, which Frampton calls *tectonic*.[33] The second principle was a minimum plot size of one acre with houses occupying 10% of the plot. Third, the lava rock was protected, and only a small amount of loose rock was used in the construction of walls and paths. And, finally, native lush vegetation was to be preserved and all new planting, roads and paths follow the natural lines of the terrain. "One should neither violate nor kill nature", said Barragán, "but it is necessary to help it and direct it through new avenues".[34]

The overall layout of the scheme takes the form of a deformed grid; composed of picturesque, meandering streets that follow the contours of the natural landscape (Figure 3.10b). Lava rocks are used as landmarks, and the streets bear the names of natural rock formations, water or trees: *Fuentes, Crater, Cascada, Lava, Colorines* and others. Most tree trunks are whitewashed with lime, which creates a very traditional Mexican feel. In addition to respecting the landscape and topography of the site, the overall design concept was also influenced by three leading theories of residential development.

First, Barragán was influenced by Le Corbusier's writings on city planning and contemporary urban form, where dwellings are situated in landscaped areas. Second, he derived some of his design ideas from the British Garden City movement. Third, both Barragán and Cetto were very much influenced by the architecture of Frank Lloyd Wright and Richard Neutra, and the ways in which these two architects integrated nature, water and topography with new built form elements. In order to promote his project, Barragán developed a powerful advertising campaign, using graphic designs and posters to attract clients. He was particularly keen to appeal the growing number of middle class families, and to draw them away from their favoured highly decorative "California Colonial Style", which Barragán hated: the style was "expressly forbidden"[35] in Pedregal.

Most of the houses and gardens are set behind lava walls, flush with the street or sidewalk. The walls are constructed of volcanic stone, with grey-white mortar inlaid with small pebbles, as in the Aztec building tradition. Some houses, built late in the construction programme, were set behind concrete walls or iron gates so as not to disturb the natural landscape. These walled streets provide a complex visual sequence, as often found in traditional Mexican neighbourhoods. Today the dark lava walls are covered with local endemic plants and vegetation, providing a dramatic contrast of colours generated by red and purple *bougainvilleas*, bright red *tricolores* and the blue flowers of *jacaranda* trees. Through the addition of railings, trees and fountains Barragán wanted to create "garden-streets" with "sex-appeal" and an "element of mystery" (Figures 3.11a–3.11c).[36]

The relationship between existing landscape and new built form elements is also evident in the design of individual houses. The housing typology designed for the Pedregal Gardens was intended to express a modern residential type, but the type itself was rooted in traditional Mexican architecture, reflecting both Aztec and Spanish influences. Although Barragán himself designed only a small number of houses in Pedregal he tried, it is believed, to control the overall design concept by developing a design "code" for the site. This "code" has never been found, however, and

Figure 3.11
(a) A typical street in the Pedregal Gardens, Mexico City designed by Luis Barragán (1945–1953). (b) A view into the courtyard of the Pedregal Gardens, Mexico City. (c) The Pedregal Gardens landscape with native plants and trees.

the only reference to it is in an article by Esther McCoy published in 1951,[37] which was based on a conversation she had had with Barragán; who believed, according to McCoy, that each house should be surrounded by walls, "giving the impression that it rose from the earth, and that each should be below the position of the rocks".[38] The residential house-type is a simple cubic form, flat roofed, solid, with often windowless street-side walls, inward-looking and centred on an open-air courtyard or patio. According to Eggener,[39] Barragán turned for inspiration to the colonial town of Pátzuaro near Morelia; known for its beautiful streets, its local vernacular buildings and its rural landscape. In the interview, Barragán said the following: "In the design of my houses, I have attempted to state new relationships between modern materials and the popular houses of the villages and forms of my country."[40] The demonstration houses that he designed were therefore not copies, but rather were re-interpretations of traditional Mexican houses and of their characteristic relationship to the landscape.

The best examples to call on to explain the architectural design principles employed in Pedregal are the two houses that Barragán designed with Max Cetto as part of their promotional campaign: they are at 130 and 140 Avenida de las Fuentes (originally 10 and 12 Fuentes). The house at No. 130 is hidden behind high stone walls. After entering a paved patio, the view of a modern house, cubic in form is visible. The house is a fusion of the earlier "functional" houses, that he built in Mexico City in the 1930s and 1940s, with the principles he developed in his own house on Francisco Ramirez street. The thick reinforced concrete walls are painted white, pink, pale-grey, pale-pink, chocolate-brown, bright-yellow, orange and green. The external walls are marked with lava rubble masonry. According to Keith Eggener "the mullions of a large, floor to ceiling griddled window, between the living room and garden are painted bright red. Beyond this, the still, blue water of the swimming pool, the pale-grey stone paths and the rugged purple-black lava formations protruding from soft green lawns complete the site's audacious mix of colours and textures".[41] The house at 140 Fuentes is even more interesting, with a spatial layering due to the rocky topography. The living room is two stories

high with bedrooms on upper levels. In these two buildings Barragán applied a concept he had previously developed in his own house: a large picture window functionally separates interior and exterior spaces, in a way which is reminiscent of Spanish colonial era convents and haciendas.

In the design of the Pedregal Gardens, Barragán achieved a harmony between on the one hand the locality's topography and landscape elements, and on the other with built form components at different scales. This scheme places Luis Barragán firmly at the roots of what Kenneth Frampton[42] calls *critical regionalism*, and is the beginning of a very distinctive line of architectural and urban design ideas shared by contemporary Mexican architects such as Ricardo Legorreta, Teodoro González de León and Diego Villaseñor.

Various ideas developed in the Pedregal scheme were taken further in Barragán's later projects, such as *San Cristobal stables* and the *Gilardi house*. At *San Christobal stables* (1967/1968) Barragán achieved a perfect harmony between the local landscape, the symbolic use of water, the spatial sequences and the built form elements. Again, one can see a clear relationship between typological references – in this case a hacienda complex – and the modern interpretation of this type through the use of contemporary construction techniques and materials. Whilst the client's residential quarter is painted white, the employment of bright colours in the stables complex is very Mexican (Figure 3.12a).

At the *Gilardi House*, completed in 1976, we can see great skill exercised in fitting a small courtyard-type house into the pre-existing morphological structure of the city. The house occupies a very tight urban plot, and measures 10×35 metres. From outside, it gives the impression of a simple cubic structure. Barragán was attracted to this project for two reasons: the presence of an old *jacaranda* tree, and the client's request to incorporate water into the design of the house. There were no architectural plans, only a sketch drawn on a napkin. Many ideas implemented in Barragán's own house as well as elements applied in some earlier schemes, such as the convent of Capucines in Tlalpan, are present here. The upper floor is recessed to provide privacy, and to create a patio courtyard on the upper level.

Figure 3.12
(a) San Cristobal stables, Mexico City, designed by Luis Barragán (1967–1968). (b) The Gilardi House, Mexico City, designed by Luis Barragán (1975–1976).

Internally, the house has intriguing spatial sequences that separate and unite the various activities of its residents. On entering, one proceeds along a hall into an inner corridor with a living room at the end. The bright-yellow painted corridor is separated from the courtyard by a transparent grill structure, which diffuses the bright sun light through a yellow-coloured glass wall, acting like the screens found in Arab houses.

The next spatial sequence is a dining area; an open plan room with a swimming pool at one end. According to Antonio Martinez; the water in the dining area had a very symbolic meaning for Barragán. It offers "the possibility of entering inside oneself, entering one's own dreams".[43] Opposite the pool is a large, glass screen, focusing attention on an old *jacaranda* tree (Figure 3.12b). Various colours are employed to construct an intimate, small and yet rich space. The wall behind the *jacaranda* is painted purple-azalea colour to contrast with the blue colour of the *jacaranda* tree when in bloom. Other walls are painted white to reflect light. The fusion of colours, light and perfumes from local plants provides a very rich sensory experience, similar to the experience of traditional Mexican courtyards.

Barragán uses memory and typological precedents to create new forms. But memory employed by Barragán "is not a return to the past but a fulfilment of an individual's potential, the reinterpretation in the present of something which belongs to the past. What counts is not what actually happened in the past but how we understand it today".[44] In this sense Barragán thought of himself as a traditional architect, that is "the individual who designs for his or her own time"[45] but provides a sense of continuity. He used tradition as a "guardian of the identity of things and their relationships as a source of consciousness",[46] or what Kenneth Frampton refers to as the Mexican *estancia*.[47]

With the Pedregal project, the Gilardi house, his own house, San Cristobal stables and many other schemes, Barragán founded a Mexican regionalism which brings together various building, cultural and landscape traditions of the Mexican people, and unites many imagined communities. Barragán's buildings and spaces are a fusion of different cultural Mexican traditions – Indian and Spanish, European and Islamic – where different concepts converge through typomorphological references, and through the relationship to and treatment of the landscape. What is characteristically Mexican about his work is the range of sources that he chose, and the fact that other architects and users also identify themselves with his work as Mexican.

Many of the ideas which Barragán developed can also be found in the work of Ricardo Legorreta. Like Barragán, Legorreta is highly sensitive to the cultural traditions and rich landscapes of Mexico. He has visited many parts of Mexico that have given him different perspectives on Mexican people, their lifestyles and their concerns. Legorreta is aware of many social situations where the poor economic situation of many Mexicans is counter-balanced by their rich spirituality.[48] According to Legorreta the key value of popular Mexican architecture lies in its natural, uninhibited and emotional approach and "it needs no reason to create forms and solutions, as opposed to academically rigid architecture where everything needs to be justified".[49] Following this approach, Legorreta says, "I let the project develop in my mind and spirit".[50]

There are four key aspects for which Legorreta's architecture is famous: the use of light, scale, geometry and form. First of all Legoretta uses light in a very original way. He is inspired by the changing luminescence found in different regions of Mexico, and by the variety of textures, shades and tonalities that are produced when sunlight hits local materials and buildings. In several of his works, including his own house and *Camino Real Hotel*, he paints a range of colours on his walls, which are then reflected to spaces below and above, thus creating a *sfumato* of different colour shades and intensities of light. What is also skilfully employed is the use of scale, geometry, colour and forms which are rooted in both pre-Hispanic and colonial Mexican architecture. This is probably best demonstrated in his *Camino Real Hotel*, completed in 1968.

Camino Real also represents another important aspect of Mexican architecture and urbanism: the building conforms to the plot system of the city grid, thus providing an important contextual link and a sense of spatial and typological continuity.

The building occupies a block near *Chapultepec Park*, and is designed as a large Mexican house with a system of courtyards, patios, communal interior spaces and private spaces guest room. The central external focus of the scheme, which also forms the main hotel entrance, is a large patio with a big fountain. This space is separated from the bustle of *Mariano Escobedo* street by a large fuchsia-coloured lattice with a bright-yellow wall next to it, providing both privacy and transparency for the hotel guests and other visitors. The main, entrance side of the hotel is a large glass wall that connects interior and exterior spaces. In contrast, suites face inner courtyard patios which provide peace and tranquillity, and project a sense of intimacy and seclusion. Here we can see the employment of similar elements to those found in *Casa Gilardi*, but at a much bigger scale and with more complex interrelationships (Figures 3.13a and 3.13b).

The remaining external walls of the hotel project different views. The *Mariano Escobedo* side has guest-rooms hidden behind a yellow wall planted with local vegetation, suggesting a very Mexican way of building houses. The guest rooms along *Calle de Victor Hugo* are screened by large concrete columns, trees and planting, whilst the side along *Calle de Leibnitz* has shops on the ground floor and blends successfully into the mixed-use block structure of the surrounding area (Figures 3.14a and 3.14b).

The main entrance lobby is also conceived as an inner courtyard that is linked both to the public and the private spaces of the hotel. The first impression is of a large, open plan space defined by richly textured surfaces, where light is theatrically projected onto walls and other surfaces, helped by Mathias Goeritz's gold painted screen. Legorreta learnt the value of light in Monte Alban in Oaxaca; where light projects mystery, elegance and spirituality. This is best experienced at dusk, when the interior spaces of the hotel are dimly lit with flickering candles, which constantly change the shades of wall textures, reflected in calm water surfaces.

Legorreta himself[51] feels that the most important elements in his work are the walls and the surfaces because these are the essential elements that define the space: they project and reflect light, give scale as well as proportion; whilst light is primordial because it confers a spatial intention.

In a 1996[52] interview, however, he said that he uses light, walls, proportions and colour only as tools. He also feels that his work encompasses the emotional and cultural dimensions of the Mexican way of life. He favours the spontaneity and magic that is part of the Mexican people, the fiesta as well as the necessary moments of peace and relaxation. He has definitely achieved that in *Camino Real*, which is basically conceived as a large house of fiestas, but also of siestas. In this scheme Legorreta expresses Mexican culture through the combination of emotion, mystery and exuberance; achieved through spatial relationships, typological elements (such as the courtyard house-type), volumes, textures, use of light, colour and above all the relationships of built form elements and the landscape. These elements are, according to Legorreta,[53] "deep-rooted" elements of Mexican culture and architectural tradition.

Thus far we have reviewed some of the key architectural and urban design directions of Mexico City's urbanisation processes. Ideas developed in Mexico City were later to influence other places. The last example in this chapter is a small scheme along the southern part of Mexico's Pacific coast known as *Punta Zicatella*, designed by Diego Villaseñor.

With Mexico's ever-increasing share in the global tourism industry, coastal sites have become highly desirable for large hotel operators attempting to create another Acapulco or Cancun. Though needed from an economic point of view, such developments are all to often insensitive towards any particular locality's ecosystem and cultural heritage. *Punta Zicatella* represents an alternative solution to large-scale coastal developments. It is located near the famous *Puerto Escondido* (Hidden Port) hideaway town, where both smugglers and surfers have enjoyed the rocky terrain, sandy beaches and big waves. A stretch of coastal land, today totalling 487 hectares, was bought by an ecological group to safeguard the area which is known for its unique flora and fauna; and in particular as a place where turtles come to lay their eggs. When Diego Villaseñor was invited to design a holiday resort here, his key references were the topography and landscape, local plants and the traditional culture of the

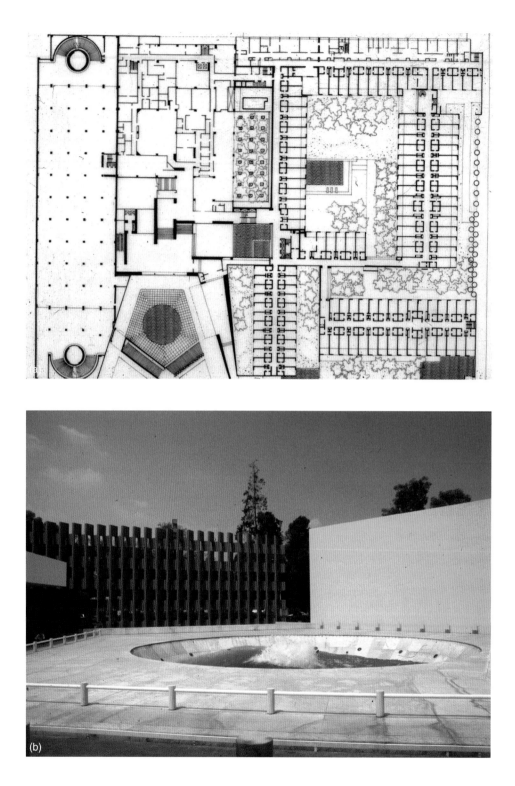

Figure 3.13
(a) The plan of Camino Real Hotel, Mexico City, designed by Ricardo Legorreta (1968). (b) Fountain and the entrance patio of Camino Real Hotel, Mexico City, designed by Ricardo Legorreta.

Figure 3.14
(a) Camino Real Hotel, the Mariano Escobedo street view, Mexico City. (b) Camino Real Hotel with mixed-use development along Calle de Leibnitz, Mexico City.

indigenous people. He rejected the holiday resort imagery of Acapulco, and proposed an alternative solution which aims, he says, "to rescue the way ancient people once lived at the seashore".[54]

Punta Zicatella is designed as a fishermen's village with 24 cottages perched on the rocks, hidden away from the sandy beach. When approaching the site, one can see only thatched roofs blending naturally into the landscape. All vegetation is native to the area; and consists of a variety of cacti, palm trees and many kinds of wild flowers. A covenant was introduced by the architect and signed by each resident which states that no "foreign" planting is to be introduced into the development.[55] Such a rich mix of plant life provides splendid support to local butterflies and other insects; whilst the sea flora and fauna attract brown pelicans, grey herons, pink storks and many varieties of sea birds that produce a rich soundscape blending harmoniously with the sound of the waves on the shore (Figure 3.15a).

All plots within Punta Zicatella are approximately the same size, and the main aspect of each cottage is a sea view, rocks and plant life. This is what Villaseñor calls "landscape framing", whereby contrast between each view is achieved by utilising a unique aspect of each cottage. Houses read as if they have grown from the site itself, and for privacy reasons no cottage overlooks another. In addition to respecting the topography, landscape, flora and fauna, Villaseñor utilised local traditional building types as a source of design ideas for the site's four dwelling types.

First, there is a complex of administrative buildings at the main entrance, designed like a *hacienda* (Figure 3.15b). One enters the complex through a large wooden door faced with palm stems; a motif that also appears on garage doors and furniture. The walls are plastered and painted pale-terracotta shades, made from pigments of the local soil, and white paint that gives the complex a very rustic character. Roofs are tiled with Roman pantiles. Pathways made of local stone, found on the site, lead to individual cottages (Figure 3.15c).

The second building type is the "common house", based on a local rural house-type. This is a large open structure, with concrete columns supporting a large roof called *palapa*, made of timber framing and covered with palm-leaf thatch. This common house is a focus of the complex; where residents and visitors eat, entertain and engage in social activities (Figures 3.16a and 3.16b).

The third and fourth types are dwellings, again based on local traditions. The first is designed as a cluster of pavilions arranged around a central living area, open towards the seaview and covered by a large *palapa* roof structure. Pavilions are built in brick, plastered and painted in terracotta colour, made of local soil and rock pigment to blend with the local stone (Figure 3.16c). The kitchen, bedrooms and bathrooms are positioned around the central living area and each bedroom has a private patio. These houses seldom have sharp corners, as according to Villaseñor "there are no corners in nature".[56] The living area furniture is largely constructed as "built in" platforms or sofas, covered by cushions. Floors are generally made of concrete, painted white to detect scorpions and other insects, with a central mosaic "rug" made of in-laid pebbles set in concrete. All other furniture, and items such as lamps and dishes, are produced by local craftsmen and craftswomen. The fourth dwelling type is based on a traditional observation or water tower, utilising sites that require height to obtain the best views. Various rooms are organised around small patios surfaced with gravel (Figure 3.17a).

The house originally designed for the architect is also a pavilion, but built in local stone rather than brick (Figure 3.17b). The approach is along a pathway, with the kitchen on the left and the main house on the right. Upon entering the main living area, one is faced with a large archway offering stunning views towards the sea and the surrounding landscape. This "framed" view is particularly spectacular at night, when the different phases of the moon's path determine the intensity of lighting in the living area (Figure 3.17c). The ceiling and the walls of the main section of the house are curved to follow the moon's path, inspired by ancient precedent; and different sections are on different levels, utilising the gentle slope of the terrain. Bedrooms are located on each side of the main living area, facing small patios covered with pebbles and offering views towards the sea and the landscape. From outside, especially from the side facing the ocean, the house resembles a cave.

Figure 3.15
(a) Punta Zicatella in its natural setting, designed by Diego Villaseñor (1980–1990). (b) The main entrance into Punta Zicatella. (c) Punta Zicatella, a paved pathway.

Figure 3.16
(a) The Common House, Punta Zicatella, the Pacific Ocean view. (b) The Common House, Punta Zicatella, a detail of the palapa roof structure. (c) A residential dwelling type based on a fisherman's cottage, Punta Zicatella.

Figure 3.17
(a) Punta Zicatella: a residential group of buildings based on a watch-tower concept. (b) Punta Zicatella: the former house of Diego Villaseñor, the architect of the scheme. (c) Punta Zicatella: the plan of the house built for the architect.

At night, the Punta Zicatella complex gives the impression of a small fishing village. Connecting pathways are dimly lit at ground level. With the lights hidden in plants, so as not to disturb the local wildlife, one can see many fire flies flickering in the air. The soundscape is even more prominent at night, with the shrieking sounds of geckos and with many night birds and insects (Figure 3.18).

The whole complex was built by local craftsmen, and is managed as a co-operative. In this scheme we can see a perfect integration of the local landscape, topography, flora and fauna together with built form patterns that continue the cultural landscape tradition initially conceived by Luis Barragán at his Pedregal Gardens. This ecological community continues to provide much needed inspiration to many other Mexican designers.

To conclude, let us highlight the lessons we have learned about designing to support users in constructing "rooted" sense of imagined communities. First of all we identified how Mexican artists, writers and designers tried to come to terms with their complex historic and cultural histories. The use of myths, legends and other forms of iconography has provided a rich source of ideas for constructing the sense of a new *Mexicanidad*

Figure 3.18
The landscape setting of Punta Zicatella.

and new Mexican place-identities. Particularly important in these processes of constructing identity by design were the genres employed by artists and writers who sought to discover how to represent the new, modern nation as a cluster of many culturally different communities. Equally important were the genres representing women and traditional Mexican ways of life situated in dramatic, landscape settings with images of volcanoes and Mexican flora and fauna. It is therefore not surprising to see Mexican architects and urban designers showing great respect for natural landscape elements in design. Here we can see a continuous and strong desire to live in harmony with natural ecological systems, evident at all scales of design and going as far back as the ancient Aztec city builders. In the design of *Punta Zicatella*, for example, we can see how at the larger, regional scale of human and non-human ecological systems we can achieve a particular kind of

imagined community and place-identity where both human and non-human systems co-exist.

At the use level, it is the connection with the geography of the locality, its topography, the water system and the natural flora that provide the underlying structure for the design of the man-made spatial connectivity systems. This principle is also used at the detailed level of design, where human and natural elements are considered as part of the same system. At the use level, human and non-human species encounter each other without threat, and both habitats co-exist in relative harmony. At the level of interpretations of meaning, the residents and visitors of *Punta Zicatella* recognise this important relationship; and construct in their minds a particular type of imagined community, offering different degrees of choice and open futures. Important views and landscape framing remind us constantly of our important links with nature, supported by rich sensory experiences.

Similar ideas were explored by the designers of UNAM, and by Luis Barragán and Ricardo Legorreta. In the Pedregal Gardens, Luis Barragán used topography and other landscape elements to construct a new cultural landscape where, again, human and non-human species can live in harmony. In a similar way to the spatial sequences in Prague, where views were directed to important buildings, in Pedregal it is the rocks, trees and other natural elements that are used to support the users' experience of legibility and place-identity.

A second important lesson is evident in the use of existing cultural landscapes in constructing a rooted sense of imagined community. This is evident at various scales. At the large scale, it is felt through the overall morphological structure; as seen in Mexico City, where different morphological layers produce a double-coded set of meanings, both Aztec and Spanish. This double-coded cultural landscape was then used by 20th century designers to construct new cultural landscapes; most obvious in the design of the public open space network, where the expansion of the existing grid pattern provided a successful tool for integrating different communities, enabling different groups of users to encounter each other. Such systems provide opportunities for fostering mixed-use developments, which in return provide safer and more economically viable neighbourhoods. At the meaning level, the grid also provides deep-rooted memories of history, and supports the users' sense of legibility. These feelings are also supported through the use of a variety of building types, as seen in the design of UNAM, *Camino Real*, or *Punta Zicatella*: buildings which can be shared by different communities because they allow different user groups to construct their own interpretations of different lifestyles. We also found useful lessons in terms of designing to support users in developing a sense of empowerment *vis a vis* their own particular imagined community. This is again evident in the design of UNAM, founded to educate and therefore empower different sectors of Mexican society and intended to be inclusive, linking high art and popular design cultures.

A third important lesson is about designing to support members of each imagined community in living harmoniously with other communities. Again,

this is evident at all scales of design intervention, from the double-coded city plan to the design of building types and public space networks. The design of UNAM illustrates well this convergence of different cultural traditions. First of all, at the large scale of urban design and town planning, this is evident in how the new spatial extensions were incorporated into the city grid. At the more detailed level of design, we can see how contemporary urban designers employed a variety of building types that were reappropriated for new needs. These architectural solutions are rooted but not stuck in the past. In this sense Mexican designers can teach us how to design for open futures.

Notes

1 Sabloff, 1989.
2 Fraser, 2000, 3–4.
3 For further discussion of these issues, see Fraser, 2000.
4 Fraser, 22.
5 Ibid., 34.
6 Kettenmann, 23.
7 Yampolsky, 1993, 40.
8 Kettenmann, 1997.
9 Haufe, 1991, 85.
10 Sabloff, 1989.
11 Martinez and Juarez, 1994.
12 Yampolski, 1993, 10.
13 Ibid., 7.
14 Miller, 1996.
15 Butina Watson, 1999.
16 Ayala, 1996.
17 For further discussion of these issues, see Yampolski, 1993.
18 Ayala, 1996.
19 Fraser, 2000, 27.
20 Ibid., 62.
21 Butina Watson, Interview with Teodoro Gonzàlez de León, March 2000.
22 Discussion between Georgia Butina Watson and Sergio Flores, April 2001.
23 Haufe, 1991, 177.
24 Craven, 2001.
25 Frampton, 1985.

26 Martinez, 1996, 8.
27 Ibid., 61.
28 Ibid., 69.
29 Eggener, 1999, 125.
30 Castillo, 1987, cited in Eggener, 1999.
31 Cited in Eggener, 1999, 126.
32 Barragán, cited in Eggener, 1999, 127.
33 Frampton, 1985.
34 Cited in Martinez, 1996, 72.
35 Eggener, 1999, 127.
36 Ibid.
37 Martinez, 1996.
38 Cited in Martinez, 1996, 76.
39 Eggener, 1999.
40 Cited in Eggener, 1999, 138.
41 Eggener, 1999, 129.
42 Frampton, 1985.
43 Cited in Martinez, 1996, 120.

44 Cited in De Anda Alanis, 1989, 175.
45 Discussion between Diego Villaseñor and Georgia Butina Watson, 1994.
46 Ibid.
47 Frampton, 1985.
48 Discussion between Georgia Butina Watson and Ricardo Legorreta, March 2000.
49 Legorreta cited in Mutlow, 1997.
50 Discussion between Georgia Butina Watson and Ricardo Legorreta, March 2000.
51 Ibid.
52 Mutlow, 1997.
53 Discussion between Georgia Butina Watson and Ricardo Legorreta, March 2000.
54 Discussion between Georgia Butina Watson and Diego Villaseñor, September 1994.
55 Ibid., September 1995, March 2000, June 2002.
56 Villaseñor, 1994.

4

The London Underground: A way for all

One key focus of the last chapter concerned ways of fostering a positive sense of co-dwelling between people and non-human natural systems. In this chapter, we shall follow this concern to a deeper level of habitation. We shall consider place-identity issues in relation to the public transport systems whose use we have to embrace if we are ever to reduce the crippling environmental damage which results from our current levels of automobile dependence.

Public transport systems will not be wholeheartedly embraced unless many people come to identify themselves as belonging to a "public transport community". How might the cultural landscapes of transport systems be designed so as to support the construction of such identities in practice? One long-running system which can offer both positive and negative lessons here is the London Underground, which this chapter explores.

During the 1860s London was the largest city in the world, with a population of some three million. In its central areas, the streets were choked with slow-moving, horse-drawn traffic. Railways offered the potential for faster movement, but dense development in the central business district made for extremely high land values there. In turn, this made it prohibitively expensive to cut new lines through those areas which most needed them.

Entrepreneurs began to see that it would pay to tunnel under these expensive areas, so that the land above could still be profitably developed. In 1863 the first tunnel was opened, and by 1870 three companies were operating. By 1907, a total of 10 were running, but economies of scale had a stern

commercial logic: through amalgamations and new developments, one US financed company, Underground Electric Railways of London, had become the major operator by 1914. The Underground's commercial success depended on encouraging as many people as possible to identify themselves as "underground users". How could the system be designed to support this identification?

First, it was important that the system could be read overall as a coherent, legible landscape; able to give shape and definition to an imagined community of "us underground users". The system's historical inheritance, however, was difficult to perceive like this. The Underground was largely disengaged – even invisible – from the city's public space: that traditional arena for supporting a sense of "us". The various constituent companies' stations were built in a variety of contrasting styles, whilst physical links between lines at common stations were often complexly disorientating. To make matters worse, the whole was made yet more confusing by indiscriminate advertisements for all sorts of commercial products fixed on every available surface. Transforming this muddle into a perceptually coherent whole would be a difficult feat of design.

Second, this was a period in which choice, manifested through a desire for all sorts of new experiences, was becoming ever more important in many people's lives. If people were to identify themselves as "underground users", therefore, the Underground's cultural landscapes would have to be perceived as offering as much experiential variety as possible. In one positive sense, the system clearly continued the expansion of life-choices earlier offered by the omnibus. This was particularly important for women, for it increased the overall offer of "unchaperoned movement" which was growing in importance in London during the 1850s and 1860s. According to Deborah Cherry, this was "part of the politics of feminism. The writings of these years testify to passages through and across London, on foot or by bus, to attend meetings and take up invitations.... Sophia Beale and her sisters delighted in wandering through London's thoroughfares, by day and by night, to sample the transitory, sensory delights and the unexpected pleasures of its ambivalent, restless spaces".[1] Sadly, however, the Underground offered far less visual variety than the overground omnibus; just at the time when, so Cherry tells us, "a diversity of paintings, prints, maps, illustrated magazines and guidebooks heightened a distinctively visual perception of the urban environment and its inhabitants".[2] Enclosure in a featureless tunnel offered passengers a relatively boring experience, which the Underground's designers would have to find ways of overcoming.

Third, the doleful experience of earlier British urban transformations as cradles of industrialisation, and the awareness of new, greener suburban or garden city potentials, had triggered a widespread desire for closer links with nature in everyday life. Again, the Underground format seemed to offer an unpromising start: the very act of leaving daylight and fresh air to descend into the bowels of the earth was all-too-easily seen as inherently unnatural, or perhaps even *deathly*. As Louisa Bain noted in her 1863 diary, "To Hatton Garden by the Metropolitan Railway … Never saw the Underground rail before … smelt rather sepulchral."[3] This situation gradually worsened. By 1879, for example, a letter to *The Times* refers to "a pharmacist in Gower Street who had for many years dispensed his own 'Metropolitan Mixture' to ease the plight of persons emerging in distress from the nearby station".[4] Particularly for those who had not gradually become inured to this state of affairs, it began to seem intolerable. By 1887, R. D. Blumenfeld noted in his diary, "I have had my first experience of Hades today … I got into the Underground railway at Baker Street … The atmosphere was a mixture of sulphur, coal dust and foul fumes from the oil lamp above; so that by the time we reached Moorgate Street I was near dead of asphyxiation and heat. I should think these Underground railways must soon be discontinued, for they are a menace to health."[5] Other dangers were also implied by this murky state of affairs. As Robert Gray points out, "the Metropolitan's cheery statement that the atmosphere in the tunnels was usually clear enough to enable the drivers to see the signals cannot have been entirely reassuring".[6]

On the other hand, however, these dangers were partly balanced by the fact that London's ground-level public spaces were also often seen as dangerous during the 1860s, as media hype whipped up a moral panic about street crime and mugging. The Underground might seem "sepulchral", but at least it opened up increased choices in many people's lives. The complex balance here was by no means all negative, so the very effort of overcoming the smoke and smells seems to have been interpreted by some users as a shared struggle against adversity, itself reinforcing a sense of imagined community. Writing in 1907, for example, Ford Madox Hueffer had this to say:

> I have known a man, dying a long way from London, sigh queerly for a sight of the gush of smoke that, on the platform of the Underground, one may see, escaping in great woolly clots up a circular opening by a grimy, rusted iron shield, into the dim upper light.[7]

This slightly masochistic identification began to give way to a broader appeal from the 1880s. For anyone willing to endure the smoke and dirt, westwards extensions of the Metropolitan line into open country offered the potential for suburban living, with all the closer links to nature which that implied. To many like Joseph Radford, even during the filthiest days of steam traction in 1906, life in *Our Suburb* made it all worthwhile:

> He had no word for its but bliss;
> He smoked his pipe; he thanked his stars;
> And, what more wonderful than this?
> He blessed the groaning, stinking cars

That made it doubly sweet to win
The respite of the hours apart
From all the broil and sin and din
Of London's damnèd money mart.[8]

The links between the Metropolitan and subsequent suburban Underground lines were intricate ones. The resulting cultural landscapes were given the name "Metroland", promoted by the Underground but appropriated by residents too. Much later, looking back to the 1950s, Julian Barnes remembered his early life there with affection:

"Où habites-tu?" they would ask year after year, drilling us for French orals; and always I would smirkingly reply, "J'habite Metroland!" It sounded better than Eastwick, stranger than Middlesex; more like a concept in the mind than a place where you shopped.[9]

This identification with Metroland was probably due in part to the new opportunities which the suburbs opened up in many residents' lives. As one "Metroland Pioneer" explained, "I was to find that residing in a suburb adds a thrill and a zest to life. It is an experience in having no tradition to live up to."[10] With plenty of cultural roots then still offered by other "traditions to live up to", Metroland offered the stimulation of open futures, to foster the construction of identities still rooted, but not stuck in the past.

Until the second world war, the Underground continued to offer these open futures to many who could never have afforded them before. Looking back on his 1930s childhood, the planner Peter Hall remembers the new opportunities for "The ordinary people like my father, who were putting down their humble £5 deposits (yes, £5 deposits) to acquire their brand new semis":[11] People who together represented "thousands of private dreams, ... all those new worlds".[12]

Positive place-identities, then, were eventually constructed from a complex set of factors, some highly negative in themselves. This successful outcome did not happen by accident. At least in part it was probably due to two key human factors: the American links of its top management, which opened the company to a rich tradition of US corporate thinking, and the presence – in the person of Frank Pick – of an energetic publicity manager.

First trained as a lawyer, Pick had previously worked for the North Eastern Railway. Here he applied his legal mind to operational issues, developing a keen interest in the use of statistics as a tool of rational management. He joined the Underground in 1906, and was given responsibility for the Company's publicity in 1908. In 1909, a new department of Traffic, Development and Advertising was set up, under his control. Responsibility for improving the quality of the service and for promoting its image to the public were now united: an arrangement with great potential for giving the Underground a more positive place-identity. Matters such as the convenience of the service, the attitudes of the staff, and the comfort and appearance of the rolling stock were crucial in constructing place-identity; but the Underground's physical design also had important roles to play, at all scales from station layouts to the design of individual graphics. Let us analyse Pick's strategy for designing all these elements, in the sequence in which it developed.

The first stage in this sequence was concerned with poster advertising. Since their earliest days, the underground lines had gained a regular income from posters on their platforms: the captive audience of commuters made these sites highly attractive to advertisers. Little design thought had been put into the positioning of these posters, so they presented a chaotic overall appearance. To make matters worse, the disorganised mass of posters made it difficult for passengers to pick out the name board of their particular destination from amongst the welter of other information on the platforms, and the consequent frustrations contributed to a further sense of disorganisation. Gunn Gwennett, himself an illustrator of railway advertisements, voiced this complaint: "It is as though the guards on the Central London Railway shouted out: 'Next station Pear's Soap, Buchan's Pills, Marblarch, Bovril.' "[13] This conflict between advertising and clear station naming would have to be overcome in the development of coherent cultural landscapes, to give shape and definition to the imagined community of underground users.

Following surface railway precedent, most stations had a relatively small number of large name signs: usually about four per platform (Figure 4.1). On the Underground, which had stations spaced far closer together than those on the surface lines, this sign system – which require passengers to crane their necks for the nearest nameplate – was far from ideal. The closeness of the stations, which meant that passengers had to make frequent identification decisions, called for station names which were easier to spot. Pick's approach was to provide a far greater number of signs, spaced approximately one carriage-length apart, so that one of them would always be in view from every position, in every carriage, wherever the train stopped (Figure 4.1).

Various experiments were made in order to decide the correct height at which the signs should be mounted. Because many of the platforms were crowded with people at peak hours, the first idea was to mount the signs above head-height, so that they would not be obscured by the crowds. However, this meant that strap-hanging passengers inside the cars could not see them at all, so a compromise

height was arrived at. This open experimental attitude, where final design decisions were made only after careful practical trials, was (and still is) extremely rare in any field of design. It stems, perhaps, from the careful construction of arguments, based on solid evidence, typical of Pick's legal training. We shall encounter this approach again and again in his work.

The first of the new signs were simple horizontal panels carrying the station's name, but these did not stand out clearly enough; partly because the competing posters and other notices were also rectangular in shape. To contrast with these, a circular bull's eye form was designed: again, this was decided upon only after practical experiments with semicircular paper cut-outs, above and below the horizontal name boards, pasted temporarily in place.

This bull's eye design was used for several years, but Pick was never really satisfied with it, feeling that it was still not sufficiently eye-catching. One day in

Figure 4.1
Early station name sign, with later version above it: Belsize Park.

1916, according to his assistant, he asked, "How does the YMCA red triangle symbol manage to hold your eye?"[14] Suspecting that the reason might be the white space at the centre of the triangle, rather than the triangular form itself, he commissioned the design of a symbol with a red ring rather than a solid bull's eye; and this gradually became the standard form used throughout the system: another example of the gradual evolution of a design, using empirical evidence of what worked well, drawn without prejudice from any available source.

Even with this highly noticeable symbol, if nothing else had been changed there might still have been a problem in making the relatively small signs stand out from the other graphic material – particularly the most eye-catching of the posters – which plastered the platform walls. Because of the Company's uncertain financial position at the time of Pick's early work, it was not possible to remove the posters altogether, for the associated advertising revenue was sorely needed. Pick, however, reasoned that each poster would become more valuable if it could be made more legible to the public; so that a smaller number of posters, if arranged in a more orderly fashion, could generate at least the same revenue as before. A suitably coherent layout was designed in Pick's usual practical way. The posters were arranged in horizontal strips, linking the station nameplates into a unified band along the platform walls. Within this strip, the posters were organised two-deep, and in modules of 4, 8, 12 or 16 posters wide. To the walls were pasted sheets of dark blue backing paper, large enough to leave dark frames round each of the standard 20 inch by 30 inch "crown" sized commercial posters. Spaces were left for other advertisements to publicise the travel facilities offered by the Underground itself: these posters were larger, at 25 inches by 40 inches, and were arranged only one-deep, so that they stood out clearly from the rest.

This arrangement, so simple to implement, revolutionised the appearance of the Underground's platforms (Figure 4.2). First, it generated a coherent image, with a place for everything and everything in its place; an impression enhanced by the fact that this layout was itself standardised for all the stations throughout the system. Second, it contrasted well with the "target" station names, whose own legibility

was thereby increased. The public responded to these changes with enthusiasm: early on in the development of Pick's ideas, The Times printed a letter from a passenger who had noted the effects of the re-organisation, and found to his delight that he could "alight at the stations required without having to hunt through all the soap, pills, whisky, milk, etc. to find the name of the stations".[15]

The individual designs of the company's own posters also had their parts to play in constructing the system's overall place-identity, by emphasising the legibility of the system as a whole, and by presenting the Underground not just as a means of transport, but rather as a life-enhancing source of varied experiences. The creation of maps, whose designs developed over the years to present the system as a unified whole, proved specially effective. The earliest Underground maps showed the positions of the various lines and stations in a graphically straightforward way (Figure 4.3a). However, a glance at such a map showed a disorganised-looking pattern of lines: just the result one might have expected from amalgamating a series of separate companies which had never been conceived as an integrated system in the first place. All-too-honestly, the map is entitled "Underground Railways of London": note the revealing plural.

Other graphics, however, were used to promote the idea that what the map showed was easily understood as a coherent whole. In 1908, for example, John Hassall's "No Need to Ask a Policeman" showed a comic country couple, presumably up to London for the day, asking a policeman for directions, and merely being pointed towards an Underground map on the wall behind him: an image of legibility reinforced by an impression of friendly authority.

By 1931, the map itself had been redrawn by Henry Beck in a far more legible way (Figure 4.3b). Instead of curving about, the lines are now all presented as straight lengths of track, running vertically, horizontally or at 45 degrees to the axis of the map; so that they seem to form a highly organised whole, with a specifically "modern" character reminiscent of the then hi-tech wiring diagram of a radio set. Distances too were altered: the gaps between the central London stations were

Figure 4.2
Poster frames integrated into design of platform space.

exaggerated, whilst the suburban stations were drawn closer together than true scale would warrant. This made it seem easy to find one's way around Central London, which was reassuring to the casual visitor: an effect which was reinforced by the way some of the individual stations were redrawn. On early maps, complex changes from one line to another, required at stations such as King's Cross and Baker Street, had been faithfully shown. The schematic later maps indicated all the stations with the same symbol: a small, neat circle; which in some cases obscured the real complexities which passengers had to negotiate. So far as anyone planning a trip to the suburbs was concerned, drawing the distances between the stations there at a smaller scale made the suburbs concerned seem more accessible than they really were.

Beck's map has remained in use, with relatively minor modifications and additions, well into the twenty-first century. When it was first produced, Peter Hall recalls how "at the age of about five, I spent many obsessed hours with coloured crayons, copying it out".[16] Its fascination as a design icon remains just as powerful to adults, three generations later: it has been pressed into service as an art museum poster, reinterpreted as a painting, and even used as the tee-shirt logo of a Jerusalem night club: broad appeal indeed.

A reinforcement of the "broad appeal" message formed the common theme of a second sort of poster. In Alfred France's "The Way for All" (1911), the message is mostly carried by the text, straight-forwardly presented as a notice built into a tiled wall, but reinforced by association with the beautiful young woman who is pointing it out to us (Figure 4.4a). Humour is used to underline a very similar message in "The Popular Service Suits All Tastes" (1913): here an overground station is rendered in the style of

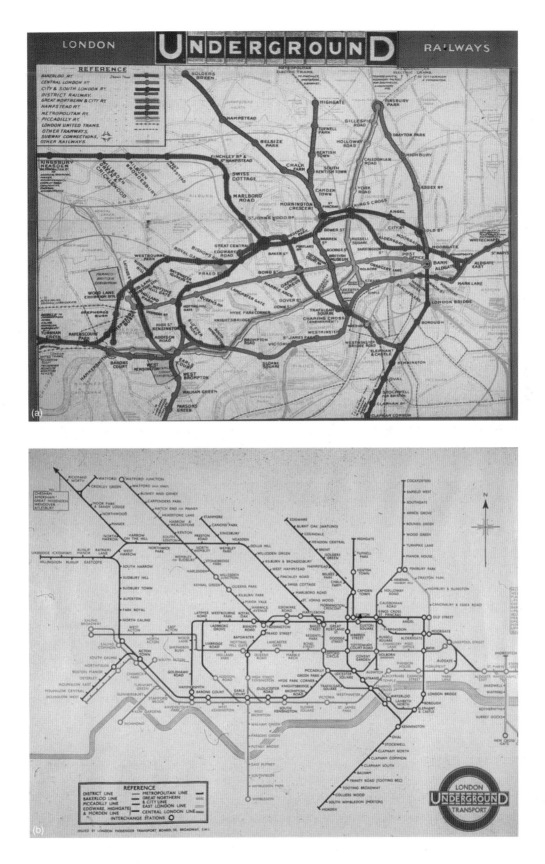

Figure 4.3
(a) Early map of Underground system. (b) Beck's revision of the Underground map.

Figure 4.4
(a) Alfred France: "The Way for All". (b) McKnight Kauffer: "Power".

a willow-pattern plate, which forms part of the "popular service" punningly referred to. A more dynamic rendering of the same theme has Alfred Leeth showing an Underground station as a great magnet, towards which people of all sorts are relentlessly drawn by "The Lure of the Underground" (1927).

A third group of posters – the largest all-told – advertised the Underground as the gateway to all that London had to offer: enjoyment, education, tranquility, excitement; the ethereal and the timeless alike. Sometimes the messages were extremely tightly focused, as with Sharland's "Boat Race" (1913): a particular event at a particular place at a particular time on a particular day. Sometimes in contrast the point was a more general one. In this vein is the splendidly titled "Winter's Discontent made Glorious" of 1909, which shows a brightly lit train with views into the warm carriage interiors, shown

as the theatre, department store and restaurant towards which the passengers are being conveyed; warm and comfortable despite a drenching downpour outside, and with the title's Shakespearean allusions adding an extra touch of class: a marriage of comfort and culture, again to generate an image of wide appeal. Or, more general still, "London's Underground lends you Wings"; as a young city clerk floats by, to capture Cupid with his umbrella: the Underground as the romantic match-maker, at least from a male perspective, which inspired the poet Richard Church to write *Strap-hanging* in 1928:

Now that we are wedged together,
Sweet stranger,
Closer than man and wife,
Why not make the best of this indignity?
Let our blood rioting together,
Murmur stories of our life's adventures,

*Just as a river in its course
Brings emblems from its source.*[17]

Finally, a further large group of posters was used to put forward a view of the Underground as powerful, fast and future orientated in character. This was an important commercial sales pitch, so the Underground's efforts here tried to push a future-orientated reading of the system – and by extension its readers – as far as possible. Because of their own associations of modernity, abstract modernist forms were often used in later posters of this type, incorporating the text as an integral part of the composition. McKnight Kauffer's "Power" (1931) is a dramatic example (Figure 4.4b).

Each of the themes which the poster campaign promoted – legibility, nature, modernity and the Underground as the key to a life-enhancing experience – was itself given a broad transcultural appeal by being presented and re-presented in ever-changing ways. Pick himself was clear about how important this was:

Everyone is different and responds to different suggestions. And so the advertiser who is enabled to publish a whole series of posters has a far better prospect of success than the advertiser who must rely on one or two.[18]

Christian Barman, Pick's publicity manager from 1935, reinforces this message:

By changing your manner from one moment to another you could appeal to every section of your audience in turn, and if you went on doing this for long enough the entire audience would end up on your side. Some people would be unable to respond to what you were doing at a particular moment but the audience would realise that, taking it all in all, nobody had been forgotten; there was something there for everybody.[19]

Avant-garde or traditional, serious or comic, low-key or dramatic: something there for everybody. And with the individual posters firmly disciplined by the layout of the platform wall surfaces, an overall sense of clear organisation too.

From organising individual wall surfaces, Pick's thinking grew to encompass the design of whole stations, as opportunities arose. The first major opportunity came with the extension of the Northern Line out to Edgware, which was completed in 1924. From what we have seen of his approach so far, we should expect him to proceed in a gradual way; one carefully tested improvement leading to the next. Following this line, the logical first step might have been gradual improvements to the design format already established for the earlier Northern Line stations, completed in 1907 (Figure 4.5). Most of these had already been designed to build up a coherent place-identity for the Northern Line by following a consistent elevational concept; each with a series of distinctive tall arches, the number varying to suit the dimensions of each particular site. As well as presenting a consistent image, these stations were mostly rather successful in standing out from their surroundings as noticeable landmarks. This was highly appropriate to their public function, and also helped to fix them in the public mind as memorable elements in the Underground identity.

There were, however, many reasons why these stations would have been inappropriate as models for developing the place-identity ideas which had been initiated by the poster campaign. The exteriors, for example, were clad in dark, liver-coloured faience, which looked almost black in dull weather, and therefore had quite inappropriate connotations for a company working hard to get away from an image of smoky gloom. The entrances were relatively narrow and dark, and led into congested ticket halls: certainly there was no sense of effortless flow from the street. The transition from pavement to platform was made even more disjointed by the need to wait for lifts, or to negotiate long spiral staircases. This effect was made especially noticeable by the topography of the area: Hampstead, for example, is still the deepest station in the whole of London. And, to complete this catalogue of inappropriate design concepts, the internal detailing of this type of station was, by the 1920s, looking extremely dated: the penalty of having been all-too-fashionable with its bottle-green art nouveau when it was built. At every level of design, from external appearance through spatial structure to internal detailing, most of the old Northern Line stations were not fit models for the new Edgware extension.

Figure 4.5
An early Northern line station: Chalk Farm.

There was, however, one exception. Golders Green – the original terminus, and a ground-level station – had been built in the neo-Georgian style. This for 1907, was quite avant-garde: Pevsner, for example, refers to it as "then very up to date".[20] Even in the 1920s, when the Edgware extension was planned, it would not have seemed old-fashioned; and, if only because classical forms had been around for a couple of thousand years, it was considerably less prone to the rapid stylistic obsolescence which had overtaken art nouveau. Given the need to promote a "modern" corporate image, with stations which would nevertheless have to last a long time, this was a considerable advantage.

Neo-Georgian, therefore, seemed a logical starting point for the design of the stations which extended the line onwards from Golders Green to Edgware (Figure 4.6a). But in other respects too these new stations represented a considerable step forward in using architectural design to promote an appropriate place-identity. For example, the idea of clearing away the old constricted ticket hall, and replacing it with a more generous space to allow the passengers a freer access, was tried out with great success at Kilburn Park. And Westminster, which was remodelled in 1924, marked the point at which the previous cumulative effects of step-by-step improvements flipped over into a new concept – the underground station as a shop – which was used in many later stations (Figure 4.6b).

There were, of course, many previous links between underground stations and shops. The major rebuilding of Baker Street in 1912 had incorporated several shops within it; and the new suburban stations, with their larger sites, often had shops associated with them in the same building complex, and sometimes within their ticket halls too. From all this, it was only a small step to see the station itself as a shop: a shop selling "access to London". And once this step had been taken it was possible to learn

Figure 4.6
(a) "Up to date" neo-Georgian. (b) The station as a shop; Brent Cross.

lessons from shop design itself, about such matters as customer access, elevational design and lighting.

At Westminster itself, the remodelling of the Victorian station produced wide, clear openings to the street, leading directly into a large, uncluttered ticket hall. However, high levels of lighting could not be achieved on this constricted urban site, at the base of an existing building; so the passer-by looking in would have seen only a large black hole. From this time on, one of the key design issues was to find ways of achieving high levels of light – preferably natural daylight – in the ticket hall spaces: the illumination of the "point of sale" in the Underground was seen to be just as important as illuminating the goods in any other kind of shop.

Westminster is also notable because here Pick first employed the architect Charles Holden who, in collaboration with Stanley Heaps and others, was to design 39 underground stations during the next 15 years. Holden was no young firebrand. He was 48 years old, and an established figure; with a considerable reputation for design in a "stripped classical" manner which was "progressive" but still kept its feet firmly on traditional ground: the "rooted but not stuck" approach so widely relevant in place-identity terms. Pick had known Holden for nearly 10 years, for they were both founder members of the Design and Industry Association. Convinced that Holden could deliver the kind of forward-looking image that he wanted, Pick nonetheless had a problem. The design of underground stations was a complex and specialised task, of which Holden knew nothing whilst Heaps was an expert: they would have to work together. In typical fashion, Pick first commissioned Holden to design one small doorway at Westminster, to see how he and Heaps would get along; and then nurtured the working relationship through two more alteration schemes before trusting Holden with a major role in the seven stations involved in extending the Northern Line south to Morden, between 1925 and 1928. As Pick himself put it, "we are going to represent the DIA (Design in Industry Association) gone mad, and in order that I may go mad in good company I have got Holden to see that we do it properly".[21] Even in the case of these new stations, design proceeded in a carefully tested way, with the construction of a full-scale mock-up of a typical entrance facade and hall, with equipment and lighting, in the Underground's Earls Court depot, so that Pick could judge its character in detail.

An analysis of the Morden terminus will show how far Holden managed to cultivate Pick's corporate identity, in terms both of spatial structure and of visual image, from the seeds sown by Heaps at Brent Cross. The spatial linkage between the street and the platforms is handled as a smooth and gradual series of transitions, both in plan and in section. Starting from the wide pavement, the traveller passes first under a wide canopy, flooded with light through its glass-block roof, and running for about 50 yards, past the row of shops which forms part of the station complex (Figure 4.7a). At its mid-point, the canopy runs into a large double-height hall. Although still an outdoor space, with the heavily used public pavement running through it, this is enclosed by walls on three sides, and by a huge window, with coloured glass bull's eye motif, facing outwards, on the fourth (Figure 4.7b). Increasing the sense of ambiguity about whether this is an indoor or an outdoor space, it is furnished with a huge electric chandelier (indoor connotations) hanging from a high sky-blue ceiling (outdoor). This indoor/outdoor hall has its long axis at right angles to the pavement; directing the traveller through a broad screen of glazed entrance doors, into a large octagonal booking hall (Figure 4.8a). This is certainly an indoor space but it has a very large octagonal skylight, and its ceiling is "dematerialised" by the daylight playing over its wave-like plaster surface. A further "outside" feeling is contributed by the newsagent's shop which opens onto one side of the octagon, helping to set up a diagonal axis which directs the traveller out of the hall, through glazed doors and down steps to a gallery in the upper level of the partly glazed train shed; whence more broad flights of steps lead down to the high, partly enclosed space of the platforms (Figure 4.8b). Finally, walking along the platform itself, one comes back into the open air once again. Overall, this spatial sequence enables the passenger to pass from the street to the train through a series of gradual and effortless transitions: every possible design decision is devoted to making the space of the Underground read as integrally linked to the public space structure within

Figure 4.7
(a) The pavement canopy and shops at Morden. (b) Inside/outside space at Morden.

Figure 4.8
(a) The Morden booking hall. (b) Platform access at Morden.

which it is set and which, as we have seen, is so crucial in identity-construction terms.

The building's surfaces and details are designed to get the same message across. An atmosphere of "lightness and brightness" is generated by the daylight which floods in through skylights and large areas of glazing, and this is reinforced by the use of white Portland stone; whilst artificial light shining out from the glazing, and continuous floodlighting along the full-length canopy, continue this "light and bright" theme even after dark. The symmetrical mass of the building, and its stripped classical Portland stone detailing, give a high-status character; whilst the plain, flat surfaces and large areas of glazing had powerful connotations of modernity in 1928. The front facade of the main hall is effectively an illuminated advertisement, of massive scale and permanence: a standard concept for all seven new stations along the line (Figure 4.9). The standard bull's eye logo, at large scale and in coloured glass, forms its central focus; whilst the same logo is used, in three-dimensional form, to make capitals for the square section battered columns which support the station name. Advertising of a more ephemeral kind, in the form of posters, is incorporated into the architecture by using poster display cases as massively squat columns to support the main canopy. This "place for everything and everything in its place" theme carries through to the platforms, where Pick's original blue paper poster frame idea is monumentalised in black, green and grey tiles: a wall treatment which is standardised for the tunnel platforms all along the line.

At every level from spatial structure to the details of its wall surfaces, the design of Morden and other Northern Line stations communicates the corporate identity which the Underground was trying to promote: an image of lightness and brightness (Figure 4.9), modern efficiency and high levels of organisation, with a place for everything and everything in its place. But these were not the only important connotations these buildings had. The way they were interpreted by the cultural establishment was also important, in terms of acquiring cultural capital which would stand the Underground in good stead when it came to government negotiations about extending the lines, to take commercial advantage of the waves of suburban expansion which

were gathering pace during the late 1920s. From the beginning, Pick's place-identity campaign had been conducted in ways which were able to generate cultural capital: his involvement with the DIA, his frequent patronage of "serious" artists for his posters and his employment of Holden as an "established" architect all had potential in this regard. Hitherto, however, he had not focused on achieving this potential in practice. From now onwards, he began to emphasise this aspect of the Underground's campaign, to great effect, in three ways.

First, he sought more "high culture" exposure for the "non-commercial" side of the work which was carried out as a normal part of the corporate identity campaign. For example, in 1928, an exhibition of selected Underground posters was held at Burlington House, clearly an "established" venue. With no accompanying text to explain their commercial purposes, the posters were presented very much as art pieces.

Second, the Underground sought association with activities which were seen to be "cultural" rather than directly "commercial" in character. For example, from 1932 onwards, exhibitions of industrial design, under the auspices of the DIA, were held in the main hall of Charing Cross Underground station.

Third, and most prominently, the "good design" aspect of the Underground's own new buildings was emphasised ever more strongly. The first opportunity came with the building of the company's new headquarters at 55 Broadway, designed by Holden and completed in 1929. To the cultural elite, the building was particularly noteworthy because it incorporated the work of "serious" sculptors like Henry Moore and Jacob Epstein. Certainly it was the "modern" character of Epstein's sculptures which hit the headlines: the *Manchester Guardian*, for example, wrote of "storms of criticism rising at times into terms of full blooded abuse that are rarely heard in art controversy in England". At first sight, this public outcry might be thought negative in terms of its impact on the Underground's corporate image; and so it might have been, if reaction to the building as a whole had been unfavourable. Luckily, however, it was not. In a context of overall positive evaluation, the outcry over Epstein's sculptures was as valuable

Figure 4.9
The importance of lighting: a contemporary photograph.

as salt in a stew: it was a signal to the cultural establishment that the Underground was not merely a crassly commercial operation, but had a real interest in fostering the arts as well. Still, it would no doubt have been better to have made this impact without stirring up negative public opinion in the process; and this would only become possible, in their later work, if Pick and Holden could somehow develop a design vocabulary which could be seen as "artistic" by the cultural elite, *and* as "proper architecture" by ordinary people. In 1930, the year after 55 Broadway was completed, Pick and Holden went on a study tour of new buildings in Germany, Holland and Scandinavia, to see what was on offer in terms of "modern" design ideas abroad.

The illustrated report on the tour which they published for private circulation on their return – itself a part of the development of cultural capital – did not deal with the corporate image implications of the design concepts they saw, but was couched exclusively in terms of "good design" in the abstract. Both text and illustrations make clear the formal innovations which interested them. First, they focused on the move away from the traditional "hole in the wall" window in much Continental modern design, in favour of what they called the "horizontal line" and the "vertical line". Second, they were complimentary about buildings which, whilst being identifiably "modern", nevertheless kept links with more traditional architecture; particularly through the use of traditional materials. The Dutch brick modernism of designers like Dudok was singled out for special praise in this report: "Dutch work, though it has rid itself almost entirely of traditional ornament, retains most of the elements of traditional design." It carried on "the spirit if not the letter ofthe old".[22]

Third, they were impressed by examples of "total design" in Denmark. The report remarks that the

characteristic of using the architect for the design of things quite other than buildings appears common in Copenhagen. At the time of our visit, several new buses and two new trams were running about the streets of the city which had been designed by the city architect. It is indeed, this extension of the principles of architectural design to things like buses and trams, and to quite small objects like tea wrappers or match boxes, which is perhaps one of Denmark's most interesting contributions to contemporary design.[23]

The Copenhagen experience, it seems, enabled Pick to focus consciously on what he had already been working towards, in practice, for more than two decades. All three of these lessons from the

Continental tour – the use of the horizontal and vertical lines as concepts for the visual organisation of buildings, the use of brick as a link with native traditions (and therefore, hopefully, public acceptance of modern design) and the "total design" integration of details into the larger whole – were to be used in the next phase of the Underground's expansion; starting with the rebuilding of Sudbury Town station from 1930 onwards.

Sudbury Town was intended as a dry-run for the new generation of stations. It was to build on all the lessons learned at Morden, but reinterpreting these in the light of what had been seen in Holland and Denmark. Pick – as we should expect from his previous track record – was particularly concerned to go in the Danish "total design" direction; and instructed the general manager and the chief civil engineer to supply Holden with a complete specification of all the station equipment which would be needed, so that "nothing shall be built which has not been specially designed to conform with the general architectural scheme".[24]

At the level of detailed integration, however, the results are not so satisfactory; partly because of the lack of experience with exposed brick and concrete used indoors, with no plaster to hide the services. Pick, when he saw the completed building, was furious: "you will note the gas piping, once more, for carrying the wiring cable. I think the whole performance unsatisfactory" he said; going on to remark that it would have been much better "if the lighting had been designed properly and at the proper time", and that "there is an entire lack of design and orderly workmanship".[25]

Given the importance of integrated details in creating an impression of "good organisation" for the Underground as a whole, this was a serious matter. The reason for it was organisational, rather than any lack of interest in detailed design on Holden's part: at the root of the problem was a division of design responsibility between Holden and the Underground engineers. Pick therefore introduced a new organisational system:

Unless some special effort is made, there is every prospect that the stations and works will have to be botched, just as Sudbury Town station had to be botched, by a failure to have a clear plan of what is required before the work is carried out. I think, therefore, we should have placed before us, at once, plans showing the lighting schemes for all the stations, and the whole of the miscellaneous equipment required; also plans showing the location and form of all signs and notices at stations, and a plan showing the water supply and any further arrangements that may be necessary for cleaning. We cannot regard a station as being approved for execution until all these various plans are agreed.[26]

Once this more integrated approach had been resolved, there followed a series of some 30 more stations, all built during the 1930s, which together represent the peak of the Underground's corporate identity approach to design. In these buildings, the vocabulary of design themes which had gradually been evolved to support the Underground's corporate identity – the landmark massing, the gradual spatial transitions between street and platform, the connotations of light and of modern efficiency, and the integrated detailing – were all freely developed to suit the unique characteristics of each particular site.

The vocabulary of external forms was extremely limited. It contained only brick, concrete and metal glazing as materials, assembled together within the disciplines of the "horizontal and vertical lines". The restricted nature of this palette was itself the key to achieving a visual expression of the unity of the Underground system as a whole, but this limited vocabulary was manipulated, with great skill, to generate a particular form for each station, which enabled it to stand out as a landmark of a type appropriate to its particular importance and its peculiar urban setting. In the larger stations, the booking hall itself was often carried up as a dramatic mass: rectangular as at Sudbury Town, octagonal as at Bounds Green, or circular at Arnos Grove. In less important situations, a smaller element would do the job, as in the illuminated towers at Osterley and Boston Manor, or the stylised statue of an archer at East Finchley. At Park Royal – a site on the main western approach road to London – a circular booking-hall drum is combined with a massive square tower, to build up a dramatic image appropriate to its "gateway to London" location (Figure 4.10). And at

Figure 4.10
Park Royal as "gateway to London".

Wood Green, by contrast, a low, curved horizontal form is enough to make the station stand out from its more conventional neighbours.

Like the restricted palette of external forms, the typical relationship of street to platform via a sequence of transitional spaces is also a constant for all the stations, but this too runs through a gamut of variations, with no two examples the same. The "deep tunnel" stations on restricted, built-up sites are often especially interesting for their handling of the transition form the station entrance to the escalators: a sequence which goes far beyond what was achieved on the Morden extension. Wood Green is a skilful example. Here the arbitrary, accidental curve of the site boundary is used to generate a symmetrical booking hall, almost boat shaped on plan, with wide entrances fanning out into the street, but with a very powerful long axis integrating directly with the escalator space. Today, in these 1930s stations, the details of the escalator spaces have often been altered for technical and safety reasons;

but contemporary posters, for example, show that the diagonally sloping escalator space's potential for generating an atmosphere of dynamism and modernity had also by now been realised (Figure 4.11).

In terms of integrated detail, the best of the new tunnel-platform spaces also went far beyond what had been achieved on the Morden line. In stations like Turnpike Lane, such items as station names, poster frames and notices were all carefully integrated into the tiled wall surfaces (Figure 4.12): the ultimate expression of the place for everything, with everything in its place; redolent of the clockwork efficiency which the Underground wished to convey. And overall, the integrated detail combines into a powerful horizontality, with its clear connotations of modernity and speed.

It seems clear that by the mid-1930s, the Underground's managers and designers had succeeded in creating cultural landscapes which offered a wide range of users a sense of solidly rooted modernity.

BRIGHTEST LONDON

IS BEST REACHED BY

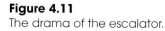

Figure 4.11
The drama of the escalator.

The historian Andrew Saint, for example, points out "the glamour and allure that the Underground has always enjoyed in the eyes of foreigners",[27] pointing to Steen Eiler Rasmussen's 1928 view that in London "The only true modern construction is, taken as a whole, not architecture: the Underground."[28] The Underground's managers, of course, saw the value of strengthening this perception; for example by contributing a mock up of their latest station ideas at the 1930 Monza Exhibition of Industrial and Decorative Art (Figure 4.13).

Closer to home, Peter Hall recalls his own childhood sense that the Underground "had a truly magical quality for any child, and for more than a few parents".[29] The stations opened up new vistas: "They seemed like modern palaces. The huge, brilliantly lit entrance halls, the extraordinary

indirect lighting on the escalators, the clean lines of the station platforms, the rivers of people flowing through the system; all made an impression of power, of simplicity, that was overwhelmingly the magical memory about my childhood."[30] With the filthy days of steam traction now long forgotten, even the smell is affectionately recalled: "Above all I remember the smell ... It has gone, vanished from the world. It hit you like a wall as you entered the station: warm, enveloping, rich, pungent."[31]

The war years, however, initiated many changes in the Underground's cultural landscapes. At one level, the system's associations with shared struggle against adversity lent it renewed meanings of national unity, through its role as communal bomb shelter. Particularly before children were evacuated to the countryside for safety, the Underground stations sometimes offered havens of safety for long periods. At Swiss Cottage, for example,

Our sleeping companions last night were a boy of six and his sister of nine. When the All Clear was sounded at 6.30 they said, "we are going home now to have a nice breakfast.""Not to sleep?""Oh yes! We go to sleep then, until twelve or half-past." Then about two o'clock we came back and wait until they let us into the station at four o'clock.[32]

Experienced directly by many, the underground's sheltering landscapes were broadcast to many more across popular and elite cultures, though films and though the powerful "shelter drawings" of the artist Henry Moore.[33]

All in all, the Second World War marked the end of an era for the Underground. Pick died in 1941, having resigned in the previous year; but more important than one individual's death – no matter how dedicated and powerful the individual – was the changed economic and political situation of the Underground after the war's end. During the late 1940s more people were using the system than ever before, so there was no need to encourage more travel. "Today our Traffic Department would actually be happier if people travelled less, especially during peak hours," wrote Harold Hutchinson, the Publicity Officer, in 1947. "The present function of our poster publicity, therefore, is different. It is to be London

Figure 4.12
The careful integration of details.

Transport's information window through which we tell the public what we do and what we hope to do."[34]

A management team which "would actually be happier if people travelled less" would hardly have a powerful driving vision for the system's future. Nonetheless, increased travel demand made extensions necessary. Unsurprisingly, the design of the consequent expansions of the Victoria and Jubilee Lines during the 1960s and 1970s took a low-key approach: "the station may be criticised for appearing visually unexciting but we consider that preferable to a transient popularity without lasting qualities", as Victoria Line designers explained.[35]

With no perceived need to attract new passengers, attention to place-identity issues was largely replaced by a rather managerialist approach to design. Architect Giles Oliver, who worked for Underground from 1977, remembers how "I was advised to remember that the fundamental design

principle was hydraulic – and to keep the involuntary passengers flowing in and out of the system without blockages or turbulence."[36] The growing dullness of this approach, regarding people as things, was wryly remembered by the writer Barbara Vine: "On the map the Victoria line became light blue. When the Jubilee Line was nearly finished there was some speculation as to what colour would be used for it. Possibilities remaining were pink, lime green, orange and mauve. London Transport Underground chose grey."[37]

Insofar as place-identity issues were addressed at all, growing concern about the worldwide erosion of local place-identities was reflected by a gradual shift of attention away from the system's overall identity towards a concern for the local identities of its constituent parts. Stations on the Victoria line, for example, had tiled panels on the backs of the platform seats, stressing local identity themes; often

Figure 4.13
The Underground as an international symbol of modernity: contemporary photo at 1930 Monza exhibition.

in rather arch ways, as in Brixton's "ton of bricks". The unconvincing nature of such a mural – I have several times heard passengers sneer at it – is unsurprising. For design strategies to have any strong potential in identity-construction terms, they have somehow to connect positively with real human desires and interests. All too often, however, travellers seem to have been thought of not as active human beings, but rather as potentially fearful sheep; so that design efforts were addressed to "taming the intestinal profiles (of the tunnels) with smooth floors, vertical walls and deceptive laminated ceilings, an illusion fixed by uniform fluorescent lights, to hold their panic at bay", as Giles Oliver remembered.[38]

The stations of Pick's golden age, with their "total art work" approach, were progressively starved of the maintenance and management required to keep them pristine. As Andrew Saint saw it, "the lasting homogenisation and order they sought were too ambitious to achieve. Perhaps they were always papering over cracks; perhaps too the golden age of

the London Underground, like most golden ages, was never quite so golden".[39] A growing sense of muddle and disorder gradually eroded the sense of safety and order which Pick and his collaborators had worked so hard to achieve during the inter-war years.

This sense of disorder grew during the 1970s. With no driving vision to channel design creativity, and with "functionalist" modernism increasingly challenged within design culture itself, the 1970s Underground became increasingly subject to arbitrary design fashions. As Giles Oliver saw it, "Here was the language of boutiques and *Starship Enterprise*."[40]

The worrying sense of disorder began to turn into outright fear with a catastrophic fire at King's Cross station in 1987, and a growing awareness of the potential for terrorist attack demonstrated by the well-publicised release of Sarin gas in the Tokyo Subway. Effectively, the Underground's place-identity potential had returned to the "sepulchral" days of a hundred years earlier. Now, however, the situation was harder to redress. Ground-level public space, just as before, was seen as dangerous through media hype; but now many people felt safe ensconced in their private cars, which now also seemed the key to life-enhancing choice. There could be no sense now of a shared "triumph over adversity" so far as the new dangers were concerned: unlike its predecessor a century before, the Underground was not seen as offering any triumphal payoff of new opportunities to balance the dangers run.

Attempts to overcome travellers' fears were first concentrated at the level of cultural meanings alone. By 1990, management had initiated the development of a Design Strategy intended "to create a calming environment of neutral colours and rationalised signage",[41] later supplemented by other initiatives such as the psychologist Charles Spence's creative attempts to use fragrances to address the perennial issue of the Underground's smellscapes. In the absence of positive change at the level of use, however, these meaning-level changes were largely perceived as mere manipulation.

Towards the end of the century, however, in new Jubilee Line extensions,[42] a more coherent design strategy began to be developed in response to new imperatives. Once again there was a need to produce cultural landscapes to encourage many people to develop identities as public transport users; this time not for commercial reasons, but in response to the manifest sustainability problems of auto-dependent urbanism.

These new cultural landscapes, however, could no longer be produced through the "total art work" approach to the system which Pick had earlier used so powerfully, for the overall cultural context was now quite different. For one thing, as we already saw, the total art work approach had proved impossible to maintain in practice. For another, negative perceptions of cultural homogenisation through globalisation had by now led to increasing demands for the sorts of cultural landscapes where local differences matter. At least implicitly, therefore, the Jubilee Line's new strategy built on the approach of emphasising the place-identity of particular local stations, which had first been signalled in details such as the tilework of the Victoria Line.

In the Jubilee Line, therefore, the earlier tentative experiments with individual station identity were carried a radical step further by appointing different designers for each station. These various designers were linked only by the facts that they were themselves London based, and that their previous work suggested that they would be able to create the new types of landscapes needed to relaunch the now tired old system.

If under this new strategy the system as a whole was no longer treated as a total art work, however, the various individual stations certainly were; and it is this which offers each the sense of order (and implicitly, therefore, of safety) which had earlier become weakened. In their various ways, the stations' designers also offer imagery which many users might interpret as forward looking, helping them to see the system as opening up new opportunities in their everyday lives (Figure 4.14). The "historical continuity" dimension of design is now shifted primarily to the level of use, for all the designs call creatively on the types of free-flowing spatial structures which had been developed long before, during the Pick regime. The sense of rootedness thus offered is further reinforced at the meaning level, by the seamless incorporation of the new stations into Beck's iconic map; by now hallowed as the Underground's equivalent of a national flag.

This new shift in the balance of design attention, away from the cultural landscape of the system as a whole towards its individual parts, is certainly not unambiguously positive. From an "outsider" perspective, for example, the Italian writer Sebastiano Bandolini suggests that "In this game of parts, something important is lost."[43] Whether the "game of parts" will prove fruitful from a more local perspective, in providing cultural raw material for constructing personal identities with an increased orientation towards public transport use, remains to be seen; but it certainly has to be taken as a serious contribution to the Underground's distinguished tradition of identity by design.

Looking back, what can we learn from this tradition overall? There are a number of important lessons we can draw out, in relation to a range of key identity-construction issues.

First, let us consider these at the level of co-dwelling with the wider ecosystem. During the Pick era, links between public transport and a sense

Figure 4.14
Forward-looking imagery at Stratford.

of co-dwelling with other aspects of nature were developed through design at several levels. At the level of use, for example, Metroland opened up new opportunities for developing contacts with "nature", both through everyday life in the transit-orientated suburb, and through making special visits to "the country". The later development of suburbs which were *not* transit-orientated, and which therefore could only foster auto-dependent lifestyles whose negative sustainability implications ultimately undermine the co-dwelling project, gave rise to new issues; which in turn called for the construction of identities with renewed public transport orientation. Recent Jubilee Line work seems promising in promoting a renewed sense of the excitements and opportunities which public transport can offer.

At the level of constructing imagined community, earlier chapters have shown the importance of public space as the key arena for "us". Despite the fact that the Underground has never itself been a truly public system, we have seen how its designers developed techniques for handling spatial axes to promote the difficult integration between the spaces of the system itself. In a current context where profit-orientated market pressures are increasingly transforming public space networks into series of disconnected enclaves,[44] the wider use of these axial planning disciplines has much to offer.

The Underground story also has much to offer in terms of transculturality across different social groups. At the process level, for example, we have seen the beginnings of attempts to go beyond the *intentions* of individual designers to discover *evidence* about the practical impacts of design decisions in users' terms. Pick's early work with mock ups of station signs, for example, can be seen as early manifestations of user involvement in design; whilst the poster campaigns also promoted transculturality by using a wide range of styles, appropriate to a wide range of different cultures, in Christian Barman's "something for everyone" approach. Further, the efforts which were made to monitor the sales of different styles of posters enabled public reactions to the image level of design to be followed up through time.

As one of the key public transport systems of a major world city, the Underground's support for transculturality had to relate to users from abroad as well as across different social groups of Londoners themselves. Pick's regime addressed the issue of achieving cultural relevance across this global/local divide: for example, his European study tour with Holden identified a detailed design vocabulary which integrated international modernism with more local, London brick traditions; and which therefore related across national boundaries in a way appropriate to a world city, but with direct "home" appeal too.

The Underground story also offers lessons in constructing cultural landscapes which can be drawn on to construct identities with increased levels of empowerment. Here, as we have seen, we are always concerned with the balance between a confidence-building sense of rootedness and an open, optimistic relationship to the future. The Underground story clearly demonstrates that what counts as an appropriate balance here must always depend on the wider context of the design situation. In practice, for example, the potentially totalitarian implications of Pick's "total art work" approach to the whole system was counterbalanced by the fact that London itself had a relatively weak *overall* place-identity. Rather than making people feel disempowered cogs in an overall machine, therefore, this approach merely helped to bind together the "city of villages" which many felt London to be.

Conversely, the powerful overall identity established through the system's underlying spatial structure, and symbolised through Beck's iconic map – the Underground's equivalent of a national flag – counterbalanced the later shift of the total art work focus, from the system as a whole to the individual station. Rather than collapsing into disempowering anarchy with no sense of us-ness at all, this shift of focus from whole to part merely deepened the empowering message that "small things matter"; which had long been carried, for example, through the graphics – incorporated *into* the architecture by the architectural frames provided for them, rather than merely "stuck on" – which played such an important role in the Underground's cultural landscapes.

At every level of design – from process to product, from use to meaning, from spatial structure to surface detail – the Underground story offers lessons about how cultural landscapes can provide raw material relevant to all our key identity-construction issues. Perhaps the most original of these insights, different from those yielded by our earlier case-studies, concern the process level: in particular, the attempts made to canvass users' reactions to experimental design ideas. These are clearly insights which deserve to be followed up more closely, to see how this user-involvement approach might be developed in more thorough-going ways. That is what our next chapter explores.

Notes

1 Cherry, 2000, 27.
2 Ibid., 28.
3 Cited in Bain, 1940.
4 *Times*, June 14, 1879.
5 Blumenfeld, 1930.
6 Gray, 1978.
7 Hueffer, 1907.
8 Radford, 1906, cited in Dyos and Wolff, 1973; Vol. 1, 300.
9 Barnes, 1981, 33.
10 Cited in Edwards and Pigram, 1986.
11 Hall, 1994, 13.
12 Ibid.: for further discussion of London Suburban dreams, see Bentley, 1981a,b.
13 Cited in Douglas, 1963.
14 Cited in Barman, 1979, 45.
15 Barman, op.cit., 29.

16   Hall, 1994, 12.
17   Church, 1928.
18   Cited in Barman, 1979, 32.
19   Ibid.
20   Pevsner, 1942, 32.
21   Cited in Barman, 1979, 118.
22   Ibid., 135.
23   Ibid., 137.
24   Ibid.
25   Ibid., 138.
26   Ibid., 138–139.
27   Saint, 1996, 24.
28   Rasmussen, 1990 (1928), 15–21.
29   Hall, 1994, 12.
30   Ibid., 13.
31   Ibid.
32   *De Profundis*, September 1940.

33   For discussion of Moore's drawings, see Sylvester (ed.), 1969 (1944).
34   Cited in Saint, 1996, 32.
35   Cited in Oliver, 1996, 35.
36   Oliver, 1996, 35.
37   Vine, 1991.
38   Oliver, 1996, 35.
39   Saint, 1996, 32.
40   Oliver, op.cit., 37.
41   Ibid., 39.
42   For more on Jubilee Line, see MacCormac and Stevens, 2002.
43   Bandolini, 1996, 5.
44   For a "cool" account of these pressures, see Bentley, 1999, Part 2. For a "hot" one, see Davis, 1990.

5

Red Bologna

In the last chapter, we explored the range of marketing and design techniques which Frank Pick and Charles Holden used to unify a fragmented underground railway system and, in the process, to promote a place identity to tie together disparate parts of London. In addition to "state of the art" marketing and design tools, Pick and Holden also consulted underground travellers and workers as "local experts", to provide inputs for constructing new imagery to make a more legible and enjoyable travel experience.

This use of "local experts" in the place-identity building process was taken much further in the libertarian communist city of Bologna, from the 1950s onwards, in order to save and rehabilitate its historic core, its *centro storico*. This was achieved through a creative partnership between local politicians, design professionals and local people. In this chapter, we shall discuss how the interweaving of imagined communities and cultural landscapes through this partnership has led to innovative conservation practices in Bologna's place-restructuring programme (Figure 5.1).

First of all, let us explain the historical and political contexts within which these place-identity ideas developed. From its foundation, the development of Bologna's urban form was underpinned by topography. Capital of the province of Emilia Romagna, Bologna stands at the crossroads of northern and southern Italy, astride *Via Aemilia*.[1] Due to its excellent location for business activities, it grew into an important Roman centre known as Bononia; laid out on a grid still visible in the deep-rooted morphological structure of the historic nucleus and surrounded by three lines of fortifications. The two main Roman streets – *decumanus maximus*

(east–west) and *cardo* (north–south) – still remain the principal streets of present day Bologna: *Vie Ugo Bassi – Rizolli (Via Aemilia)* and *Vie d'Azeglio Galliera – val d'Aposa.*

By the eleventh century, the city began a period of economic and demographic boom; and was extended to six times its original size.[2] With a Law School already established, Bologna founded the first European University specialising in legal studies.

In 1164, when the Bolognese citizens joined the Lombard League, an alliance of Italian *commune*, and urban historians Fanti and Sussini[3] attribute this shift in political alliance to the presence of many teachers and students of law, who aspired to a more democratic system of city government. By 1256 the city housed some 50,000 people, and increasing wealth underpinned a large building programme. The city proper was encircled by three successive walls, the last being completed as a 7.5-kilometre polygon. Some 180 towers and fortresses provided not only strong defensive support, but also became a visual trademark of Bologna, and a key place-identity factor (Figure 5.2).

Within the three lines of mediaeval walls, the city's spatial structure continued to be defined by a grid system of streets and blocks, intersected by canals which provided water for generating power to support the city's local manufacturing industry – mainly paper products for books and manuscripts – for transport, for water supply and for drainage. Even today, this mediaeval morphological structure still plays an important role in place-identity terms (Figure 5.3).

A major urban design intervention, carried out by the Commune of Bologna between 1200 and 1203,

Figure 5.1
Morphological layers of Bologna.

was the forming of the *Piazza Maggiore* (Figure 5.4a). During the thirteenth century the *piazza* was enlarged to become the city's main open-air theatre where carnivals, *palio* (horse races) and major political events took place.[4] Since mediaeval times, the square has represented the city's collective imagined community.

Today, the key building which defines the west part of the space is the Basilica of San Petronio, started in 1390 and never finished. According to local urban historians,[5] the Basilica has always been considered a symbol of local power, expressed through the impressive size of the edifice: 132 metres long, 57 metres wide and 44 metres high in the central nave.[6] The Basilica's importance is also emphasised by its raised position with nine long steps elevating its entrance above the level of the *piazza*. Opposite the

basilica is *Palazzo dei Podesta*, on a site bought by the *comune* in 1200 to build its own offices (Figure 5.4b). The central tower *Torre dell'Arengo*, built in 1212, connects to King Enzo's Palace at the back; and stands as a landmark, symbolising the city's power, on the *piazza*'s eastern side. To the north is the Town Hall and the Hall of the Notaries. Finally, the southern edge is defined by an elegant, arcaded building, built in 1412. Its name – *Palazzo dei Banchi* – indicates its ground floor activities: bankers and moneylenders had their stalls under the arcades. The building was renovated between 1563 and 1568 by Vignola; unifying several earlier buildings with an elegant new facade, but leaving two arched passage ways to connect the piazza with the complex of Roman and mediaeval streets.

The city's distinct character is also enriched by many other historic building types. The eleventh

Figure 5.2
Mediaeval towers of Bologna.

century's most significant typological introduction was the *portico* (Figures 5.5a and 5.5b). It is estimated that, when combined, *porticos* stretch to 75 kilometres. They were built as private structures, supporting rooms above the public passageways, to provide extra space for the residents and to supply much needed accommodation for some 2000 students. According to historian Carlo de Angelis "the ground floors of mediaeval dwellings were often studios or boutiques, although severe punishments were dispensed for those who built permanent structures in the porticos. During the day, craftwork was permitted on condition that space was left for pedestrians".[7] One of the oldest porticos surviving, still forming an important landmark, is that of the *Palazzo Sanguinetti* in *Strada Maggiore*.

Materials, too, are important here. Early mediaeval buildings were constructed of wood; but fire problems led to wood being replaced over time by red brick, made from local terracotta soil, whilst stone, often recycled from the Roman ruins, was used for the more important public buildings. The terracotta red brick colour of the buildings, the towers and the porticos contributes strongly to the Red Bologna identity.

A second important wave of city building took place during the fourteenth, fifteenth and sixteenth centuries; particularly under the influence of the Bentivoglio family, who promoted large urban construction programmes. From the sixteenth century, the city council decreed that all new porticos have to be built of brick or stone. This led to the construction of new building types closely linked to the socio-economic status and occupation of its residents, which further transformed the city's image (Figure 5.6a).

Figure 5.3
Bologna's mediaeval plan.

Figure 5.4
(a) Bologna's Piazza Maggiore with Basilica of San Petronio and Palazzo dei Banchi. (b) Palazzo dei Podesta and Torre dell'Arengo, built in 1212.

Figure 5.5
(a) Old porticos of Bologna. (b) Palazzo Sanguinetti in Strada Maggiore.

In 1553[8] the Inquisition arrived in Bologna; expelling all the Jewish families to a ghetto, where they suffered economically and socially.[9] Though centuries apart, we can see here the same negative side of imagined community that we encountered in nineteenth century Prague. Later, we shall see how these negative historic pressures have been addressed in Bologna's more recent rehabilitation programmes.

During the nineteenth century, there were many class clashes; but from about 1889 internal conflicts calmed down, and renewed efforts went into the improvement of the city fabric. According to Roberto Scannavini, "with the adoption of the 1889 plan and the demolition of the third wall in 1902, the fourth and last formal addition of the post-unification city (1861) was born. Boulevards, public gardens (those of Minghetti and Cavour), belvederes (of the Hill of San Michele in Bosco), French-style expansion (Via Farini, 1870; Via Independenza, 1875; Via Ugo Bassi, 1909, etc.) and the little villas of the public gardens all exemplify this modern transformation of Bologna" (Figure 5.6b).[10] Whilst the infrastructure plan was influenced by Haussman's ideas, to accommodate fast-growing industry, conservation was also focused on the restoration of historic monuments.

In the aftermath of the Second World War Bologna, like many other Italian cities – especially those in the north – entered a period of economic and political transition, after a spell of fascist government between the wars. Considerable problems, linked to the political restructuring of the city government, corruption and land speculation,

Figure 5.6
(a) Bologna's porticos. (b) Via Ugo Bassi with Torre Garisenda and Torre Asinelli in the background.

were experienced in the early post-war period and the historic core of the city was greatly transformed as many historic buildings were pulled down without permission.[11] The Italian people had to come to terms with their turbulent past, and with the negative impacts of Mussolini's Fascist government. A redefinition of Italian national identity began to be manifested in arts, literature and cinema, and through national, regional and local administrative structures.

Early post-war Italian town planning practice was not well developed. Until 1942 most planning decisions had been made centrally, giving very little power to the local administration. During the period of fascist government, all the contemporary town planning ideas developed elsewhere in Europe were banned. As a result many Italian cities,

including Bologna, had difficulties in coping with the need for post-war restructuring.[12] The liberal left communist party, which had first come into power before the First World War but had fallen victim to Fascism, therefore had to work hard during the 1940s and 1950s to develop its powers and spheres of influence; aiming to decentralise some of the city's political and administrative functions, and to introduce a democratic system of decision-making based on public participation in local governance. These ideas were not totally new to Bologna, as its first *comune* (commune) had been founded in the eleventh century.

The first post-war plan was a reconstruction plan known as *Piano di Recostruzione*, produced in 1948.[13] This contained proposals for the reconstruction of

133

areas demolished by bombing, but failed to address the future growth and infrastructure needs of the city. Fast urban growth took place during the 1950s, largely associated with the influx of migrants from poorer southern regions of Italy, seeking better employment and housing opportunities. In 1958 a new plan was approved, based on the 1889 and 1937 master plans, it was already out-dated by the time it came into force. In addition, weak fiscal and implementation mechanisms meant that Bologna continued to sprawl in a piecemeal, unplanned fashion with no proper infrastructure provision. At the same time the historic core of Bologna was in social and economic decline because of the closure of manufacturing industries and the eviction of working-class families from their historic neighbourhoods: a spatial redistribution of the urban population, known as the "sack" of Italian cities,[14] which was largely due to land speculation and to the unauthorised demolition of historic buildings in the core of the city.

In order to combat these problems, a number of new initiatives were developed. First, unemployed blue-collar workers began to form small entrepreneurial businesses with a very positive impacts on the city's economy. According to Simon Parker, these new worker–entrepreneurs "were later to provide a vital link between the social-communist subculture and the productive middle class"[15]: that is, a new united imagined community. Second, many farmers became members of the communist party, "forging links between workers and small producers".[16]

The Bologna Communist party prospered under Mayor Giuseppe Dozza, who oversaw a liberal form of Communism with an efficient, honest and innovative municipal government: many social building programmes were implemented, and Bologna acquired new hospitals, schools, play areas and a subsidised public transport system. The city was organised into 18 local neighbourhood councils known as *Consigli Quartiere*, each representing some 30,000 residents, with all members democratically elected. The historic core of the city had 4 councils together representing some 80,000 residents.[17] The new city administration took on board all city planning functions, and appointed two leading experts: Leonardo Benevolo as City Planner and Pier Luigi Cervellati as City Architect.[18]

All town planning and administrative policies developed during the second half of the 1950s were formalised and consolidated in a new master plan of 1960, approved by central government in 1965. The plan's key objectives were to oppose speculative gains in the land and housing markets, to increase the role of public housing agencies, to improve the housing conditions of low-income and working-class people, to rebalance development trends in the metropolitan area by controlling the location of industrial plants and safeguarding agricultural land, and to protect the historic heritage of the city centre.[19]

In order to achieve these goals, the city administration used three mechanisms: a public housing programme, a service location programme and a new system of land controls. Attention was given to the provision of low-income housing within the city boundary, rather than on the outskirts as was the practice in other Italian cities. A new housing policy known as *Piano di Edilizia Economica e Popolare (PEEP)* was prepared at the beginning of the 1960s, and was employed in the acquisition of city land for housing and other public facilities such as schools, hospitals, and cultural and social centres. Although the city could not solve all its housing problems, because housing funds were controlled by central government, Francesco Bandarin claims that during the 1960s Bologna was "the only city in Italy with a large stock of newly built public housing in proximity to the urban centre".[20] A more balanced urban growth strategy was implemented in 1968 through the Metropolitan Plan for Bologna, which slowed down immigration from rural areas. The Metropolitan Plan also incorporated strategies for reshaping the transportation system, for land control and for transforming the functions of the historic core.

In addition to controlling new urban expansion, the rehabilitation and preservation of the historic core was high on the agenda of both the city administration and local neighbourhood councils. The driver for conservation and rehabilitation was the belief that "the ancient city was not only a collective expression; it was also the property of its inhabitants".[21] The rehabilitation programme became a revolutionary act, where conservation signified the social reappropriation of the city.

This idea of social reappropriation was not only politically driven. There was much ideological material in Italy at that time linked to the cultural work of the Italian Neo-Realists. Themes of social marginalisation and exploitation were vividly expressed through cinematic realism, in masterpieces depicting urban life such as Roberto Rossellini's *Roma Città Aperta* (1945) and Vittorio de Sica's *Ladri di Biciclette*, released in 1948.[22] Parallels can be found in the writings of Alberto Moravia and Giorgio Bassani with dominant themes centred on working-class people and their struggles for survival. The squalid tenements and desolate outskirts of northern Italian cities were also captured by Alberto Lattanda's photographic works.

Similar ideas began to be explored by city planners and architects. According to Peter Rowe "in architecture, neorealism was also asserted as an appropriate way of identifying with the mass movements sweeping Italy after the war, and of creating dwelling environments in a familiar, commonplace way".[23] This was achieved in overall development layouts which both respected topography and reflected the building practices of older rural towns; making typological references to traditional building structures with pitched roofs, stuccoed walls and shuttered windows.[24] Such houses were designed both to appeal to their future occupiers – young families from rural areas – and to forge a transculturality from the traditional roots of popular culture to high art, as we already saw in Prague and in Plečnik's Ljubljana buildings.

Particularly, influential was the Neo-Rationalist architectural movement *La Tendenza*, which opposed speculative development trends. According to Kenneth Frampton, the protagonists of *La Tendenza* wanted "to save both architecture and the city from being overrun by the all-pervasive forces of megalopolitan consumerism".[25] Some architectural theorists, such as Manfredo Tafuri, saw the salvage of the historic city as a revolutionary act; through which architecture and urbanism could change the socio-political order of the country. At the same time architects such as Aldo Rossi and Giorgio Grassi were concerned with the development of theories of architecture and urbanism that promoted new methods of analysis, classification and design; rooted in the past but also responding to changing, everyday needs. In addition, architects and town planners began to develop a new generation of city plans, which respected existing morphological structures whilst accommodating new needs. They supported the employment of architectural and town planning devices that were familiar to users, and therefore – as Peter G. Rowe sees it – "could be embraced broadly with affection".[26]

Neo-Realism was also rooted in traditional and participatory city building practices that support an intimate relationship between culture, shelter and the individual; thus supporting the construction of a particular type of imagined community. Mario Ridolfi and others set out to document traditional construction techniques, to assist builders and craftsmen in restoration work. These studies led to the development of the Italian school of urban morphology, whose key protagonists were Severio Muratori, Gianfranco Cannigia, Leonardo Benevolo, Pier Luigi Cervellati and Aldo Rossi.[27] This approach was founded on the understanding that a city can be read through its physical form elements. These elements can be analysed at different levels of resolution: the buildings, the plot units, the open spaces, the street/block system, the overall settlement morphology and the region.

In addition to these physical levels, the morphologists claimed that it is also important to understand the socio-economic and cultural aspects of urban form, and the way these are transformed over time. Severio Muratori, the key protagonist of this approach in Italy, also introduced the concept of "operational histories", based on understanding the relationship between urban form and the time of building. Equally significant is the concept of *tessuto* or urban tissue: the characteristic overall pattern of relationship between land subdivision, plots and streets, as well as groups of buildings and open spaces and their associated patterns of use. The Italian morphologists used characteristic tissues, composed of morphological elements either built at the same time or belonging to the same set of morphological rules, both for analysis and for design.[28]

Gianfranco Caniggia developed the Italian morphological school of thought even further. He introduced the concept of *procedural typology*, which focuses on the classification of *building types*, their origins and their mutations over time. When a new building type is constructed it is known as a *leading type*. A leading type can be modified over time to become a *mutation type* (Figure 5.7). Building types and their relationships to urban tissues were seen as important for understanding place-identity over time, and building types were considered by Caniggia to be "elemental roots of urban form".[29] This concept allowed architects to use traditional tissues and typological references as sources of ideas for constructing either new types or mutation types. In using these approaches, neo-realists and morphologists were attempting to produce an antidote to the sense of alienation which they associated with schemes designed in the international modernist style.

Once this attitude towards Bologna's historic centre, its people, and its inherited patterns of built form had been established, the next step was to carry out a systematic analysis of the evolution of the city, and to make an inventory of its built form elements.[30] Using the morphological and typological classification methods outlined above, systematic studies of the historic built form were carried out between 1962 and 1965. This huge task was co-ordinated by Leonardo Benevolo, Bologna's City Planner and "one of the most prominent Italian planners and architecture historians".[31] He was assisted by a team of well-known architects and urbanists such as City Architect Pier Luigi Cervellati, Gianfranco Caniggia and Roberto Scannavini. First, the overall city plan was analysed and presented in a number of morphological maps. These contained important information about how the overall spatial structure of Bologna had been formed over centuries of the city building process (Figure 5.8). These morphological layers show that the ancient grid layout has changed little over time. The overall urban plan is therefore an important deep-rooted structure, a skeleton that holds many building types together, and it is therefore critical to retain it in any new interventions in the historic city core. The morphological maps also contained information

about the city's services and infrastructure; periods of tissue formation and their transformations over time; patterns of characteristic land use; and the socio-economic profiles of particular neighbourhoods (Figure 5.9).

In addition to these overall morphological analyses, individual buildings and open spaces were analysed, using Gianfranco Caniggia's typomorphological classifications. Four main typological categories and subcategories were identified:

- *Category A* includes large building types, called *contenitori* (containers) including convents, palaces, and industrial units which have a great potential for accommodating public facilities such as schools, theatres, libraries and other functions.
- *Category B* includes courtyard complexes of 10–20 metre building depth with mixed-use developments on the ground floor.
- *Category C* consists of private buildings with narrow frontage (4, 8, 10 metres wide) and deep plot coverage, which were identified by the professionals as a potential source for public housing schemes.
- *Category D* included larger residential dwellings suitable to house larger families or in private ownership (Figures 5.10a and 5.10b).

Each building was also analysed in terms of its physical condition, socio-economic potential, level and type of repair needed, and potential use. All these aspects were integrated to form a methodology of urban renovation, attributed to professor Leonardo Benevolo. According to Francesco Bandarin "the essential concept of the Benevolo proposal was that the architectural typology is, as well as the facade or the style of buildings, a characteristic to be preserved as part of the historic heritage".[32] Similar attention was given to both hard and green open spaces, as they were considered important for the daily lives of the Bolognese citizens. Each typological group and its typological sub-components were then translated into building codes, which were subsequently used in the development of specific rehabilitation proposals.

Once the morphological elements had been described and analysed by professional teams, it was

TERRACE HOUSES

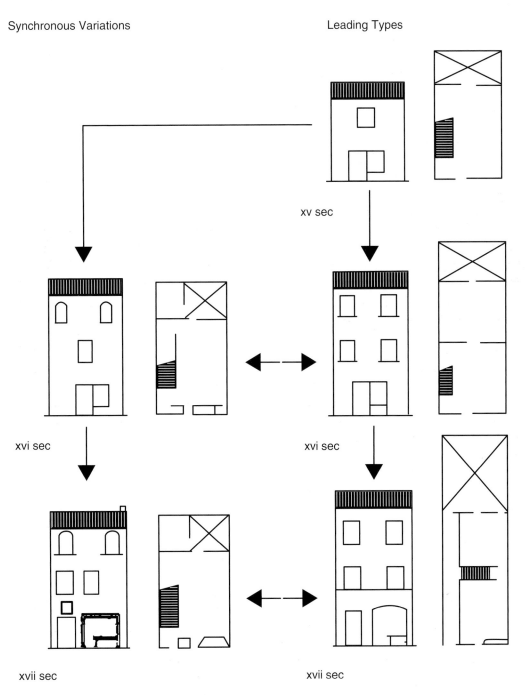

Synchronous Variations

Leading Types

xv sec

xvi sec   xvi sec

xvii sec   xvii sec

Figure 5.7
A typological classification method of Bologna's leading mutation types.

Figure 5.8
Bologna's historic layers.

necessary to identify what counted as *important* in place-identity terms. Since place-identity is linked to the meanings that users attribute to places, it was important to engage different user groups in this process, because morphological classifications are not value free. They only provide a source of data; and therefore what counts as important to whom, in place-identity terms, has to be interpreted by users themselves. User-participation practices were also supported by the city council, who wished to establish a more democratic system of decision-making, of which city planning was an important aspect. The key underlying message is clear from Francesco Bandarin's question: "For whom are we going to restore and preserve this historic heritage?"[33] The answer was both obvious and important, it was to be for the citizens of Bologna.

The process of place-identification and restoration was therefore based on public participation and consultation, which developed over time into one of the biggest participatory exercises amongst recent urban intervention programmes. This complex approach to historic city restoration is based on the premise that the historic city is the collective property of its inhabitants, where all social classes are integrated. By adopting this position, the conservation approach "signifies the social reappropriation of the city"[34]; returning it back to its *comune*, its social and political conscience, and its deeply rooted sense of imagined community.

A starting point for constructing a positive place-identity for Bologna was therefore an all-inclusive method through which the city's cultural landscape could be identified as "ours": as the property of the

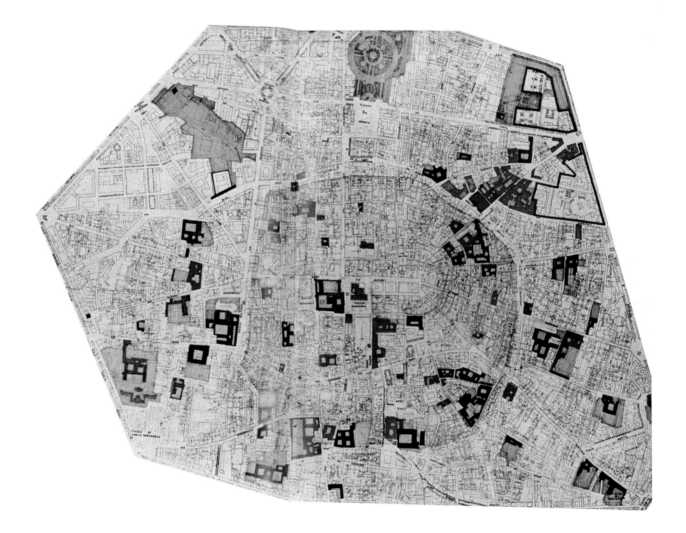

Figure 5.9
An analytical record of Bologna's inventory showing the location of key monuments.

Bolognese residents, shared by as many different social groups as possible. By working collaboratively with professionals and politicians, local citizens began to forge a new integrated form of imagined community, which they expressed through a variety of ideological and built form material.

The method chosen for this collaborative process of place-identity construction is generally known today as "Inquiry by Design", as defined by John Zeisel in 1981.[35] In this approach, design solutions are tested with different user groups; and through various stages of elimination, shared and mutually supported design solutions are developed, as common visions. These common shared visions then form the starting points for developing implementation strategies.

The first important aspect of this collaborative place-identity process concerned relationships to nature. These were approached at two different scales of intervention. At the micro scale, a positive attitude to nature is expressed through many "tiny oases"[36] scattered among the rooftops, courtyards and city, and neighbourhood parks. The macro scale concerned the relationship between the city's compact urban form, with its tightly grouped street sequences and buildings, and its topography and natural landscape elements. Particularly important

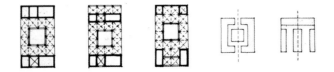

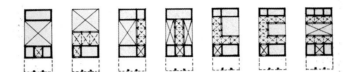

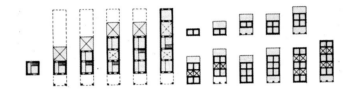

(a)

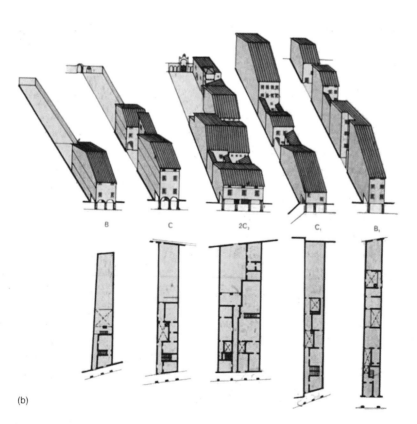

(b)

Figure 5.10
(a) Typological classifications of Bologna's residential dwelling plans. (b) Three-dimensional classifications of Bologna's residential dwelling types.

here were the hills that surround the city, so protecting these had many important meanings. First, the hills provide a certain degree of protection from the expansion of development. Second, the hills symbolise important links between urban and rural communities: wooded or planted with a variety of crops, they provide a rich supply of produce for the Bolognese citizens. The hills also form the foothills of the Appenines: a particularly well-protected scenic area composed of meadows, hedges, farms and vineyards; full of local plant and bird species, as well as having a rich supply of underground water courses which flow into the river Reno. Without this rich natural supply, life in the city would have been poorer (Figures 5.11a and 5.11b). In order to safeguard this "nature–city partnership", a new Metropolitan plan known as *Piano Intercomunale Bolognese*, approved in 1968, helps to protect and guide the urban expansion of the Emilia Romagna region. The plan covers 17 municipalities, a total of 700,000 inhabitants and an area of some 390 square miles.

A second important aspect, in place-identity terms, was the cultural landscape of the city itself, embodied in its overall morphology and spatial sequences. We have seen how the historic core of Bologna was formed over time, and how it was linked to the socio-cultural and political life of the *comune*. These deep-rooted links became important in the redefinition of the imagined Bolognese community of residents, traders, students, academics and other visitors. Again through regular consultation and engagement with community representatives, the city's overall spatial structure was redefined. Although most of the discussions took place at the local neighbourhood councils, the city-wide aspects of place-identity construction took place in the main city square, *Piazza Maggiore*. On the occasion when the main strategies were discussed in 1966, some 150,000 Bolognese citizens participated in the exposition of the ideas,[37] which were then further discussed in the Town Hall and in the local councils.

In order to overcome the divide between professionals and users, large-scale models and axonometric drawings of neighbourhood blocks were prepared by the professionals to facilitate better-informed discussions with the "local

experts" – residents, traders and others – about the types of interventions needed in individual streets and buildings. Together, professionals and users were developing a *common vision*, of an open and optimistic imagined community; rooted in the past but not frozen in the past, and offering a wide range of choices in the everyday lives of as many Bolognese people as possible. This inclusive participatory approach to rehabilitating neighbourhoods also engaged the residents of the former ghetto, correcting the harsh destiny of the people who in 1553 were marginalised and "gated" so as not to spoil the rest of the city (Figures 5.12a and 5.12b).

After much discussion, key proposals for the city were officially adopted in 1966. Further studies led to the identification of methods of designation and intervention for 13 rehabilitation projects. These ideas were consolidated into an overall plan for the historic centre known as *Piano per L'Edilizia Economica e Popolare/Centro Storico*,[38] approved in 1973. With new housing reform, funding and legal mechanisms in place, the City Council, professionals and residents began to implement the plan, through three methods of intervention: restoration of monuments and buildings of great historic value; renovation and conservation of urban tissues and building typology, and reconstruction of buildings that could not be preserved. Some of the buildings which were demolished were not replaced, in order to create more open space in the city; much of it contained within urban courtyards. Of the 13 planning areas originally designated, known as *comparti urbanistica*, five were selected for the first phase of the implementation process; either because of their typological and social homogeneity, or because of their overall importance in historic terms.

In order to implement the rehabilitation plan, a form of co-operative management structure was set up. This was based on several important principles. First, all projects became collective properties with clear management structures, and public and private responsibilities. Second, each member of this collective was guaranteed the security of an apartment for life. Third, each family was guaranteed fair rent. In addition, some of the repair work was paid for from the rents collected, and the rest – about 80% of the rehabilitation cost – was paid for

Figure 5.11
(a) A panoramic view of Bologna. (b) Bologna's rooftop mini oases.

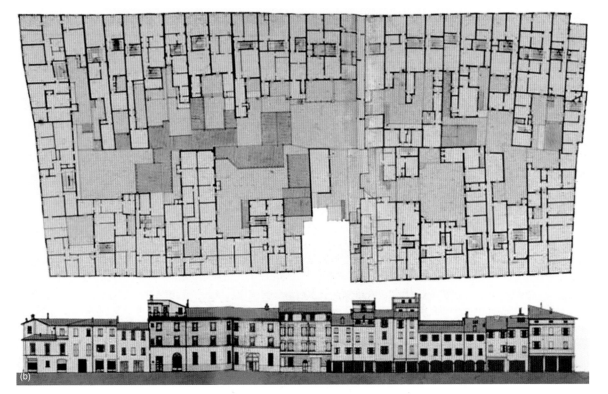

Figure 5.12
(a) Exhibition panels and a model of neighbourhood rehabilitation proposals. (b) A plan and facade elevations of restoration proposals for Via Maggiore street.

by the City Council. The co-operative system and the collective ownership of the rehabilitated buildings was set up to allow members a certain degree of flexible tenancy. Residents are able to move from one tenanted property to another within their co-operative system, in order to satisfy individual families' changing needs. Local neighbourhood councils are also responsible for the approval of rehabilitation budgets, for the regulation of commercial activities and for the management of social, cultural, education and health facilities.

But how did all this work out on the ground? Let us now explore the partially rehabilitated historic core, in order to understand how the cultural landscape and community ideology have produced a particular type of imagined community, and reinforced Bologna's place-identity. Through this process of collaborative engagement we are discussing what David Novitz[39] calls the construction of participatory art and appreciative practice. This kind of art can best be understood through kinaesthetic spatial experiences – journeys through the city – since the viewer is then physically involved in the artwork and intellectually engaged in negotiating the meanings that streets, spaces and architectural elements offer.

The starting point of our own journey is the central space of *Piazza Maggiore*. We have already explained how the space was formed, and how it has played a key role in the daily lives of Bologna's citizens since its foundation in 1200 (Figure 5.13a). The *piazza* is located in the heart of the historic core, and its present day shape is the result of successive transformations. The space carries many historic meanings, both from ancient and recent times. During the more recent past, in particular, not all its associations have been pleasant ones. The place is therefore imbued with strong feelings with many relics built into the arcaded walkways recalling the city's turbulent past.

Today the *piazza*, which is pedestrianised, is used for a variety of daily and special functions, for strolling up-and-down on Sundays and in the evenings; for concerts and political debates; or for children running around and playing. A well-known phrase "*andare i piazza*" or "going to the square" is still used by Bologna's citizens visiting the space for their daily *passeggiata*.[40] As passers-by venture into the *piazza*

they "look up to" the Basilica, and to an impressively large mosaic figure of San Petronio, which gives messages similar to those associated with the National Museum in Prague, discussed in Chapter 1. The steps, on the other hand, provide interesting and comfortable platforms used by many as conversation corners or observatories, from which they can watch the world go by (Figure 5.13b). The *piazza*'s central zone is slightly raised, giving the impression of a stage-set and the whole space has recently been repaved as part of the rehabilitation programme.[41] The paving was designed firstly to unify the *Basilica* and the *piazza* colour scheme of pale-grey and pink marble slabs, and secondly to define a varied range of activity zones.

The *piazza*'s walls are formed by important and recently restored public buildings (Figures 5.14a and 5.14b). The Town Hall has a similar importance to the Basilica, being the seat of the local administration.[42] In its entrance hall one can view a large axonometric drawing of the city, as a reminder of the efforts which have been invested in improving both the city's fabric and its citizens' quality of life. The Town Hall and the *Palazzo dei Podesta* define a smaller space, *Piazza del Nettuno*; built between 1564 and 1566, by Pope Julius II, to show off a huge statue of Neptune by the Flemish sculptor Jean Boulogne (or Giambologna) from Flanders, itself placed on top of a fountain designed by Tommaso Laureti of Palermo. The steps surrounding the fountain are used as resting places, and the whole sculptural complex provides a functional and visual sense of enclosure to the *piazza*, separating busy *Via Ugo Bassi* from the quieter space of the *piazza* itself.

Continuing our spatial sequence, we enter through the *Quadrilatero*, known as "Bologna's Belly" because of the number of shops and the variety of merchandise on sale. This maze of tiny alleys and streets is "full of grocers, butchers, cheese and fishmongers, bakers and confectioners, all masters of good food, their tidy shop-windows packed with mouth-watering victuals. Here, too, are found skilled artisans such as goldsmiths, postcard-sellers and drapers".[43] The names of the streets give clues to the types of merchandise on sale: *Via Clavature* for locksmiths, *Via Pescherie Vecchie* where fishmongers used to be, and *Via Drapperie* where drapers used to sell their wares. Today most of the streets sell a

Figure 5.13

(a) Restored Piazza Maggiore with beige and pink marble slabs. (b) A detail of Basilica of San Petronio.

Figure 5.14
(a) The Town Hall and the Hall of the Notaries located in the northern side of Piazza Maggiore. (b) A view into *Piazza Maggiore* from *Palazzo dei Podesta*.

146

Figure 5.15
(a) A display of rich local produce in *Quadrilatero*. (b) A view of *Piazza Maggiore, Via Vitale, Strada Maggiore* and *Via San Stefano*.

variety of goods; providing a richness of visual, sonic, tactile and olfactory sensory experience. Through this rich experience, we can see how creative rehabilitation solutions linked to employment and services provision have helped in the formation of the Bolognese imagined community, constructed both from physical form elements and from patterns of use. This offers a powerful lesson for other cities that have either sanitised or gentrified their historic cores (Figure 5.15a).

Leaving the Quadrilatero at *Piazza Mercanzia,* an irregularly shaped open space, three streets fan out: *Via Vitale, Strada Maggiore* and *Via San Stefano. Via Castiglione* defines the edge of the *Quadrilatero*

quarter, and leads into the *Piazza Mercanzia* (Figure 5.15b). The name of the *piazza* is linked with the *Loggia della Mercanzia,* erected between 1384 and 1391: according to Renzo Renzi and Otello Sangiorgi the "building is a gem of international gothic architecture".[44] Again, this is building closely linked with the affairs of the Bolognese *comuni,* being used as their customs house. Built in Bologna's characteristic red stone, it strongly supports the city's distinctive "red" image. *Loggia della Mercanzia* used to be called *Trebbo dei Banchi* which means a place of lively meetings, due to associations with foreign students exchanging many different international currencies. The building

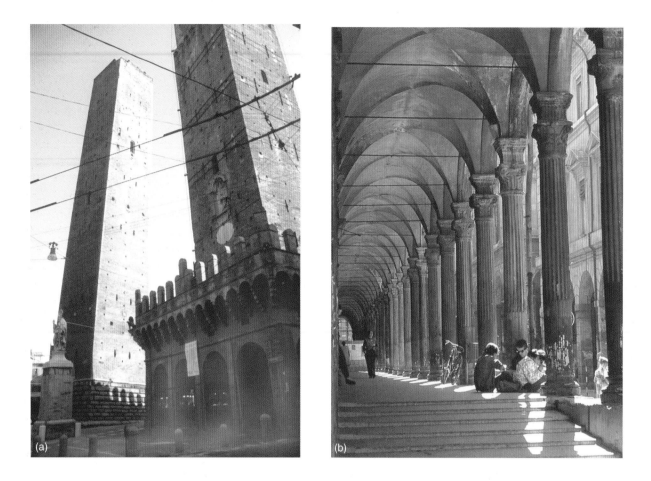

Figure 5.16
(a) *Torre degli Asinelli* and *Torre Garisenda.* (b) Arcaded walkways in the University District.

presently houses the Chamber of Commerce, Industry, Craft and Agriculture, and symbolises close links between the city's commerce and its rural activities.

The most visible buildings here, however, are two leaning towers: *Torre degli Asinelli* and *Torre Garisenda* (Figure 5.16a). The Asinelli tower is the tallest structure in the city, 97 metres high, built by Gherardo Asinelli, completed in 1109 and, like the remaining hundred medieval towers, built for defensive purposes. It was bought by the *commune* in the twelfth century as a watch tower. *Torre Garisenda* is half the height, "sways tipsily to the south",[45] and is made famous through Dante's *Inferno*. If one climbs Asinelli's five hundred steps, the views of the city are truly rewarding. From here we can see, all together, the different layers of morphological elements which

represent collective historical efforts in the construction of Bologna's cultural landscape, its past and present imagined community and place-identity. Restored roofscapes, buildings and public spaces signify the efforts that have been made by professionals, politicians and residents alike in reappropriating the historic heritage.

The dramatic views from the Asinelli tower reveal important links between the city and its nearby hills. As we take in these views, deep-rooted place-identity elements are clearly displayed. The city's central core has a fairly regular grid pattern, whilst the nearby neighbourhoods are connected to the core by a system of streets that fan out, forming a sequence of triangular tissues. Although the overall pattern of building within each "slice" has a fairly uniform overall height, neighbourhoods are easily differentiated by their local churches or towers, most of them now restored, providing important clues for the interpretations of the city's legibility and place identity.

From the top of the Asinelli tower, the eastern section of the walled city is a true stretch of terracotta and greenery, and seems to be deeply cut into by the straight "canyon" of Strada Maggiore.[46]

The trace of the more recent morphological and typological methods used in place-identity construction is also evident in the rehabilitation schemes of individual neighbourhoods and buildings. Using Gianfranco Cannigia's tissue studies and procedural typology, which we earlier explored, several interventions have been completed. Where urban tissues had been radically altered, individual plot subdivisions were traced from the historic maps, and reinstated in order to restore the original land subdivision pattern. Corresponding building types were then also re-introduced in order to repair neighbourhood place-identity, following the "code" approach, explained earlier. Socio-economic and demographic profiles were also considered, in order to avoid gentrification and "to preserve the original cultural characteristics of the city".[47] Even industrial buildings such as the old gas factory are being reused for more contemporary functions such as offices and housing. According to Pier Luigi Cervellati, who is working on such a proposal, it is critical to address industrial buildings, as they play essential roles in place-identity terms.

The overall purpose of the neighbourhood restoration plans was, says Francesco Bandarin:

an ability to function as a good (methodologically correct) restoration plan and an intention to protect the interests of the working-classes living in the historic centre, and in so doing, to be a programme of integral conservation of the social, cultural, economic and artistic characteristics of a city.[48]

The success of this large-scale rehabilitation programme would not have been possible without a co-operative management structure which controls the ownership, rents, maintenance and the allocation of properties to individual tenants; achieved through 15–25-year covenants that ensure that the original ideas are preserved.

The first neighbourhood rehabilitation project to be explored here lies along the *Via San Leonardo*, located between via *San Vitale* and *Via Trombetti*, in *Dallo Studium al Fiera* District, on the edge of the University District. Restored, working-class houses, with arcaded walkways at ground level, are painted in rich terracotta colours. Wooden shutters unify narrow three-storey buildings, forming a beautiful example of what we referred to earlier as a "commonplace landscape". Here we can also see the local attitude to nature with local trees and other plants such as pomegranate and azaleas providing rich, colourful and lush textures to otherwise densely packed built form tissue. Similar restoration work can be seen in nearby *Via Sant'Appolonia* and *Via Vinazzetti*. The area as a whole is full of life and everyday activity, and demonstrates the success of the local neighbourhood initiative (Figures 5.16b and 5.17).

Cutting across to *Via Zamboni* we enter the University District, the city's "Latin Quarter", and home to some 100,000 students "who gather to eat here, plaster leaflets on the walls and browse in the specialised bookshops and in the many museums which boast of ancient and modern culture".[49] Various historic palaces are beautifully restored, and house a variety of university, cultural and entertainment facilities. At the edge of the University District is the old Ghetto, built during mediaeval times to house the many Jewish families expelled from the core of the city. Today, the area is receiving similar attention to other parts of the city; here we can see how the Bolognese citizens are coming to terms with their dark past, in a constructive and positive way. Today, this part of the city is full of artisan shops, workshops and restaurants.

Two other neighbourhoods are worth mentioning. The first is south of *Piazza Maggiore*, *Via Farini* and *Piazza San Domenico*, comprising several streets with rehabilitated houses. The most interesting are *Via Mirasole* and *Miramonte* with their combination of working- and middle-class houses above stretches of porticoed walkways, housing local grocery shops and many types of craft and services premises. Again the restored houses, terracotta colour scheme and wooden shutters reinforce local place-identity through physical form (Figures 5.18a and

Figure 5.17
Restored houses in *Via San Leonardo,* near the University District.

5.18b). Here we can see how principles "rooted in the past but not stuck in the past" have skilfully been employed. Those buildings in relatively good condition were restored, using the same type of built form elements and detailing as when originally built. What was changed in such cases was the internal organisation of apartments and family houses, improved to meet modern requirements. On the other hand, those buildings that were beyond repair were replaced by new constructions, based on the codes established for individual blocks. These newly built houses therefore constitute mutation types; based on earlier edifices but re-interpreted to meet modern requirements. This "progressive" attitude to rehabilitation is also evident in the

socio-economic and cultural composition of the neighbourhood, allowing old tissues to be rejuvenated for use by young families, professionals and students.

Equally rewarding are walks through the Marconi District, particularly *Via del Porta* and its surrounding streets. The range of different types of arcaded walkways carry a great variety of building types, which support a rich socio-cultural diversity of inhabitants. A range of churches, towers and small neighbourhood parks give the neighbourhood an aura of community success. What all these neighbourhood rehabilitation schemes show is design methods that demonstrate the relationship between the overall collective place-identity, expressed in the

Figure 5.18
(a) Restored houses in *Via Mirasole*. (b) A view into the restored *Via Mirasole*. (c) Houses and shops in *Via del Porta*.

major spatial sequences of the city, and the local place-identity expressed through a local network of streets, building types and open spaces (Figure 5.18c).

To conclude, the methods employed in the rehabilitation of the historic centre of Bologna offer many important lessons for designing cultural landscapes from the place-identity perspective, at various levels of cultural meaning. First of all, we can see a continuous desire to coexist with nature. At the use level here we can see a close relationship between the city's open space network and its regional transportation routes, where the urban street *Strada Maggiore* continues as the ancient regional route *Via Aemilia*. The links between city and landscape are also protected by the Metropolitan Plan, which serves as a powerful device to control urban sprawl. The protection of the hills and their flora, fauna and water courses are important for the very survival of the Bolognese citizens, whilst at the meaning level, views of the Bolognese hills remind the citizens of powerful relationships between rural and urban imagined communities, and between human and non-human species. A similar attitude to nature is also evident at the micro scale of design; where city parks, neighbourhood courtyards and small rooftop oases provide breathing spaces within the city's compact urban form, where residents can relax and children can play; whilst such spaces can also support a variety of non-human species.

A second important lesson is evident in the reuse of Bologna's existing cultural landscape, which supports a sense of rooted imagined community. At the use level here, the urban grid and the city's numerous arcaded walkways provide many opportunities for different communities to encounter each other. At the core is *Piazza Maggiore* where major events and numerous daily activities take place. Major and minor streets provide a subtle differentiation between more public or private neighbourhood activities. A variety of shops and other urban functions are also important elements for ensuring the vitality and safety of the city's many streets. At the meaning level various morphological layers, from the city's walls to its numerous monuments, provide rich sources of ideological material for many imagined communities and place-identity interpretations. They

also give clues to legibility for achieving a sense of orientation. The use of red and other earthy colours also supports a very strong feeling of distinct place-identity, rooted in Bologna's natural soil, but also coloured by its historic political events.

A third important lesson concerns designing to support members of each imagined community in living harmoniously with other communities, which is strongly evident in both the overall city form and in its democratic processes of city governance. At the use level here, the physical form facilitates residents and visitors encountering each other. This is achieved via the open space network and the fine-grained system of different house and apartment types, which support the socio-economic and cultural integration of different imagined communities.

This leads us to a fourth key design lesson in relation to community empowerment. "Enquiry by design" tools, together with a democratic participatory process of design facilitate this in practice; whilst at the meaning level, the city thereby becomes the collective property of its many imagined communities, where place-identity and human identities are intertwined.

The overall methodology used in the rehabilitation of Bologna demonstrates an integrated approach, where the city's morphological and typological components are engaged together with socio-economic and cultural aspects. The process overall is governed by what Francesco Bandarin calls "the three faces of planning in Bologna".[50] The first face is contained in the Metropolitan Plan which is used by the planners as a device to control urban growth and for the co-ordination of the whole metropolitan area. The second is the decentralised and democratic system of decision-making implemented through the local neighbourhood councils. The third is formed by the rehabilitation proposals developed from the architectural typologies and the cultural aspects of conservation.

One main criticism, however, is that despite a carefully worked out method, the rehabilitation programmes have not delivered the quantity of social housing required. There were also political problems which caused the fall of the Bologna's Communist government in 1997. Nonetheless the new liberal right-wing government continues the rehabilitation programme with similar aspirations. In conclusion, Bandarin claims that Bologna's experience:

> *... clearly opposes all the ideological principles and the speculative aims of the dominant classes, since, while it plans a conservation of the historical urban structure, it establishes the necessity of public control of the renovation process as a condition to preserve the social classes that now live in it.*[51]

Taken together, the three faces of planning are clearly forward looking, protecting the interests of all Bolognese citizens – particularly working classes – against the ideology and interests of speculative economic forces.

Notes

1   Fanti and Susini, 1995.
2   Ibid.
3   Ibid.
4   Renzi, 1995.
5   Bellettini et al., 1995.
6   Renzi, 1995.
7   De Angelis, 1995, 66.
8   Fanti and Susini, 1995.
9   Lanzarini, Piombini and Renzo, 1995, 135.
10 Scannavini, 1995, 61.
11 Breveglieri, 2000.
12 Bandarin, 1978.
13 Ibid.
14 Hinrichs, 1995.
15 Parker, 2001, 288.
16 Ibid.
17 Bandarin, 1978.
18 Discussion between Georgia Butina Watson and Pier Luigi Cervellati in Bologna, October 2001.
19 Bandarin, 1978.
20 Ibid., 190.
21 Ibid.: from Accame, *Conoscenza e conscienza della città*, pp. 190–191.
22 Rowe, 1997.
23 Ibid., 101.
24 Rowe, 1997.
25 Frampton, 1985, 294.
26 Rowe, 1997, 100.
27 Moudon, 1997.
28 Ibid.
29 Discussion between Georgia Butina Watson and Gianfranco Caniggia, Oxford, 1983.
30 Interview with Cervellati, Bologna, October 2001.
31 Bandarin, 1978, 192.
32 Ibid.
33 Ibid.
34 Cited in Bandarin (from Accame, Conoscenza e Coscienza della città, pp. 100–101).
35 Zeisel, 1981.
36 Rubbi et al., 1996, cited in Bandarin, Acame, Conoscenza e Conscienza della città, pp. 100–101.
37 Bandarin, 1979.
38 Ibid.
39 Novitz, 2001, 153–166.
40 Renzi, 1995.
41 Belodi, 1999.
42 Renzi, 1995.
43 Ibid., 122.
44 Ibid., 159.
45 Facaros and Pauls, 2000, 174.
46 Renzi, 1995, 42.
47 Bandarin, 1978, 193.
48 Ibid.
49 Lanzarini, 133.
50 Bandarin, Ibid.
51 Bandarin, Ibid., 193.

6

Rossi in Perugia: Designing with layers of history

Both the morphological approach and the *La Tendenza* movement, which we encountered in the last chapter, have been widely influential. Some of this influence came directly from the Bologna team, whose members became involved in other projects and taught at various universities. Particularly influential were Gianfranco Caniggia and Leonardo Benevolo, both of whom held a number of visiting professorships and thereby influenced many young designers, particularly in the Spanish speaking countries. Benevolo, for example, made frequent lecturing visits to the School of Architecture in Cuzco in Peru, so it is not surprising to see that the rehabilitation of the historic part of Cuzco results from a conservation strategy similar to that developed earlier in Bologna.[1] In Italy, this tradition has been carried forward through the design projects of Pier Luigi Cervellati,[2] Roberto Scannavini, Giancarlo Cataldi, Gian Luigi Maffei, Maria Grazia Corsini, Paolo Marretto, Giuseppe Strappa and others, who teach and practice in Bologna, Florence, Rome, Genoa and Sienna. Aldo Rossi, one of the most notable designers of the *La Tendenza* movement, departed from the Muratori school of urban morphology to develop his own body of theoretical and design work, which forms the focus of this chapter. We shall first discuss Rossi's theses on urbanism, and then go on to explain how he used these ideas in the design of *Centro Direzionale* in Perugia, in an attempt to reinforce that city's place-identity.

Before we introduce Rossi's ideas on urbanism, it is important to locate Rossi himself within the socio-political framework and design culture in Italy, and to discuss his own personal development. Rossi was born in Milan in 1931, and spent his childhood years there; subsequently enrolling at the *Milan Politecnico* to study architecture, receiving his degree in 1959. Whilst still a student, he started to work on the architectural magazine *Casabella – Continuita*. From 1961 to 1964 he was the editor of the magazine, which had a leading role in Italian design culture.[3] Rossi's connection with *Casabella* introduced him to advanced ideas on architecture and urbanism, and gave him many opportunities to develop his writing skills and to express his own views.

In 1963 Rossi began his teaching career, first by assisting Ludovico Guaroni's urbanism course in Arezzo, and then between 1963 and 1965 working as an assistant on Carlo Aymonino's course on *Organizational Characteristics of Buildings* at the *Istituto Universitario di Architettura* in Venice. In 1965 he joined the faculty of the School of Architecture in Milan, where he also set up his own design studio. Whilst teaching at Milan, Rossi became involved in the Italian socialist student movement, which influenced his political maturation and his ideas on urbanism. From 1972 he held teaching positions at various institutions, including the *Eidgenössische Technische Hochschule* in Zurich; and in 1975 he was made Professor of Design at the *Istituto Universitario di Architettura* in Venice. From then on Rossi continued to develop his ideas, both through writing and practical design. Attested by Vitruvius, Alberti, Serlio, Palladio, Aymonino and Tafuri, the tradition of architect-writer is well established in Italy. According to Peter Eisenman,[4] we need to understand Rossi's architectural and urban design writing if we are to understand his design work. We shall therefore briefly discuss his main ideas about urbanism, to locate him within the broader Italian and international cultural scenes.

First, what new material did Rossi call on in constructing his own position? We have already explored Rossi's connections with the urban morphologists and with the *La Tendenza* movement. Involvement with *La Tendenza* introduced him also to the Rationalist architects of the 1930s, who initially constituted themselves as an official body in the *Movimento Italiano per l'Architettura Razionale* (MIAR) and had brief associations with the Mussolini government. Some of the ideas developed by the Rationalists, especially by those known as the *Gruppo 7*, can be traced in the development of Rossi's own ideas; particularly through the use of typological classifications, and reinterpretations of traditional urban form elements combined with modern idioms of the machine age. Through such work Rossi also became aware of the much earlier ideas of the *Deutscher Werkbund* and the Russian Constructivists. As we shall see later, Rossi was also influenced by other schools of thought; primarily French urban geographers and urbanists, but also theorists such as Louis Mumford, Homer Hoyt and Kevin Lynch. Also influential were the political circumstances of 1960s Italy: which were "the traumatic years of student discontent as a polemical critique of the Modern Movement position on the city."[5] It is during this period of political and intellectual discontent that Rossi's thoughts on urbanism were shaped, communicated initially through his lectures and seminars at the Milan Politecnico, and published, in Italian, as *L'architettura della citta*, in 1966. A second edition was published in 1970, and was translated into Spanish, German and Portuguese. A fourth, illustrated Italian edition came out in 1973, and the first English edition was published in 1982 with subsequent republications in 1984 and 1986. According to Mary McLeod's review of *The Architecture of the City*, published as the back cover of the 1986 edition, she states that Rossi's book is:

> In part a protest against functionalism and the Modern Movement, in part an attempt to restore the craft of architecture to its position as the only valid object of architectural study, and in part an

analysis of the rules and forms of the city's construction.

From this we can see that Rossi is against those ideas of the city proposed by the advocates of Modernism, although he is not against Modernism as an architectural style. Rossi proposes an alternative approach: an "analogous city" which he arrives at through a complex, *rationalist* approach, based on a study of geography, economics, history and the city's constituent morphological elements. According to Peter Eisenman,[7] Rossi approached the discipline of urban study from the position of a scientist or an archaeologist, who systematically examines the city in an objective, scientific manner. The results of this type of study enable the designer to intervene, in the most appropriate manner, in the repair or design of new urban tissues and artefacts. The urban form elements are used in this design approach as a source of "verifiable" data, and become the starting point in the design process.

In the introduction to the *Architecture of the City*, Rossi says:

> The city, which is the subject of this book, is to be understood here as architecture. By architecture I mean not only the visible image of the city and the sum of its different architectures, but architecture as construction, the construction of the city over time. I believe that this point of view, objectively speaking, constitutes the most comprehensive way of analysing the city; it addresses the ultimate and definitive fact in the life of the collective, the creation of the environment in which it lives.[8]

In this paragraph, Rossi introduces the key ideas that he explores in the body of the book. In his exposition, he also states where he is coming from in terms of other influences on his ideas, which he discusses in four parts. Part One introduces the concepts of description and classification. Part Two explains the structure of the city in terms of its different elements. In Part Three Rossi explains the architecture of the city and the *locus* on which it is imprinted, and therefore urban history. The final part introduces concepts of urban dynamics and the problem of politics as choice. We shall now discuss these concepts in more detail, to understand the implications they have for the design of *Centro Direzionale* in Perugia.

According to Rossi, "architecture came into being along with the first traces of the city; it is deeply rooted in the formation of civilisation and is a permanent, universal and necessary artefact."[9] In the creation of the city, built-form elements have both utilitarian and aesthetic intention. These elements also have an intimate connection with nature, and over time the city acquires a consciousness and memory. Rossi tells us that the

> *contrast between particular and universal, between individual and collective, emerges from the city and from its construction, its architecture.*[10] *It manifests itself in different ways: in the relationship between the public and private sphere, between public and private buildings, between the rational design of urban architecture and the values of* locus *or* place.[11]

Rossi argues that we should study cities both qualitatively and quantitatively, and that his method is presented as a theory of urban artefacts which "stems from the identification of the city itself as an artefact and from its division into individual buildings and dwelling areas."[12] The city is both collective and private; and is "composed of many people seeking a general order that is consistent with their own particular environment."[13] Any regular changes that we observe in the city bear imprints of the daily life of its citizens; and we can trace and understand these different layers through a systematic, analytical method. Cities are not static, they change all the time, they are part of what Rossi calls *urban dynamics*. It is therefore important not only to accommodate present needs but also to allow for transformation to take place over time. Rossi's position is that the city is a source of verifiable data, an archaeological artefact; and the architect is an unheroic, autonomous researcher. The key focus of his method is the concept of process – that is, urban transformations over time – which enables him to make sense of the past, present and future. In order to operationalise this method, Rossi introduces four further concepts:

– The concept of urban *skeleton* or urban plan.
– The concept of *typology*.

– The concept of *locus* and *history*.
– The concept of *urban dynamics*.

First of all, we shall explain Rossi's understanding of urban history. History, according to Rossi, is analogous to a "skeleton" whose condition serves as a measure of time, and is measured by time. This skeleton bears the imprint of collective actions, and links the city to history. The urban skeleton is like a human body, it grows over time. If certain parts are broken, or distorted, we try to repair them. In this repair process, however, we should bear in mind the appropriateness of new elements, so that they fit into the existing skeleton. In its basic form, the urban skeleton means the urban plan; it is the underlying morphological structure of the city. This urban skeleton is very important for our understanding of a city and for our ability to orientate ourselves.

In addition to the urban plan, or skeleton, we also need to understand the nature and character of individual artefacts or *types* as Rossi calls them. A type is an analytical instrument, or "apparatus". It is an individual cell, a basic organising element, a sort of *gene* or DNA, that cannot be reduced any further. A type possesses basic characteristics that can be transformed over time. When types are transformed, they become "mutation types", as explained in the chapter on Bologna. Types have important implications for the interpretation of place-identity: as they not only represent physical entities but also carry associations with "a way of life", and therefore represent a particular kind of imagined community. When similar types are bound by sets of similar rules, they form characteristic tissue formations, and become *typology*. Rossi refers to mediaeval housing districts as good examples of this concept. Here he acknowledges Lynch's work on districts as a key source of his own ideas.

Types can be further classified into *primary* and *secondary* elements. Primary elements are those that are also *permanent*, as their physical forms and patterns of use last for a long time. Primary elements can further be classified by Rossi as *monuments* and *districts*. Amongst monuments we can place, for example, public buildings such as Town Halls, Churches and Market Halls. Monuments have, Rossi claims, by their nature a symbolic function, and thus a function related to time. As permanent and primary elements in the city, monuments are dialectically related to the city's growth. Monuments provide a sense of the continuity of urban life, and support feelings of rootedness.

Equally, districts also form *primary* and *permanent* elements in the city. Although individual buildings may change over time, the basic underlying tissue structure remains. In this context, permanent elements have deep-rooted meanings, and are important for place-identity interpretations.

Permanent elements can have further characteristics. They can be *propelling* or *retarding*. If they are propelling, they can be catalytic in helping to repair and regenerate particular parts of a city. Rossi refers to the Theatre at Arles and *Pallazzo della Regione* in Padua as good examples of propelling monuments, as they were able to accommodate changing needs over time. On the other hand, when certain monuments stop being active, when they are turned into museums – as in the case of the Alhambra in Granada – they become *pathological*, dead; and appear to us "like an embalmed body".[14] In that state, they become *urban memories*. However, pathological monuments can be revived and rejuvenated, by being given new functions. Therefore, according to Rossi, monuments that have retarding properties can become propelling; and they can bring the past into the present and future.

Types, both primary and secondary, have both specific and generic values. They have specific value when they belong to their context, that is they are part of the original tissue formation. Certain types can also have a generic value and can be used in other locations and places: in this case they need to be adjusted to their new context, to define some new place-identity. If they are not adjusted then, Rossi claims,[15] we can end up with empty formalism, which we can see both in modern movement solutions and in *figure-ground* approaches and other design concepts which take into consideration only physical form elements, disregarding the socio-economic and cultural contexts which are essential to the construction of imagined communities.

Rossi's third theoretical concept is *locus*: "the place in which urban artefacts are manifested, that is, the area in which they can be seen, the physical ground they occupy."[16] In developing the concept of *locus* Rossi uses theories of place, or *genius loci*, developed by French geographers such as Maximilien Sorre and Henry Paul Eydoux,[17] and ideas from architecture and art historians such as Henry Focillon and Pier Lavedan. Focillon speaks of psychological places, which project the spirit of a place; which he describes as artistic landscapes offering a notion of "art as place".[18] Rossi states that the underlying principle of any place stems from its location, its topography and other natural elements. Physical forms of cities and socio-cultural processes form characteristic imprints on the locality: cities are very complex, they are the sum of many parts and they cannot be reduced to a single, basic idea.

In his definition of *locus*, Rossi refers to the practice of building cities during the classical world where "the situation, the site, was governed by the *genius loci*, the local divinity, an intermediary who presided over all that was to unfold in it."[19] We can find similar ideas in the work of the Roman engineer Vitruvius, and in the theories of the Renaissance urbanists.

A site or *locus* contains a succession of events, both ancient and recent. Any particular locus is a theatre of events, a deposit of memories. When a particular place is an event in itself, it becomes a unique place, or what Rossi calls *locus solus*. Such a place "absorbs events and feelings, and every new event contains within it a memory of the past and a potential memory of the future."[20] The passage of time leaves many traces of different events. Whilst the place is in the original use, it is part of living history. When the place is no longer in its original use, it shifts into the realm of memory. Here Rossi refers to the city of Split in Croatia, where new activities within the walls of the Roman Diocletian palace gave new uses and new meanings to unchangeable forms.[21] The process by which the city is formed over time is part of urban history, but the succession of events constitutes its memory. Just as with types and monuments, we can use urban memories to construct new places. Urban memories form a "collective unconscious life", and through the apparatus of type and memory we can construct future places: memory can imagine and reconstruct a future time of imagination.

The final concept that Rossi uses in his operational design approach is the concept of *urban dynamics*, which refers to the processes of urban change and transformation. These are the result of many factors: political, social, technological, aesthetic and economic. These factors influence the growth or rejuvenation of particular districts, and allow new functions and needs to be accommodated within the urban skeleton. On average, Rossi claims, a city changes every 50 years. However, there are forces that bring about faster and more radical transformations. Paris under Napoleon III is a good example of such transformation, brought about by political and other reasons. More regular and incremental changes are often the result of economic factors. We need to understand the specific way in which these produce transformations.[22]

Equally significant for our understanding of urban transformations are the planning laws and regulations administered by local municipalities or other such groups. Land ownership is also critical, since it gives powers to individuals to change the city through development processes.

An analysis of the city also allows us to see how these forces are applied; for example, by studying the history of property through deed registries we can bring to light the sequence of landholdings and trace certain economic tendencies.[23]

Through the concept of urban dynamics we can see how Rossi comes to terms with modern architecture, but not with modernist urbanism. As an urbanist he is securely rooted in the past; as an architect, he is forward looking.

Having explained the basic principles that underlie Rossi's theory of the city, we shall now explore how he uses these concepts in his design work in Perugia. Until 1981, when he was awarded first prize for the *Friedrichstadt* housing project in Berlin by the International Berlin Architecture (IBA) body, almost all Rossi's architectural work was in northern Italy, and consisted predominantly of small-scale schemes. Despite the interest that he received after the publication of his book, larger schemes did not come his way: he needed a project to operationalise his discourse on urbanism. He was given this opportunity in 1981, after winning the Pritzker Prize, when he was invited by the City Council to design a new civic centre for Perugia, the capital of Umbria; in the

district of Fontivegge which is located between the historic hilltop heart of the city and its post-war modernist business area.

The brief was very specific as to what Rossi had to achieve. The new development was to house 850,000 square feet of new space[24] to accommodate a new civic and administrative centre containing the *Palazzo Regionale*, a theatre, offices, housing, retail units with underground car parking facilities and a fountain. Other criteria were that the new scheme ought to support Perugia's identity, whilst reflecting a modern and progressive image. According to Lucia Vasak,[25] who carried out interviews with members of the City Council in 1989, Rossi was chosen for this project because of the ideas he had expressed in *L'architettura della citta*.

The development site is the former location of the Perugina chocolate factory opposite the main railway station, and the scheme is a joint venture between the City Council and the pasta manufacturer Buitoni. The site was bisected by a main distributor road, and the new scheme was to be designed to integrate the two parts, and to act as the heart of the district of Fontivegge. The City Council also wanted the new development to respect the hill town topography, and the sociological pattern of the everyday life of the region. The new architectural elements had to reflect the city's existing typologies.[26]

Before we explore the method that Rossi used in the design of *Centro Direzionale*, it is important to explain briefly the city's history and its morphological structure, to understand the elements Rossi used as typological references when designing the new scheme. From its beginning, Perugia's development was underpinned by its hilly topography above a green and swampy valley (Figure 6.1). Perugia's early settlement, located on a hill 493 metres above sea level is linked to the ancient tribes known as Umbrii. They used the hilltop locations for defensive purposes, and farmed the fertile land in the valley below. Early Umbrii tribes spoke an Italic language which was similar to Latin, and from their arrival in the region they fought hard to preserve their identity and political independence. During the seventh century BC, however the Etruscans settled in the territory and the two groups began to merge into a united culture. The Etruscans, who arrived from

Figure 6.1
A panoramic view of Perugia.

Lydia in Asia Minor were experienced builders of citadels; a skill they usefully applied in the building of *Pieresa*, a hilltop fortress formation overlooking the river Tiber. The remains of their walls and fortresses can still be found in Perugia today.

The early Etruscan settlement of some 40,000 inhabitants was taken over by Roman troops in 309 BC, but the original tribes were never content under Roman administration and staged several revolts during the Republican era, which destroyed much of the town's original fabric. The town was subsequently rebuilt by the Emperor Augustus who gave it the new name of *Augusta Perusia*.[27] The Romans also built *Via Flaminia*, a major regional road that connected Rome to Rimini. After the collapse of the Roman Empire, Perugia became part of the strip of territorial land connecting Rome to Ravenna known as the Byzantine province. Its crossroad location rendered it liable to many invasions and conflicts, which escalated around 1000 AD when many towns fought each other for political supremacy. The *Perugini* citizens were known for their fighting spirit, and they frequently attacked smaller, nearby towns whilst making useful alliances

with larger cities such as Florence and Siena. Nevertheless, they never managed to attain city-state status. Politically, Perugia retained a fair degree of independence, reaching its Golden Age between eleventh and fourteenth centuries. During this period the town flourished economically and culturally, as evidenced by the many buildings and monuments constructed during this period. Particularly prevalent was the construction of churches and convents, as the region was noted for birthplace of saints and martyrs – the most famous was St Francis, from the nearby town of Assisi, who used to "talk to the birds" on the nearby lake *Lago Trasimeno* (Figures 6.2a and 6.2b).

In the absence of central authority from Rome, local church dignitaries organised councils of men from noble families to govern the town's internal affairs. These informal associations led to the formation of secular political groups, known as *commune*, which were based on the ancient Greek city-state model, with the town's central urban space serving as *Agora-Forum*. During the mediaeval period, professional umpires known as *podestàs* were appointed by the Council, usually from men of

Figure 6.2
(a) A view of the old Etruscan *Porta Marzia*, incorporated into the defensive system by Antonio and Aristotile da Sangallo (1530–1543). (b) The Etruscan Arch, also known as Arch of Augustus, one of the seven gates into the ancient city of *Perugia*.

reputation from other towns, to keep the fighting clans under control. *Podestàs* had counsel from judges and notaries, housed in the *Pallazzo del Comune* also known as the *Pallazzo dei Priori*.

By 1300 Perugia had reached a peak in wealth and prestige, housing some 28,000 residents and 41 artisan guilds. Streets and squares were paved, aqueducts and fountains were constructed, wooden houses were rebuilt in stone and markets were established. The town was proud of its strong defensive system, and the town proper was organised into five quarters or *rioni* clustered around five city gates of *Sole*, *San Pietro*, *Eburnea*, *Santa Susana* and *San Angelo*. The University, which specialised in legal studies, was founded in 1307; and many churches

and palaces were built. By 1347 the town began to suffer economically and culturally, and its social life was drained by internal fights for political governance.

Despite three centuries of political turmoil, the town began to be visited by tourists during the last quarter of the eighteenth century: there was a renewed interest in St Francis, whilst many writers and artists stayed in the city to gain inspiration for their work. In 1861 Umbria joined the rest of Italy, and Perugia experienced another economic decline. Gradually the economy began to recover with the introduction of steel, jute, chemical and food factories, which promoted the city's urban growth. Today Perugia is an important administrative, university and cultural centre, with some 155,000 residents. Despite

Figure 6.3
San Lorenzo Duomo, the *Great Fountain* and the *Piazza IV Novembre,* in the heart of Perugia.

its regional resemblance to other Umbrian hilltop towns such as Assissi, Gubbio, Orvieto, Todi and Spoleto, Perugia stands out because of its size and to its administrative function, as the regional capital.

Because of its complex history Perugia is composed of several distinct cultural landscapes, like a patchwork of elements held together by its hilly geography through which winds the river Tiber. The first impressions of Perugia today reveal a semi-fortified hill town whose many towers and *campanili* project a religious character: both characteristics are very important in the construction of Perugian place-identity and imagined community. At the crown of the hill is *San Lorenzo Duomo,* standing out from the rest of the townscape elements (Figure 6.3). Pink and cream-coloured houses, built of local Umbrian stone, provide a memorable image; especially in evening light. At the bottom of the hill, a mass of vegetation separates the old core from the modern quarters.

To understand the sources of Rossi's ideas for designing the *Centro Direzionale* we shall first explain Perugia's spatial structure and the key building types which give the space its unique character, its place-identity. We shall start our journey at the ancient hilltop area, and descend into the more recent neighbourhoods. At the heart of old Perugia is the main space known as *Platea Comunis* or *Platea Magna* but now called *Piazza IV Novembre* (Figure 6.4). The space holds memories of many riots and fights for independence, including also the "War of the Stones", an annual festive punch-up which used to cause many deaths each year. The *piazza* is defined by several important buildings. At its southern edge is *Palazzo dei Priori,* the mediaeval town hall built around 1270 in local Travertine and white and red Bettona stone. It is believed that the building is the work of the local master builders Giacommo di Servadio and Giovanello di Benvenuto. The present structure is

Figure 6.4
Piazza IV Novembre, the *Great Fountain, Palazzo dei Priori* and *Corso Vannucci.*

the result of many building additions and alterations carried out between the thirteenth and sixteenth centuries, during which time several individual buildings were united by a facade that follows the curved spine of the *Corso,* the city's main pedestrian street. The overall composition of the building is asymmetrical, an effect which is accentuated by the off-centre bell-tower.

The ground floor has Roman arches leading to various shops, and the main entrance into the building is richly decorated with 58 animal and plant-like decorative motifs; paid for from the proceeds of the butcher's trade. The rest of the facade is perforated by oblong and arched windows, whilst the cornice consists of a castellated structure which served as a defence platform during times of political turbulence. In 1902, the facade facing the fountain and the cathedral acquired a semi-circular staircase, connected to the fourteenth century portico and arcade. Both the steps and the arcade provide a

refuge and a seating area for tourists and for Perugini citizens during hot summer months. The whole first floor of the *Piazza IV Novembre* section is occupied by the *Sala dei Notari,* a remarkable room divided into bays by huge round arches, and decorated with early thirteenth century frescoes of the Old Testament, local legends and biblical stories of the people of Perugia.

The northern section of the *piazza* is defined by the Cathedral of San Lorenzo, the tallest building of the old town which figures large in Perugia's characteristic silhouette. The cornerstone was laid in 1345,[28] but it took many years to complete the building as the Perugians used it for defensive purposes. Even today, only the lower parts have the intended lattice-like pink facing, whilst the upper parts remain bare. The Cathedral's steps are regularly used by residents and visitors as a seating area, and as a viewing platform for watching the world go by on the main *piazza* (Figures 6.5a and 6.5b).

163

Figure 6.5
(a) A view into the *Piazza IV Novembre* and arcaded passageways of *San Lorenzo Duomo.* (b) The steps heading into the *San Lorenzo Duomo,* used also as a seating area.

In the centre of the large, oblong *piazza* is the pink and white *Fontana Maggiore*, designed by Fra Bevignate in 1270 to provide water for the city. The fountain has 48 double-relief panels around the lower basin, executed by Nicolo Pisano and his son Giovanni, and depicting both secular and religious themes from Perugian history. Adjoining the *piazza* at its southern edge is the main street *Corso Vannucci*, named after Pietro Vannucci, Perugia's most famous son, Perugino (Figure 6.6a). The *Corso* is pedestrianised, slightly raised towards the *Piazza IV Novembre*, paved in local stone and defined by mediaeval and Renaissance palaces housing shops, galleries, hotels and residential accommodation. Every evening the *corso* is transformed into one of the loveliest *passeggiatas* in Italy. At the southern edge the *Corso* adjoins *Piazza Italia*, with a belvedere offering stunning views into the valley and the modern parts of the city.

The ancient streets around the Cathedral are full of old, grim buildings with overhanging arches, "some incorporating bits of Gothic palaces and Etruscan walls, a set no film director could possibly improve upon (Figure 6.6b)."[29] According to travel writers Dana Facaros and Michael Pauls, "mediaeval Perugia must have seemed like one continuous building, all linked by arches and passageways (Figure 6.6c)."[30] Its ancient layers are continuously revealed by the presence of Etruscan ruins, Roman mosaics and gates and other built-form elements. From the top, long green views suggest important links between the city and the countryside which surrounds it.

Figure 6.6
(a) A famous *passeggiata* along *Corso Vannucci*, Perugia's most important social street. (b) Ancient layers of old Perugia, incorporating a part of Via Apia and the old aqueduct. (c) One of many Perugia's arcaded passageways.

The rest of the mediaeval spatial structure is formed by meandering streets sloping down the hill, creating smaller *piazzas* in front of churches, convents and other institutional buildings (Figure 6.7a). The most significant set of secular buildings, in the north-west part of the old town, is the University complex. The University forms an interesting complex of mediaeval streets and houses, and includes the mediaeval aqueduct that used to bring water from nearby *Monte Pacciano* into the *Fontana Maggiore* (Figures 6.7b and 6.7c). A stairway descends through Roman-Etruscan walls into the *Borgo Sant'Angelo*, once a working class quarter and the centre of Perugian resistance to Papal administration.

The streets in the south-east part of the town are also very old, with more ancient vaulted tunnels underneath. Parallel to and below *Corso Vannucci* is *Piazza Matteotti*, the former market place and "field for burning witches".[31] Descending from the mediaeval core one finds many arches, gates, mosaics and other artefacts that remind us of the town's complex and rich history, where each layer represents a particular type of imagined community. Lower down, beneath the hilltop formation, is the modern city of Perugia with its many nineteenth and twentieth century buildings (Figures 6.8a and 6.8b). Parts of the nineteenth century development are built on top of a mediaeval suburb which was

Figure 6.7
(a) *Piazza Cavallotti* leading into many ancient arcaded passageways with a church facade incorporated into the fabric of the city. (b) A view of Saint Luke's Gate showing parts of the old aqueduct. (c) The Church of St. Theresa and the Sciri Tower.

Figure 6.8
(a) A panoramic view of new parts of Perugia. (b) Contrasting of old and new Perugia seen from *Via Baglioni*.

destroyed by Pope Paul III during the "Salt War", and rebuilt between 1530 and 1543 by Aristotle and Antonio da Sangallo and others as Roca Paolina, a defensive fortress which incorporated parts of the old Etruscan wall. More recent developments are typical modernist structures that offers a contemporary place-identity character.

Before Rossi began to design *Centro Direzionale* he tried to become familiar with this rich tapestry of morphological layers, monuments, topography and transformational processes. Rossi collected his "sources of verifiable data" from old city plans and other documentary sources, from the city itself by studying various morphological layers, and by experiencing its dynamic life. According to Severio Fiori,[32] Rossi's collaborator on the project, Rossi's design approach for the new civic and administrative centre was very much embedded in his theory of urbanism, explained earlier in this chapter. Rossi first analysed the city's constituent parts using his concepts of city structure, typology, locus and history and urban dynamics. The key urban elements which Rossi identified as important sources of old Perugia's place-identity were its historic spaces and monuments such as *Piazza IV Novembre*, *Palazzo dei Priori*, the *Duomo* or Cathedral, *Fontana Maggiore* and *Corso Vannucci*. These monuments, being the most permanent and socially important types, are key carriers of place-identity meanings and offer support for the city's legibility. In contrast, Perugia's contemporary image is comprised of modern administrative and residential complexes, symbolising its more progressive character. The Fontivegge site offered a unique opportunity to unite these two areas: the new scheme, according to the requirements of the City Council, had to be rooted in the past but be forward looking and progressive.

After Rossi completed his morphological and typological analysis, he began to design the *Centro Direzionale* using his "analogous" design approach. According to Lucia Vasak, the City Council's aims were to create a truly urban centre which would serve a variety of public functions.

Such a development should be organised in a way which would be of benefit to the city as a whole in function and support its local identity.[33]

Severio Fiori claims[34] that the first principle of both analysis and design that Rossi employed drew on the concepts of *type* and *typology*. Given the functional requirements specified in the development brief, both Rossi and the City Council felt that the focal point of *Centro Direzionale* ought to be a *piazza*; and that *Piazza IV Novembre* could be a useful reference. Its location, size and spatial relationship with key city monuments make it Perugia's most important public space at the local level: the new civic space, Rossi and the Councillors felt, should have a similar function at the larger scale of the city and the region. The old town piazza was translated by Rossi into a new civic space named *Piazza Nuova*, an "analogous" interpretation achieved through a rational design solution (Figures 6.9a–6.9c).

The next stage in the design process was to identify typological sources for designing other building types for the new scheme. The most important building type in relation to *Centro Direzionale* was the *Palazzo Regionale* to house various administrative offices. Rossi's idea was to create a new "*Broletto*", a generic type of edifice with arcaded ground floor areas, frequently used in Italy for administrative buildings. However, in order to design a Perugian version of such a building, Rossi used *Palazzo dei Priori* as a source (Figures 6.10a and 6.10b). Although modified to meet the requirement for a modern, progressive image, typological references are obvious in the volume, scale, proportions and spatial positions that both buildings have in common. Once the basic typological elements were established, Rossi began to add other, smaller-scale typological references, such as the use of a pediment in the main facade of the new *Broletto*, typical of the facade of the Cathedral and other Perugian churches. The *University Palazzo* (Figure 6.10c) and the abundance of mediaeval streets and narrow passages provided design sources for the new Broletto's arcaded passageways (Figures 6.11a–6.11c).

The second principle that Rossi employed in his design was the concept of *history of locus*. In his book Rossi states[35] that the underlying principle of any place is its location, its topography and other natural elements. Morphological layers of cities and their socio-cultural life leave deep imprints on the locality: they create a unique *genius loci*, a particular

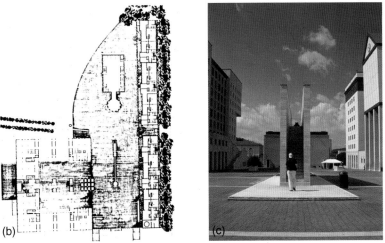

Figure 6.9
(a) Piazza IV Novembre, the Great Fountain and a complex of residential and commercial buildings. (b) Aldo Rossi's conceptual design for *Centro Direzionale* and *Piazza Nuova* in Perugia. (c) Piazza Nouva with the fountain looking towards the shopping centre.

Figure 6.10
(a) Palazzo dei Priori, Perugia. (b) A detail of the central section of Palazzo dei Priori, Perugia. (c) The old University building, Perugia.

Figure 6.11
(a) Aldo Rossi's Centro Direzionale with its new Broletto, Perugia. (b) A detail of new Broletto in Perugia. (c) The main entrance into the government offices building, Perugia.

kind of cultural landscape. The succession of events creates urban memories; and these memories, Rossi states,[36] can be used to construct future places.

We can see much evidence of the use of such concepts in the design of *Centro Direzionale*. We find reference to the same group of monuments that Rossi used in his typological classifications: here *Palazzo dei Priori*, and the Cathedral and *Piazza IV Novembre* bear memories of important historic events. These references were therefore important

to include and refine at each stage of the design process. The town's hilly topography and its regional road network were also included in the new scheme. First, the multi-level new scheme with its elevated sloping new *piazza*, connected by many steps, evokes the kinaesthetic experience of old Perugia (Figure 6.12a). Second, the existing road network is incorporated into the design of the scheme, connecting the site to the larger whole. The regional road is tunnelled through the building

Figure 6.12
(a) A detail of the government offices building, with one of the staircases leading to the upper level. (b) A view of the regional road charging through the Broletto. (c) The regional road connecting residential neighbourhoods and *Centro Direzionale*. (d) A view of *Centro Direzionale* in its context.

complex in a similar way to other hilly areas of the region; reflecting the importance of the new scheme in its regional context, and its regional sense of place identity (Figures 6.12b–6.12d). Third, characteristic pediments, memories from old Perugia and the Cathedral, are made more explicit in the development of new individual building types (Figures 6.13a–6.13c). An underground car park is also included to satisfy modern city requirements, but in symbolic terms this underground space also evokes memories of the underground maze of passages underneath the mediaeval core. An old Perugina Chocolate Factory

chimney that Rossi incorporated into the new scheme is also a reminder of the former function of the site; and Rossi used it as a landmark, and a focal point for the alignment of a new avenue leading into the complex.

The third principle that helped Rossi to "adjust" and further refine his design came from Perugia's *city structure*, and its constituent elements that provide the "skeleton" of the overall city form. The city structure or "skeleton", according to Rossi, bears imprints of the passage of time, and allows the city to grow. If the "skeleton" has broken parts, it must

Figure 6.13
(a) *Piazza della Republica* with an old church turned into a commercial outlet. (b) A detail of Centro Direzionale, Perugia. (c) A framed view of the new shopping centre in *Piazza Nouva*.

be mended; but new elements must fit into the existing skeleton. The Fontivegge site was very much a broken part, and needed to be repaired so that old and new Perugia could be connected.

Following Rossi's analogous design process, we can see how these ideas contributed to the further refinement of the new scheme. In addition to the new *Broletto*, Rossi had to incorporate other functions to complete his "skeleton" structure. For that purpose Rossi examined *Corso Vannucci*, the main pedestrian precinct in old Perugia, defined by

a characteristic typology of mixed residential and retail units (Figure 6.14a). The typology and the pedestrian street were then translated into the design solution. The new *piazza* was finally enclosed by the mixed residential and retail scheme, which bears typological references to old palaces along Corso Vannucci. In the design of the mixed residential and retail unit, Rossi made reference to old shutters and colour schemes whilst giving it a very modern look; what Peter G. Rowe defined in other Italian schemes as the creation of commonplace urban

Figure 6.14
(a) *Corso Vannucci* leading to the Cathedral *San Lorenzo*. (b) Old residential buildings near *Porta Trasimena*, Perugia. (c) New residential complex with shops underneath arcades in *Piazza Nuova*.

landscape (Figures 6.14b and 6.14c)[37] At this stage of design, three other elements were added to the scheme. At one side of the new *piazza* Rossi proposed a theatre/community centre with a conical tower marking its entrance (Figure 6.15a). When built this new theatre would have a similar position in the scheme to that occupied by the Cathedral in its old counterpart. At the southern edge of the *piazza*, there is a shopping centre; again showing typological resemblance to an old religious building in *Piazza della Republica*, used today as a retail unit (Figure 6.15b). One last element that Rossi added to the new civic centre is a fountain, which though designed as a modern form, bears typological reference both to *Fontana Maggiore* and to the old viaduct (Figure 6.15c). The new space gently slopes,

following the natural contours of the site. It is paved in red bricks which evoke old Etruscan and Roman streets and open spaces. We do question here why Rossi did not use the same type of paved surfaces as in *Piazza IV Novembre*, which would make the two spaces, old and new, more united.

The final principle that Rossi applied in the design of *Centro Direzionale* was that of *urban dynamics* and politics. So far we have seen how Rossi used existing types as initiators and precedents for new design. There are, however, other needs that Rossi and the City Council had to cater for. This is where the use of ideas "rooted but not stuck" in the past are most obvious. Perugia is more than just a mediaeval town, and the new civic centre also had to reflect the modern part of Perugia's place-identity.

Figure 6.15
(a) Aldo Rossi's design concept for *Piazza Nuova,* Perugia. (b) The main entrance into the new shopping complex in Piazza Nuova. (c) A detail of Piazza Nuova with its new fountain.

The principle of urban dynamics is largely evident in the provision of a shopping centre and the underground car park, the use of construction materials and detailed, smaller-scale aspects of design: the windows, surface textures, the colours and other detailed elements (Figure 6.16a). At this scale of design, Rossi relied heavily on his own architectural culture and its neo-rationalist interpretation of built-form elements. The windows of the civic centre, for example, are simple square openings instead of the highly decorative and stylised windows typical of the old buildings. Modern materials reflect the "progressive" identity, through the use of concrete, stone, brick, metal and glass surfaces. Beige,

dark-brown and pink coloured surfaces also blend well with both old and new Perugian buildings; as is obvious when viewing *Centro Direzionale* from the old town. The new civic centre reflects the old town building types, but also blends well with modern Perugia; reinforcing both old and new place-identity characters (Figure 6.16b).

Having explored Rossi's method for designing *Centro Direzionale,* it is apparent that the "scientific approach" that he used was very much embedded in an understanding of the town's topography and geography, its historical roots as well as its modern tissues and progressive image. As we have seen, such an approach relies on the ability of a designer

Figure 6.16
(a) A small courtyard of Centro Direzionale. (b) A panoramic view of new Perugia and Centro Direzionale.

to understand the morphological and typological components of a place, and then to use that knowledge in the construction of a new scheme. One problem with this method is that it is not "value free". It is therefore important to discover what kind of messages and meanings such newly designed places actually convey to different actors and user groups. We shall try to map out the views of the Perugia City Council and local planners and architects, as well as everyday users and visitors to the city, to see how successful Rossi has been in his attempt to design a scheme that would reinforce Perugia's place-identity.

We shall first discuss the views of Perugia City Council who commissioned the project. According to Lucia Vasak,[38] who interviewed the Councillors, opinions here are very positive. The Councillors felt that *Centro Direzionale* "is harmonious with the character of the old and new parts of the city."[39] This harmony, they said, had been achieved through the spatial organisation of the new *piazza*, the building structures and the relationships between buildings and topography. Particularly successful, they felt, was the reference to building types such as the *Palazzo dei Priori*, the Cathedral, the University buildings, *Fontana Maggiore* and *Corso Vannucci*. Reference was also made to the smaller-scale elements such as steps, windows, entrances and arcades, re-interpreted by Rossi to reflect the modern progressive image of Perugia.

Similar views were also presented by Francisco Angellili and Nazzasesso Gambasacci, two City Council architects and city planners, whilst Morris Adjami, an architecture historian, claims that the scheme is typical of the squares in central Italy and its design composition and elements provide a great setting for cultural, civic and political gatherings.[40] We can see that the professionals felt positive about the new scheme, but this may be because they share Rossi's professional values. It is therefore equally important to understand the everyday users' views, as they represent their own kind of imagined community.

According to Lucia Vasak, who carried out interviews with the residents and citizens of Perugia,[41] it is clear that they all recognised the elements that constitute the place-identity of Perugia. They all agreed that Perugia had a very strong and

definite character but they also stated that the city was typical of other Umbrian hill towns, with "a closely knit" urban form structure, with narrow passages, steps, alleys and arches.

One of the respondents described:

> *A home town you return to because of its small spaces and routes that are like secret passages, always leading to surprising places and piazzas.*[42]

Residents and visitors were also able to identify key monuments and public open spaces as important elements in the city's place-identity construct. When explaining Perugia's place-identity they referred to *Piazza IV Novembre*, *Palazzo dei Priori*, *Cathedral* and *Fontana Maggiore*, the same group of monuments that Rossi used as "analogous" elements for his design. Residents and visitors also noted the importance of the local materials that gave the city its distinctive "beige and pink" tonality. Equally important, they felt, was the city's topography. One of the residents observed that "the city grows out of the hill and conforms to the different parts of it."[43] It is obvious, therefore, that the elements identified by the residents and visitors of Perugia as important for place-identity represented the same set of components that Rossi found important for his design reference. We shall now discuss the meanings and interpretations that the city users made of *Centro Direzionale*, to see the extent to which Rossi managed to achieve the qualities that users felt were important in place-identity terms.

The respondents were asked to identify which of the new design elements supported the place-identity of Perugia, and prioritise their importance. At the larger scale of design, residents and visitors felt that it was the respect for topography, the design concept of the new *Piazza*, the new Civic Centre and the new Fountain which supported the Perugian character most strongly. However, respondents had mixed feelings about the smaller, more detailed aspects of design. They felt that Rossi made good choices in the use of local stone, steps and colours; and that these were important for reinforcing the Perugian character. However, the overall balance between the old Perugian elements and the new ones are perhaps too radical. Respondents observed that Rossi could have used more local stone, to blend with the old Perugian character. New corridors and passages, though described as "interesting and pleasant", were "not narrow and dark enough", and ceilings were too low in the new scheme. Some of the respondents noted that the rhythm and the use of entrances along the ground floor of the main *Broletto* were similar to the elements of the *Palazzo dei Priori*, but questioned the absence of rounded arches. Several residents also wished that Rossi had used even more steps, to recreate the hilly topography of the old city.

A number of people also noted that *Centro Direzionale* was "new", and naturally required some time to become part of the rest of the city. They also felt that "although it was important to be harmonious and in sympathy with the old city, it was necessary to be 'modern' and to show 'progress'."[44] One of the respondents remarked that:

> In ten years time, or even one hundred years, because it was modelled after the old city in many ways, the piazza, the size, and use of land, that it recognises the chimney, the road (passing through it), and other surroundings, it will be considered a natural part of Perugia.[45]

Taken together, these observations suggest that users felt that new designs ought to support existing place-identities and that *Centro Direzionale* had been very successful in its use of large-scale elements but less so in the design of small-scale detailing. It therefore appears that when designing new schemes from a place-identity perspective designers ought to focus on both large- and small-scale elements. Despite some reservations, we can argue that an overall success from a place-identity perspective can be judged by the ways in which *Centro Direzionale* is described to visitors: it is now included in several tourist guide-books, and described as an evocation of the Umbrian character and as a force that marks the new millennium.

It seems to us that Rossi's method has great potential for use by other designers. First, his concept of *locus* and history provides a powerful tool for understanding nature, topography and other geographical properties of a site. In Perugia we have seen how topography promotes a particular kind of

kinaesthetic experience, which contributes to the legibility of a locality. Rossi also used water in his design to make powerful links between urban and rural landscapes, and incorporated local trees which, as we saw in Ljubljana and in Mexico, are also important in place-identity terms.

The second important factor in Rossi's method is the overall spatial structure, the skeleton of a place, which has to be designed to connect into the existing context. This "skeleton", however, has to allow growth over time so that new elements can be added on, to allow the urban form to expand. Rossi has achieved that by integrating old routes into the new scheme.

The third, and in Rossi's terms, most important factor concerns the concepts of *type* and *typology*. It is useful to note that types and typological elements can be used as a source of design ideas. However, when we use types we need to bear in mind that they are not only physical elements; they also carry important messages in terms of their use and function. When we design new types, they need to be robust enough to accommodate changing socio-economic and cultural needs. We also need to remember to consider both large- and small-scale detailed elements, as identified by the users of Perugia.

The fourth aspect of Rossi's method, his concept of *urban dynamics*, is also important to incorporate in the design process, so that finished projects are rooted but not stuck in the past. The key question here is how big is the leap between the contextual reference and the new, progressive built-form elements. In the case of *Centro Direzionale* this leap was perhaps too radical, too abstract, for residents to connect to all levels of design. This suggests that a closer working relationship with all key actors is desirable, so that these issues are discussed at the different stages of the design process in order to achieve the best trade-offs between different imagined communities.

Rossi's method, also connects many different groups through the concept of urban memories deposited in urban artefacts, spatial systems and the sequence of events that form characteristic layers of human histories imprinted on natural landscapes. These urban memories therefore represent the collective subconsciousness of many imagined communities. Through consideration of urban memory, the skeleton, types and typology Rossi designed a scheme able to project many new meanings, and therefore able to support many communities. Through the design of the new Civic Centre and its new *piazza*, the city's new *genius loci* becomes an important new place where different communities can interact and participate in the construction of new events.

Let us now discuss Rossi's approach in designing *Centro Direzionale* in relation to our four key place-identity issues. First, what useful lessons have we learned about designing to support a rooted sense of imagined community? At the use level, Rossi's concepts of *skeleton*, *types*, *locus* and *history* are all based on the understanding of deep-rooted urban form elements and their spatial relationships, that are interpreted an employed by a designer, in an "analogous" way, to create new places, new place-identities. Particularly, useful here is the concept of skeleton, or urban structure, used in design to expand existing places and to allow them to grow in a consistent way, where each part follows a similar pattern of rules. At the most practical level of design we can create integrated public open space networks, regional and local. Such open space networks allow different users to encounter each other. Similarly, the use of types and typology, rooted in the past but modified to meet the present and future needs through the employment of the concept of *urban dynamics*, become useful tools for designing new developments that meet the users' needs and offer opportunities for a range of human encounters. At the meaning level, Rossi's method connects many different groups through the concept of urban memories that are deposited in urban artefacts and spatial systems, and form characteristic layers of human histories imprinted on natural landscapes. These urban memories therefore represent the collective subconsciousness of many imagined communities. Through the employment of the concepts of urban memory, the skeleton, types and typology Rossi designed a scheme able to project many new meanings, therefore able to support many communities. Through the design of the Civic Centre and its new piazza, the city's new *genius loci* is given an important new role where different communities can interact and

participate in the construction of new events. Such elements also support our interpretation of legibility.

Rossi's approach can also offer useful lessons in designing to support harmonious living with members of other communities. At the level of use, this is achieved through the positive sense of safety *vis-à-vis* "others". The scheme shows how Rossi's approach can be used to design an integrated public open space network with mixed use developments providing support for different user groups. At the level of meaning, the use of urban memories allows us to conceptualise deep-rooted structures and our own sense of identity.

A third important lesson is about designing to support users' sense of empowerment. At the use level, Rossi's design approach promotes integration of different tissues and public open space networks, offering different communities choice of routes, patterns of activities and lifestyles. At the meaning level, users' interpretations of new places that are rooted in old familiar settings, reinforces users' own sense of themselves and their sense of belonging to a particular type of imagined community.

Finally, what can Rossi's design approach offer in terms of designing to support the development of a sense of harmonious co-dwelling with the wider ecosystem? At the use level, this is achieved by respecting the site's topography and geography, by uniting the old and new Perugia. At the detailed level of design, Rossi's use of water, local trees and other plant life provides rich habitat for birds, insects, and other types of non-human species. At the meaning level, users' perceptions and inter-pretations of *Centro Direzionale*, reveal deep-rooted meaning of the site's topographic and kinaesthetic richness; again linking old and new Perugia into a unified sense of place-identity, its *genius loci*.

Notes

1 Seminar presentation by Nullo Belodi, Lisbon, 1999.
2 Interview with Pier Luigi Cervellati by Georgia Butina Watson, Bologna, 2001.
3 Biographical note on Rossi, in Rossi, 1986.
4 Eisenman, Editor's Preface in Rossi, 1986.

5   Ibid.
6   McLeod, in Rossi, 1986.
7   Eisenman, Ibid.
8   Rossi, 1986, 21.
9   Ibid.
10 Ibid.
11 Ibid.
12 Ibid., 21–22.
13 Ibid., 22.
14 Rossi, 1986, 6.
15 Rossi, 1986.
16 Ibid., 63.
17 For further information refer to Chapter 3 of Rossi's book.
18 Ibid.
19 Rossi, 1986, 103.
20 Eisenman in Rossi, 1986, 7.
21 Rossi, 1986.
22 Ibid.
23 Rossi, 1986, 139.
24 Vasak, 1989.
25 Ibid.
26 Ibid.
27 Facaros and Pauls, 2002.
28 Ibid., 2002.
29 Ibid., 106.
30 Ibid.
31 Ibid.
32 Interview with Lucia Vasak, 1989.
33 Vasak, interview with the City Council of Perugia members, Perugia, July, 1989.
34 Interview carried out by Lucia Vasak, Perugia, July, 1989.
35 Rossi, 1982.
36 Ibid.
37 Rowe, 1997.
38 Vasak, 1989.
39 Ibid., 124.
40 Adjami, 1994.
41 Vasak, 1989.
42 A resident of Perugia, quoted in Vasak, 1989, 134.
43 Ibid., 135.
44 Vasak, 1989, 143.
45 A Perugian resident quoted in Vasak, 1989, 143.

7

Malaysia: Layering ecology and culture

In the last chapter we explored Aldo Rossi's approach to designing the *Centro Direzionale* in Perugia; where natural landscape, the town's topography and inherited morphological and typological elements played key roles in the design. We also saw how Rossi managed to build a sense of rootedness into the *Centro Direzionale* scheme, whilst incorporating progressive new design ideas. We saw how Rossi was successfully guided in this challenging task by his own theoretical approach, by the strong morphological structure of old Perugia, and by the progressive attitudes of the Perugini citizens and professionals.

Whilst the city of Perugia had undergone a relatively slow and steady growth over several centuries, resulting in a strong sense of Perugian identity, there are many places where fast development trends pose new, challenging questions when it comes to designing contemporary place-identities. This is particularly evident in countries such as Malaysia, where the rapid growth of cities such as Kuala Lumpur generates strong images through development types associated with the globalised world economy, whilst also raising complex multicultural design issues. Before we explore how appropriate place-identities might be formed in such situations, it is important to explain the context within which these ideas are being developed (Figures 7.1a and 7.1b).

First of all, Malaysian identity is strongly affected by geography. Malaysia's 14 states are geographically and topographically varied, and together comprise the main Peninsular Malaysia, which stretches 132,000 square kilometres, and Sabah and Sarawak which

occupy a part of Borneo Island with a territory of 333,000 square kilometres.[1] Most of the urban development of the country occupies the western parts of the Malay Peninsula, due to ancient maritime trading routes and a relatively flat topography: in contrast, the central zone is mountainous, and the eastern parts have long stretches of fine, sandy beaches. Equally rich is the geography of Sabah and Sarawak, with mountain ranges including the mysterious Mount Kinabalu, and placid meanders which feed into the blue, island-studded South China Sea. Malaysia's islands are covered by primeval rain forests, with rich flora and fauna. The country's hot (35°C average) and humid climate, with plenty of rainfall, has also contributed to the production of a unique cultural landscape. Particularly important for the process of place-identity construction is a rich supply of timber; which has traditionally been used in the building of houses, mosques, shophouses and other building types.

In addition to the effects of natural topography and landscape, the country's historic, political and cultural events have also played important roles in place-identity terms. The original people of Malaysia – Bumiputras – include Malays and other indigenous groups; who today total some 58% of the overall population. The second largest ethnic group is Chinese, representing some 32%; whilst Indians account for most of the rest.

During the thirteenth century, Muslim traders from India introduced Islam: today some 45% of the Malaysian population belong to this main religious group. Other groups practise Buddhism, Hinduism and

Christianity. The main languages spoken today are Malay, Chinese, Tamil and English.[2]

Between the seventh and the fourteenth centuries the area was governed as Indian Kingdoms, ruled by Indo-Buddhist dynasties.[3] Between the fifteenth and mid-twentieth centuries the country was successively ruled by the Portuguese (1511–1641), the Dutch (1641–1785) and the British (1785–1957).[4] Successive waves of political and administrative change also introduced a rich tapestry of cultural influences, still evident in the country's socio-economic, architectural and urban design character. The latest stage of the country's political, socio-economic and cultural transformation began in 1957, when Malaysia gained independence from Britain.

Malaysia's transition to independence, known as Merdeka, is in many ways a great success story. This is partly due to rapid economic growth, associated with a rich supply of primary commodities such as rubber, tin, oil and palm oil. Malaysia's geographic position, and her good trading relationships with other countries, have also played important roles in the growth of the globalised economy. At the same time educational programmes, promoted by successive governments, enabled a constant supply of highly educated workers. The most challenging issue in building the new Malaysian nation has been the need to involve the country's varied socio-cultural groups; each holding strong feelings and perceptions of itself as a unique imagined community, whilst at the same time belonging to a modern nation-state with strong beliefs in an overall Malaysian identity. Such complex structures were not achieved overnight, nor without strong emotions and occasional

Figure 7.1
(a) Kuala Lumpur's landmarks of progressive place-identity image. (b) Kuala Lumpur's contrasting morphologies.

conflicts; which from time to time create inter-racial tensions. These tensions seem to have become weaker in recent years, as a result of a common, progressive search for a more united sense of nationhood.

If we are to understand how Malaysian designers have tried to work with this complex tapestry of cultural traditions, we have to explain how built form elements evolved over time, to understand the origins of particular place-identity ideas. There have been two main historical building sources to draw on in contemporary place-identity construction processes: on the one hand traditional rural timber-framed houses, built on stilts with very characteristic roofs;[5] and on the other, urban design traditions developed in the larger urban centres such as Kuala Lumpur, Malacca and Georgetown (Figure 7.2a).

The indigenous Malay house, according to Lim Jee Yuan, "is one of the richest components of Malaysia's cultural heritage. Designed and built by ordinary villagers themselves, it manifests the creative and aesthetic skills of the Malays".[6] It also provides, says Chris Abel, "a good example of one-to-one relations between social and built forms typical of traditional cultures".[7] Many architectural theorists and vernacular building experts claim that the traditional, rural Malay house responds well to the socio-cultural needs of its occupants, and is at the same time a perfect response to the hot and humid climate. With a direct dependence on nature

Figure 7.2
(a) A traditional timber-framed Malay house. (b) A traditional Malay Kampong. (c) Malacca's old waterfront buildings. (d) Malacca's eclectic shophouses.

for its resources, and embedding a deep knowledge of ecological balances, the house is efficiently designed to suit the local climatic requirements; using a range of ventilation and solar-control devices, and low thermal capacity building materials.[8]

In its basic form the rural Malay house is a "post and lintel structure with wooden and bamboo walls and a thatched roof";[9] allowing a large number of windows to provide good ventilation and views. This basic house unit can be extended to suit the needs of its residents. Internally, houses contain one large open space to allow the flow of cool breezes. The floor is at various levels, to provide functional separation between family activities such as cooking, eating, sleeping or entertaining.

Over a long history, this basic house-type has evolved into many sub-types; distinguished by decorative elements of walls, shutters and doors, and particularly by variations of roof-shape. Lim Jee Yuan claims that:

From a distance, the Malay house seems to merge naturally with the environment. The roof, which is large, dominates the low walls and the open stilted bottom of the house. The juxtaposition of the roofs of the house with different sizes and at different orientations creates an interesting visual form.[10]

Malay house types are classified according to their roof forms and shapes, the basic and most common being *bambung panjang*, *bambung lima*, *bambung perak* and *bambung limas*.[11] *Bambung panjang* has a characteristic long gable roof, and can be found all over Peninsular Malaysia. The roof material is known as *attap*, a thatch made from *nipah* and other palm trees found locally. More recently, thatched roofs are being replaced by modern materials such as zinc and slates, which mostly do not perform as well in this hot climate. The funnel-shaped roof has ventilation grilles at its gable ends, called *tebar layer*; and the use of ventilation gaps provides a very efficient cooling system. Large roof eaves usually project beyond the house walls, to provide protection from sun and rain.

Despite its simple construction, the Malay house can be very elaborate in decorative terms: some houses display a very interesting mix of local traditional and eclectic colonial influences, largely Dutch and British. In Malacca, for example, they are often richly decorated, with colourful tiles at the entrance and in courtyard spaces. Some houses have Chinese influence evident in carvings, tiles and porcelain balustrades. Some larger houses, composed of several basic units, have tiled, interior courtyards and timber verandahs. Most other regional types are less colourful, but sometimes have rich carvings on their timber surfaces. Roofs and walls are made of the beautifully patterned bark of the bertam tree and of bertam leaves.

Traditionally, rural Malay houses sit in a compound; usually defined by trees and shrubs. A group of houses and compounds together comprise a *Kampong*, a larger village territory. Individual compounds define a private residential domain and are usually planted with fruit trees and shrubs, which provide food and give shelter against scorching sun or heavy rain. Palm trees are particularly well suited for modifying the local climate: the top, leafy sections provide an "umbrella-like" shelter from the sun and rain, whilst lower trunks allow the circulation of air. The spatial arrangement of compounds within a Kampong, which defines the village social space, is determined by the site's topography and climate (Figure 7.2b). According to Lim Jee Yuan, traditional Malay houses are randomly arranged. This ensures that the wind velocity in downwind houses will not be substantially reduced.[12] Taken together, this pattern of spatial organisation and building techniques provides a very efficient system; ecologically and climatically responsive to residents' needs.

In addition to the traditional rural Malay house form, Malaysian designers have also inherited other more urban dwelling types and settlement patterns to draw on when designing contemporary Malaysian place-identities. The best examples are found in the larger urban centres, such as Kuala Lumpur, Malacca and Georgetown.

According to historical sources,[13] the first urban developments on the Malaysian Peninsula began in the province of Kedah, between the seventh and fourteenth century. The city of Malacca was established during this period as an important port, where Arab, Indian and Chinese merchants came to collect spices from the region. With economic growth, other early townships were formed around main administrative trading and cultural centres such as Georgetown (Penang) and Kuala Lumpur.

Between the fifteenth and twentieth centuries, Chinese merchants introduced various patterns of shophouses; the basic type consisting of two dwellings, front and back, with an open-air courtyard between them. In morphological terms these houses were arranged in rows on narrow plots of land. Anthony Too states that:

> A panoptic overview of the existing built form, planning and image of any of the major cities and towns of Malaysia like Malacca, Georgetown, Ipoh and Kuala Lumpur will reveal a marked degree of coherent taxonomy and civic unity in their old town centres and traditional business districts. A closer focus reveals relatively uniform grid-patterns created by interesting streets and lanes, intricately textured and interweaved to form the basic legible component that facilitates spatial and formal continuum within the delicate urban fabric.[14]

Shophouses are generally two or three storeys high. The front part is a business or "shop" unit, with a five foot wide arcaded walkway at ground level. Behind the walkway is a business area with offices above. The second, back dwelling – separated from the shop by a courtyard – is for the family's private use. Such a building type forms a very robust unit, which is also climatically responsive as it allows air to circulate through different parts of the building complex. Particularly interesting are the shophouses of Malacca where, according to Anthony Too, "the earliest prototype and typological variation of the local shophouse is found".[15] Over time, depending on other architectural and cultural influences, the shophouse type has acquired many decorative elements from Portuguese, Dutch and British influences which resulted, as is evident in Malacca, in a distinctive Straits Eclectic Style[16] (Figures 7.2c and 7.2d).

> Designed on narrow plots separated by party walls, they have a covered loggia on the street front which pre-dates the five-foot verandah way. Most of these houses with their characteristic red tile roofs, are subdivided into sections along a single axis, separated by airwells.[17]

Variations of this typology can also be found in Kuala Lumpur and Georgetown Penang (Figure 7.3a).

In addition to the rural Malay house types and the urban Chinese shophouse examples, much of the place-identity of cities such as Kuala Lumpur and Georgetown was the result of British colonial urbanisation processes; which started with the introduction of the British administration in 1795, following an initial invitation by the Sultan of Selangor in 1779 to provide law and order in the region. The most significant leap in terms of urban growth came through the expansion of a little village at the confluence of two rivers – the Gombak and the Klang – when the muddy estuary of Kuala Lumpur began to function as a tin-trading post and later, in 1819, became the seat of the British administration. The original Chinese tin trading port was a ramshackle clutch of wooden buildings and attap huts within which, according to Chay, each ethnic group had its own "quarter".[18] The Malays settled in villages upstream from the confluence of the two rivers, towards *Bukit Nanas* (Pineapple Hill). The Chinese, on the other hand, located downstream, along what is today *Jalan Petaling*. In 1880 Kuala Lumpur (muddy river) was made the capital of the State of Selangor.

As a result of a fire that spread from an opium shop in 1881,[19] some 220 wooden houses were destroyed. This gave a clean sheet for the new Resident, Frank Swettenham, to build the city of bricks and tiles and to widen the roads and improve infrastructure: the streets were laid out on a simple gridiron plan, still evident today in the Chinese Quarter. According to Ken Yeang, Swettenham also introduced Building Regulations in 1884; decreeing that the original attap hut settlement was to be rebuilt in brick or wattle, with tiled roofs and allowance for a five-foot covered passageway alongside the road.[20]

During the British administration Kuala Lumpur acquired many colonial buildings, built in an eclectic mixture of styles. Most representative are the Government Buildings designed by A. C. Norman in 1894; Masjid Jame Mosque, a replica of a North Indian mosque designed by A. B. Hubbock in 1909; and the Railway Station, based on a North Indian pattern, built in 1910.[21] According to Chris Abel all these public buildings embody a hybrid of European (British Palladian) and Indian Islamic architectural

Figure 7.3
(a) Kuala Lumpur's restored shophouses. (b) Contrasting images of modern Kuala Lumpur: Masjid Jame Mosque with modern buildings in the background. (c) Kuala Lumpur's Railway Station, based on a North Indian pattern, built in 1910. (d) The Law Courts in Kuala Lumpur, part of the British colonial inheritance.

principles, which together with local building traditions produced the first Malaysian architecture (Figures 7.3b–7.3d).

There were many other cross-cultural influences in both public and domestic architecture. During the 1930s, for example, modern European architectural influences began to shape the Kuala Lumpur skyline. The most significant landmark building from this period is Central Market, an art-deco structure built along the river Klang, designed by engineer and architect T. Y. Lee in 1937. According to Peter Chay, "this was where KL housewives came for fresh meat, vegetables and fruits"[22] (Figure 7.4a). An eclectic mix of different architectural styles initially continued

after Malaysia's independence in 1957, due to the presence of the many western town planning and architectural firms still working in the region. Most famous was the building of the Merdeka Stadium, constructed to celebrate the historical event of the proclamation of independence, witnessed by some 22,000 citizens with Tunku Abdul Rahman Putra Al-Haj as the first Prime Minister of modern Malaysia.

The first post-Merdeka building programme, between 1957 and 1967, focused on the commercial and administrative development of Kuala Lumpur; which served as a model for other Malaysian centres. In addition to banks, commercial outlets and government buildings, there were also many housing

Figure 7.4
(a) Central Market, an art-deco structure, designed by T. Y. Lee in 1937. (b) Ken Young's Plaza IBM, Kuala Lumpur.

projects constructed on Western models, to deal with the rapid increase in population, largely formed from rural migrants, who often found these new high-rise apartment dwellings inappropriate both for socio-cultural and for climatic reasons.

Western architectural influences are also evident in the construction of low-rise residential suburbs such as Petaling Jaya, popularly referred to by local residents as PJ, planned as a dormitory satellite district of Kuala Lumpur. Early houses here were single or two-storey dwellings resembling some of the first generation new towns in England. Similar ideas continued to be implemented during the second post-Merdeka period, between 1967 and 1977. These trends are most evident in the design of Shah Alam, the new capital of the state of Selangor, built to take over administrative and state government functions, and to release some of the development pressures of Kuala Lumpur, which became the Federal capital in 1974.

Once Kuala Lumpur became the capital of modern Malaysia, politicians, investors, designers and city planners started to focus their attention on shaping the city's place-identity. This was initially expressed through the design of individual buildings rather than through the city's overall spatial structure. It can be

argued that this is largely due to complex political and historical circumstances, and to a very strong link with the colonial past, where deep-rooted spatial structures represent colonial ties. It is, therefore, not surprising to find that many of the sources for constructing modern Malaysian place-identities were drawn from international building types.

As a result, western influences were particularly strong during the 1980s economic boom, when many high-rise business and apartment dwellings were built in Kuala Lumpur to accommodate a variety of new needs. During this period, most new buildings followed standard high-rise design and construction principles that could be found almost anywhere in the world. Many of these developments did not respect the local topography: building sites were often flattened to accommodate easier and faster construction methods. Such thoughtless interventions brought about land erosion, deforestation and in some cases flooding. Equally negative are shopping malls with their numerous trading avenues enclosed by large citadel-like structures that have many negative impacts on the microclimate and vitality of open spaces.

In order to connect these newly developed buildings, a new infrastructure system was built. First, an elevated road system was introduced in the 1980s, to facilitate fast moving vehicular traffic. Second, an elevated light-rail system was built to reduce the need for car journeys. Together, these systems have created a form of dual city, where pockets of traditional neighbourhoods such as those of Chinatown and Kampong Bahru are in stark contrast to the high-rise buildings of the Golden Triangle area.

Whilst Chinatown is full of life due to the variety of businesses, shops, markets, temples and eating places, connected by five-foot verandah ways that provide shelter for traders and visitors to the area, modern high-rise developments are served by the elevated road system. Many local and international critics question such modern development trends, as they lack the sense of rootedness and contextual reference that the modern Malaysian nation is aspiring to achieve.

According to Chris Abel, some of the key problems associated with such developments stem from the preponderance of rural rather than urban design traditions in Malaysia, causing "a lack of appropriate models equivalent to Western theoretical tools".[23] Even the introduction of several development plans, between 1957 and 1985, did not resolve Kuala Lumpur's spatial integration problems. Many of these interventions were short-term responses to pressures for rapid growth, rather than making planned, strategic responses to its morphological transformation processes. Another shortcoming of these development plans was that they focused largely on two-dimensional aspects of planning, and lacked any urban design guidelines to shape three-dimensional public space networks.

Despite the preponderance of Western influences during the 1980s, a number of new ideas began to be explored by Malaysian, rather than Western architects. Although mostly trained either in the United Kingdom or in Australia, young architects started to explore alternative, specifically Malaysian design solutions. Architectural and design critics began to support these ideas: Chris Abel, for example, suggests that:

Any conscious effort by Asian urbanists to break out of this impasse and create an alternative approach to planning and design born of their own cultures and histories, if only in part, is therefore to be greatly welcomed.[24]

Several lines of these new design ideas can be traced, though not all of them have yet been implemented. The first line centred around the design of individual high-rise buildings; where the use of local iconography and symbolism on the one hand, and eco-friendly design on the other, started to appear in the design of office blocks, banks and other public buildings. The best-known building from this group is Ken Yeang's Plaza IBM, enveloped by landscaped balconies to cool the building mass (Figure 7.4b). Another good example is the Dayabumi Complex in Kuala Lumpur, designed by BEP and MAA Akitek group. Here we find the use of Islamic arches and geometrically patterned grilles, employed both as elements in a new symbolic iconography and as energy-efficient devices to filter the strong sun and therefore cool the inside of the building (Figures 7.5a–7.5c). A key departure from earlier developments is that this complex of buildings is organised to create a small public space for pedestrians to rest under the shade of palm trees, to absorb the views of the Central Market and the modern Kuala Lumpur townscape; whilst a small pedestrian bridge links the two banks of the narrow, muddy Klang river, to extend the spatial sequence into the Central Market area.

Issues of conservation also began to surface during the 1980s, with growing concerns about the loss of built form heritage. This debate helped to rescue many Malay timber houses, as well as groups of shophouses in Kuala Lumpur, Malacca and Georgetown. In addition, the first national Design Discourse, organised by PAM (Pertubuhan Akitek Malay) in 1983 focused on questions of architectural and regional identity, and on issues of architecture's reference to place and time. The subject of the first major conservationist intervention in Kuala Lumpur was the Central Market area. The Market building itself was scheduled for demolition in the early 1980s to allow the site to be redeveloped, but due to conservationist pressures it was saved and refurbished in 1986, and this triggered other, smaller-scale urban design improvement schemes. The space surrounding the Central Market building was

Figure 7.5
(a) Dayabumi Complex, designed by BEP and MAA Akitek group. (b) Dayabumi Complex with a view of the Islamic Centre building. (c) A detail view of the Dayabumi office block.

pedestrianised, and is today one of the most popular public spaces in Kuala Lumpur. The Central Market building itself was turned into a craft outlet, to provide selling spaces for traditional Malaysian craft merchandise, and is today very popular with tourists as well as with local people. In such conservationist interventions it is always sad to see the loss of a traditional market; however, the presence of old shophouses in the area provides colourful and important selling units for everything that residents may need for their everyday supply of goods. During the 1980s a number of other historic buildings were restored, which made it a turning point in place-identity terms, as local professionals and other key actors began to recognise the complex nature of Malaysian identity (Figures 7.6a and 7.6b).

In addition to the efforts made by Malaysian architects to preserve and restore historic buildings, the 1980s also saw the beginning of a body of academic research designed to explore the new kind of urbanism that Kuala Lumpur was experiencing. Particularly rich were studies in city legibility and in the character of open space networks. These studies began to draw attention to the "dual city" problem, already outlined.[25]

The most coherent 1980s discourse on urbanism was Ken Yeang's *Tropical Verandah City*.[26] The underlying concept of the *Verandah City* is a system of arcaded, pedestrian walkways that bind the buildings together. Such walkways could provide shelter and support streetlife, as with traditional shophouses. Yeang suggests that verandah ways could potentially

Figure 7.6
(a) The Central Market complex, Kuala Lumpur. (b) Traditional shophouses in the Central Market area, Kuala Lumpur.

integrate old and new buildings in the city, and could also be connected with natural landscape elements; improving both climatic and legibility aspects of urban form (Figure 7.7). Some critics see this as a very useful concept through which infrastructure, climate control and urban aesthetics could be resolved with the same device.[27]

However, most other Malaysian urban developments during the 1980s, particularly in Kuala Lumpur as the nation's capital, continued to reflect global rather than local design practices. The rate of urban growth eluded the grasp of any urban design intervention, and the most visible outcome was the transformation of the Kuala Lumpur skyline with high-rise office, hotel and residential towers constructed at enormous speed against a backdrop of historic mosques and other building types.

This promotes the modern, progressive side of Kuala Lumpur's cultural landscape; where modern business, administration, shopping centres and luxury hotels compete for key locations, and are distinguished from each other by their height and by their architectural imagery. In contrast, another type of imagined community is represented by the traditional pattern of streets, shophouses, mosques and other historic buildings. Both types of imagined

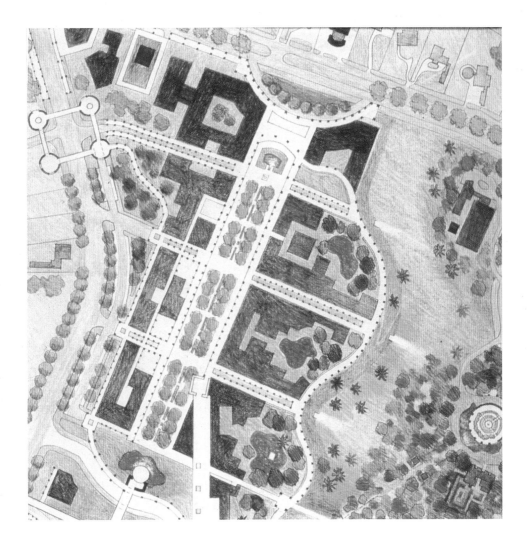

Figure 7.7
Ken Young's The Tropical Verandah concept.

community seem important, and the key question for contemporary Malaysian architects and urban designers is how to embrace both; to construct a new type of place-identity which would be rooted in the past but be modern, progressive and forward looking.

In the absence of an integrated urban design framework for Kuala Lumpur some of the most creative solutions, in place-identity terms, can be found at the smaller, architectural scales of design. The most significant architect here is Jimmy Lim who, with his architectural office CSK Associates, has developed a contemporary interpretation of the traditional timber Malay house and has begun to work on the idea of a tropical city.[28] Before we discuss examples of Lim's work, it is important to explore the theoretical body of ideas and design principles that underpin it.

Jimmy Lim was born in Penang, and images of the area's distinctive landscapes and traditional Malay roofscapes were amongst early influences on his choice of career, and in shaping his architectural direction. He trained and worked in New South Wales before returning to Kuala Lumpur in 1972; since when he has tried to design buildings that would be responsive to the tropical climate whilst reflecting the socio-cultural aspects of both traditional and modern Malaysian built form.

Lim's approach to constructing Malaysian place-identity is organised around five key factors which broadly correspond to our own place-identity agenda. These are climatic factors, environmental influences, cultural and traditional influences, traditional structural concepts and spiritual metaphor.[29]

In terms of climatic factors Malaysia's warm, humid climate, intense tropical sunshine, heavy seasonal rainfall and prevailing winds are critical for the design of dwellings. Sunshading, rain throw-off and ventilation therefore have to be considered as major issues in the design process. The traditional Malay timber house, as we already saw, is a good example of how to solve these issues.

Lim's second key factor concerns environmental influences. First of all, he suggests:

The characteristic features peculiar to a site have to be perceived and retained as much as possible

as they contribute to the "uniqueness" or "oneness" of the site as a whole.[30]

Lim also believes in harmonising nature's landscape with the architecture, so that "a hill should remain a hill and a valley should remain a valley, and any structure designed should harmonise with the environment".[31] It is also important, he feels, to consider water, both surface and subterranean, as it has important symbolic implications in terms of energy, luck and continuity:

To be able to optimise this feature, the architect should seek to obtain a clearer insight into its value and integrate it with his design in his search for a total architecture whereby the building extends beyond the physical structure to include the spiritual aspirations of the occupant of the building.[32]

Wind direction is another important environmental aspect, as the proper orientation of a dwelling provides occupants with cooling breezes. The relationship between wind and water, according to the Chinese tradition of "feng-shui", plays a vital role in the siting and orientation of a dwelling. Overall, Lim approaches the landscape with humility; using a particular kind of "Tai-Chi", where the designer works *with* rather than against nature:

My approach to architectural design is simple: understand your context to create the architecture that is suitable for the environment that you live in; understand the place, where you are, who you are. There are two aspects of architecture that influence my thinking as an architect. One is what I term "Architecture of Humility" and the other, the "Tai Chi" of Architecture. When I talk about humility I am referring to the suppression of one's ego in the face of the situation, and how it wants to be resolved.[33]

Lim also believes that architects must build to preserve the natural balance, the "yin yang" of the land. He also works with a sensory experience of places, which he calls "the rites of the tropics". He takes careful account of the colours, sounds, smells, kinaesthetic and visual experiences "tantalised by the different layering of shapes, light and shade, variety of hues and the mysticism of the unseen and unanticipated".[34] Tropical architecture allows a symbiotic relationship between man-made elements and nature, and evokes emotions and memories. Architectural interventions, if properly articulated, also provide the opportunity for "framing" nature, a concept that we also discussed in relation to Mexico, in Chapter 3. Lim suggests that:

> *The mysticism of transparency, layering of forms, light, shade, structural texture, – accentuates the visual surrealism of the space – blurs the distinction between space, distance and time.*[35]

The third principle that Lim considers in developing his design ideas concerns cultural and traditional influences. Here he tries to incorporate appropriate cultural and social factors, in order to preserve and promote the continuity of values embedded in different imagined communities, their lifestyles and building traditions. He often uses the concept of a traditional *Kampong* layout in the design of his interior spaces, where the living area is a symbolic reinterpretation of the Kampong square, and individual rooms are re-interpretations of individual Kampong dwellings.

The house type that Lim frequently uses in his residential design solutions is a re-interpretation of the traditional Malay house on stilts, which is based on his fourth design principle: the use of traditional structural concepts. Here the reference to traditional building techniques is particularly evident in the layered design of roof structures that he has employed so skilfully in many of his award-winning projects. In order to support his layered, fin-like roof structures, "Lim had devised a unique support system based on a bracketing technique inspired by traditional examples like the column capital brackets used in traditional Chinese architecture".[36] Lim often also employs traditional building materials, such as wood (often recycled), bamboo blinds and other components; frequently rescued from abandoned traditional Malay houses. Chris Abel explains that:

> *Lim emphasises the virtues of local materials and techniques and building in harmony with natural and cultural ecologies. The primary model for his houses is the traditional Malay house-on-stilts, one of a family of timber-framed dwelling*

types found throughout South-East Asia. Yet his inventive structural and spatial configurations are also evidence of a free-wheeling creative spirit, challenging hackneyed oppositions between "modern" and "traditional" architecture.[37]

The fifth design principle relates to the concept of *spiritual metaphor*. When Lim designs houses he thinks of them as places where a person can find spiritual solace, as one would in a temple: "a house is a temple to oneself". Lim feels that:

> *It is a place where we try to elevate ourselves spiritually to meet with God. It is a place where He dwells, symbolically. A place where we go for solace, to communicate with Him, a place where you feel most at ease and His presence will be most felt.*[38]

In this personal temple, the various internal spaces provide shelter, social interaction and solace. As one moves through one of these houses, one follows a "processional route", starting from public and moving to private spaces.

Lim, like Plečnik and Barragán discussed in earlier chapters, draws inspiration from the landscape and its sense of place, local cultures and lifestyles, and building traditions. It is therefore not surprising to find that all three architects were influenced by the architecture of Frank Lloyd Wright.

Jimmy Lim has tried out many of these principles in his own house. Located in Taman Seputeh in Kuala Lumpur, the house is an ongoing personal project, which has evolved around a pre-existing dwelling which now forms the core of a much extended building. Extensions have been built gradually, to accommodate changing family needs (Figures 7.8a and 7.8b). Lim feels that:

> *A house is like a tree – each new addition is like a branch – each new room is like a crest of a branch – each new detail is like a delicate leaf – a tree grows vertically into beautiful proportions.*[39]

Lim's house sits comfortably in its hilly location, and forms a local landmark that stands out from the rest of the residential dwellings in the neighbourhood. The house is made up of two units, one for the family and one for the guests. The space

193

Figure 7.8
(a) Lim's residence in Taman Seputeh, Kuala Lumpur, designed by CSK Associates. (b) A covered extension in Lim's residence.

in-between is an open-plan lounge, and the overall sequence of external and internal spaces is arranged to create the "processional" experience explained earlier. A number of opening devices in the large, umbrella-like timber roof act as "sails" to catch the wind and assist in cooling the interior.[40] These openings have two additional advantages. They face westward so that cool breezes enter into the house during the early evening hours, flowing around and through the house to cool the rooms and courtyards. They also provide stunning views of Kuala Lumpur and of the valley below the house: the height of these openings was determined by the height of the architect's rocking chair, and the views offered when sitting down in it.[41] The sides of the living area are also left open, to allow breezes to circulate freely; producing a cooling effect which is further enhanced by the sound of a small waterfall.

Typologically, the house is a very successful fusion of a traditional Malay house type and a modern residential dwelling. Various extensions were built from recycled wood and local *chengal* hardwood, whilst salvaged bricks came from Penang. The original part of the house is largely unaltered, and contains various domestic rooms; whilst the Guest House, an extension of the original dwelling, is built of carved timber. Another addition is a small "Music House", which is air-conditioned in order to sustain the levels of humidity needed for the musical instruments: it sits comfortably in the shaded garden area, with timber and glass walls which can be opened to create an instant stage for musical performances. "A typical problem resulting from the air-conditioned spaces in this tropical climate is water discharged from a dehumidification mechanism. However, in Jimmy Lim's house he has improvised by collecting and routing the discharged water to a large basin, irrigating the trees in the centre of the house."[42] Behind the house is a plot of land full of local plants and trees, intended to provide the necessary cooling environment for the living complex, but also to be used in the construction and landscaping of other houses that Lim designs and builds for his clients. In this way, he is giving back to nature what earlier generations of house builders have taken away.

A key feature of the house is that, like a tree, it evolves over time: present, past and future are all part of the same evolving history. Many of the artefacts, furniture and building materials that Lim utilises in each phase of the house expansion bear memories of other families, of other houses and other lifestyles within them.

It is not surprising to find that many of the ideas which Lim tests in his own house have been utilised, and further perfected, in other houses that he has designed over the last 30 years for a variety of clients. Although most are based on the generic principles explained earlier, each house is unique due to the specific properties of the site, the local *feng-shui* and the requirements of each client. Each new house makes an important contribution to an evolving sense of place-identity, in a similar way to the building of place-identity in a traditional Kampong. We have chosen three houses to explore this process in more detail. Each marks a different type of challenge in the architect's professional development, and represents a landmark in the maturation of his creative ideas.

First we shall explore the well-known *Precima House* at Jalan Ara in Bangsar, Kuala Lumpur. The house occupies a steep-sloping site, which Lim saw as having great potential for testing his five principles. Instead of altering the terrain of the site, Lim uses it as a starting point in his design. As in all his other houses, he "sensed" the site first; to establish its *feng-shui*, its geomorphic, topographic and planting formation properties. The house occupies a narrow plot and faces north-east. The clients' brief called for a tropical house which would be comfortable yet informal, and would cater for a contemporary lifestyle whilst remaining in touch with tradition. This idea of being traditional was very important to the clients, who needed to house many artefacts that they had collected whilst living and working in various countries in South-East Asia.[43] Lim also wanted to integrate the house with nature. A traditional Malay house type offered a perfect solution to accommodate the sloping terrain and to meet all the other requirements.

The spatial organisation of the house and the courtyard complex suggest a "processional sequencing": as we move through the house we become aware of different spatial spheres and experiences. The urban edge, with its entrance into the complex along Jalan Ara Street, is through an ordinary wall with glass openings, which blends well with the neighbouring properties (Figure 7.9a). Once we enter the front courtyard we become aware of the relationship between the house proper and the natural landscape. The low planting and ground cover, formed from a variety of local plants, offer a pleasing and calming scented backdrop.

> *There are no corners or blank walls to obstruct one's view as one enters the house. The stunning interior, the pool, the outdoors and the Kuala Lumpur skyline as the background view are all there for the visitor to behold. Everywhere, the richness of timber, the glitter of the rippling pool water as it reflects the sun's rays, the exotic décor and the unclaustrophobic openness of the living area are tantalising.*[44]

There is immediate contact with nature, with few boundaries between "inside" and "outside". The main house follows a symmetrical U-shaped plan, and is arranged around a central pool, which flows into the living area:

> *a swimming pool, acting as the nucleus of activity, gives the house a "rural spirit" likened to a house by a river where one gets up in the morning and bathe in the river.*[45] (Figure 7.9b)

The water in the swimming pool also cools the interior and provides rich visual and audio experiences, enhanced by a small waterfall incorporated at one end of the pool amongst the rocks and plant life (Figure 7.10).

> *The pool area terminates at the cliff-side end with built-in timber benches doubling as balustrading, a vantage point where one could get a panorama of the city and the only point from where the glory of the house can be visually appreciated in full.*[46]

Visual richness is particularly potent at night when the pool surface reflects the flickering lights of candles and Chinese lanterns (Figure 7.11).

The central part of the house is two storeys high, with a large timber roof structure. The main core is a large open-plan living area, which holds all the other parts of the house together, as does the central space in a rural Kampong. The section of the living room which connects into the swimming pool

area has no walls but wooden blinds; and projecting, umbrella-like roof components and overhanging eaves provide shelter from the sun and rain (Figures 7.12 and 7.13); so that the house is pleasantly cool, with air circulating freely through.

Access to the upper floor is via a wooden spiral staircase, which ends in a drum-like pulpit projecting into the main living area. The upper floor houses a den and a guest bedroom with a bathroom.

> *It brings to mind a scenario of a room in a typical Malay "Kampong" house devoid of any contemporary furniture and carpets with only the warmth of timber as a sole luxury.*[47]

There is a very strong relationship between the design of the house and the various artefacts it houses: we can see the merging of high and popular art objects, creating a sense of transculturality. The entrance to the guest bedroom, for example, incorporates a pair of authentic Balinese doors: a possession of the clients who wanted to incorporate their own cultural experiences into the house's design. It is from this upper deck guest area that the full splendour of the timber roof structure is revealed; masterfully executed in stained chengal beams and white cemboard, this offers both a shelter from external weather conditions and a "temple-like" feel of solitude and spiritual meditation. Coloured glass, wooden shutters, bamboo roller blinds and translucent material filter through just enough light for carrying out daily activities.

On the ground level two bedroom wings face the swimming pool, and provide privacy for its users. As the site slopes, these two wings are built on stilts, like a traditional Malay house; allowing native plants and insects to cohabit with humans in this urban habitat. Symbolic reference to nature is also evident in the detailed design of the building: the trusses supporting the roof structure are carved to simulate the wings of a bird in full flight, suggesting the "lightness" of the structure; which is then counterbalanced by "water-drop" details implying gravitational balance.

Similar design principles can be found in Lim's other buildings, though each is unique in responding to particular site characteristics and the needs of its occupants. Ideally, Lim would like to have a large

Figure 7.9
(a) Precima House in Jalan Ara in Bangsar, Kuala Lumpur, designed by Jimmy Lim and CSK Associates.
(b) Precima House, a bedroom wing.

Figure 7.10
Precima House, the courtyard view.

Figure 7.11
Precima House at night.

Figure 7.12
Interior view of the Precima House.

plot of land where he could put such houses together to form a new, contemporary Kampong. A step on the way here was taken when the owner of the Precima House, Rolf Schnyder, purchased land next door to meet his need for more space, and invited Jimmy Lim to design a new house in such a way as to complement the earlier one next door: the client's brief was to connect the two sites so that he can move seamlessly from one house to the other (Figures 7.14a and 7.14b).

The building is again based on the principles of a traditional Malay house, utilising the sloping site as part of the design concept. Lim's idea was to design a large three-storey pavilion, with a master bedroom

Figure 7.13
Interior and roof detail of the Precima House.

located on the top floor, like "the eagle's nest". The house follows a semi-circular form, offering stunning 180 degrees views over Kuala Lumpur. In order to counter the traffic noise of busy Jalan Ara Street, the house is sunk below road level to allow the creation of a waterfall which flows into the swimming pool. Large plants, ferns and shrubs are planted around the house for climatic and ecological reasons, and again the house is built on stilts to allow nature to become part of the dwelling itself.

Probably the most challenging of Lim's houses in topographic terms is the house for Peter Eu, built in the Damansara hills which surround the valley in which the central core of Kuala Lumpur is located.

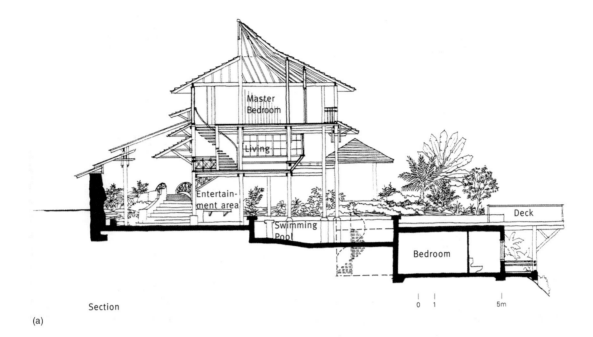

Section

(a)

(b)

Figure 7.14
(a) A cross-section of the Rolf Schnyder's House, Kuala Lumpur, Jimmy Lim and CSK Associates. (b) A courtyard view of the Rolf Schnyder's House.

Figure 7.15
Interior of the Peter Eu House, Kuala Lumpur, designed by Jimmy Lim and CSK Associates.

This house, which won the 1989 PAM Architectural Award, is like a huge umbrella, with a stairwell in the centre. The stairwell plays an important role in holding the rooms together; forming a central "hinge" for the radiating fins of the pitched roof which shelters a deck for resting and views.[48] Spatially, the house demonstrates once again the "processional" sequencing of spaces: the higher up we go, the more secluded. A "temple-like" house emerges, where solitude and contemplation can be practiced (Figures 7.15, 7.16a and 7.16b).

The re-interpretation of traditional Malay and Chinese types also features in the design of houses in other locations. Particularly interesting, in

Figure 7.16
(a) Layering of roof structure in Peter Eu's House. (b) A detail of roof structure in Peter Eu's House.

place-identity terms, are those designed for rural locations, where much damage has been done by extensive alterations to the natural landscapes and the overexploitation of natural resources. For example, the Selanger House, located some 30 miles south-east of Kuala Lumpur in Ulu Langat, Kajang, is an excellent example of transculturality and of creating a symbiotic relationship to the landscape. The house sits in a fairly flat rectangular plot, on high land with a commanding valley view. It is surrounded by rich local flora and fauna, with tall trees providing privacy; and has a natural cooling system, with breezes freely circulating through trees and penetrating inside the house. The site is full of surprises, including sizeable yellow lizards, sun bathing amidst the trees and shrubs; whilst the sounds of birds are amazing.

The design is again a re-interpretation of a traditional Malay house on stilts. A three-pointed, triangular plan is Lim's response to the client's requirements "for a trilogy of special usage for living, dining and study".[49] A hexagonal central core, made of rubble stone, encloses the main stairwell. Each corner of the triangle is designated for a different use and, like the raised deck, they all open onto an open, sheltered *wakaf* or corridor. The master bedroom occupies the top level, again designed as a temple. The building has a multi-layered roof structure, with openings to allow hot air to spill out; whilst the raised first floor platform directs cooler air into the house, to circulate freely through grilled partition walls and covered terraces and walkways. The house is built of new and recycled timber and rubble stone, and incorporates many

Figure 7.17
The Selanger House, Ulu Langat Kjang, the 1998 Aga Khan Award for architecture, designed by Jimmy Lim and CSK Associates.

elements rescued from old houses. The overall image suggests a "large bird in restful poise". The house, a winner of the 1998 Aga Khan Award for Architecture, is a beautiful example of the hybridisation of Malay traditional and modern concepts in housing design. It demonstrates "a symbolic relationship between man-made elements and nature, a cerebral relationship laced with emotions and memories. It embraces totally all one's senses"[50] (Figures 7.17, 7.18a and 7.18b).

Working within denser urban contexts is still a major challenge for Jimmy Lim. He is as sensitive to the socio-economic and cultural challenges of traditional urban shophouse neighbourhoods as he is to the traditional Malay Kampong. This sensitivity is evident in the restoration of several shophouses, where he has created two office spaces for his firm, each with a particular emphasis on the inherited structures of the buildings he occupies. Amongst his

dreams is a scheme where he could acquire a whole block of traditional shophouses that would be restored to their original glory but be adapted for modern urban living.[51] He is exploring similar ideas through the concept of what he calls a "Kampongminium": a fusion of a traditional Malay Kampong development, a shophouse and a modern condominium. Such a development could offer a radical alternative to residential current development patterns, and could potentially help save the remaining landscapes of Kuala Lumpur and other Malaysian cities.

Lim is also exploring the idea of a new Tropical City. He states that "the main preoccupation when designing for the tropics is to keep the sun and rain out; and to allow as much cross-ventilation as possible".[52] Ideally, therefore, the tropical city should have an urban build-up that is set in a forest. If there are to be any tall buildings, these should be energy

Figure 7.18
(a) The main entrance into the Selanger House. (b) A side view of the Selanger House.

generators which are sustainable, and will make it obvious even to the casual observer that these are buildings with their origin in the tropics.[53]

These large-scale urban visions of a tropical city are also being explored by a new generation of urban designers. There are some beginnings of small-scale urban design interventions, at the pedestrian scale of use. With the introduction of pavements, tree planted avenues and some mixed-use developments Kuala Lumpur might become a more user-friendly city with stronger place-identity, and serve as a model to other South-East Asian cities.

To conclude, then, what can we learn from Malaysian architects when designing to support different types of imagined communities and place-identities? First of all, we have seen how a modern nation-state is coming to terms with its rich tapestry of different cultural groups, each with their own historic and cultural traditions, in the formation of a progressive and future-orientated nation. The sense of "rootedness" brings out all kinds of feelings and complex meanings amongst Malaysian people when defining what counts as "theirs", what it means to be Malaysian, whilst at the same time belonging to a particular local cultural group. Issues of place-identity are sometimes difficult to resolve, as different spatial and morphological layers support the interests of different imagined communities.

Our analysis of Kuala Lumpur and its constituent parts brings out a range of useful lessons for designing cultural landscapes from the place-identity perspective, where east meets west. First of all, there is a very strong positive attitude to nature, as seen in Jimmy Lim's work. Lim's attitude to nature operates at all scales of design intervention and can be interpreted at both the use and meaning levels. At the use level we can see how Lim connects natural and built-form cultural landscapes, when working with the site's geography, topography, wind, water and a range of natural habitats. These natural, environmental influences provide an important underlying structure, where both human and non-human species can co-habit in harmony. This harmonious relationship is also important at the detailed level of design, where internal and external spaces are united to offer rich sensory experiences. In such habitats, human and non-human species can

encounter each other without threat. Lim also helps natural habitats by planting new trees and other vegetation, to restore and rejuvenate damaged landscapes. At the level of meaning, Lim uses a fusion of symbolic interpretations of cultural landscapes; these range from the Chinese geomancy and feng-shui, to the Malaysian idea of co-dwelling with nature in a traditional Kampong. At the more individual, personal level, we also see how ideas of humility and *Tai Chi* provide strong symbolic meanings of human–non-human symbiotic relationship.

A second important lesson can be learned from the use of existing cultural landscapes in constructing a rooted sense of imagined community. At the use level, as seen in the spatial structure of Kuala Lumpur, we have different morphological layers that support the interests of various imagined communities, traditional and modern. This works well at the local level through the overall spatial integration of individual neighbourhoods where the traditional cultural landscapes support a variety of uses and the pedestrian movement patterns. Such cultural landscapes provide many opportunities for different communities to encounter each other in their pedestrian journeys whilst enjoying varied cultural experiences. However, at the city-wide scale of design, co-ordinated by the Kuala Lumpur Planning Department, the modern road system represents another kind of imagined community largely linked to the global systems of cultural landscapes and to fast patterns of movement which do not connect well with the traditional neighbourhoods. These two systems need to be united, as suggested by Jimmy Lim in his "Tropical City" concept, or in Ken Yeang's "Verandah City" ideas.

At the smaller scale of design intervention we can find useful lessons in Jimmy Lim's interpretation of deep-rooted traditional influences, largely evident in his residential buildings. Here we see the skilful re-interpretation of a range of traditional design ideas from Kampong to Chinese and Indian influences, to create Malay house types designed to be traditional but at the same time modern and progressive.

At the meaning level, different morphological and typological layers provide rich sources of ideological material for different communities to interpret different parts of the city as theirs, whilst at the same time belonging to a modern, progressive, Malaysian cultural landscape.

We also saw the value of conservation initiatives where historically important buildings such as the Central Market and the shophouses are adapted for new uses. These new uses, such as the craft centre for example, provide support for traditional crafts to be sold whilst old shophouses sell products to suit the tastes of different cultural groups.

The use of recycled timber and other building components provide symbolic links with Malaysia's rich cultural traditions, as does the relationship between buildings and their natural settings, where sensory experiences offer many layers of cultural meanings.

A third important lesson we can learn about designing to support members of each imagined community is in living harmoniously with other communities. At the use level, this is evident in the way that some of the smaller scale spatial sequences have been introduced to support linkages between various traditional neighbourhoods as in the area around the Central Market building and in the old Chinatown. At the individual, building level of design, it is obvious in Lim's utilisation of multiple cultural traditions in the new housing developments and his ideas of Kampongminium. At the meaning level, this is particularly evident in the fusion of, what Lim calls "traditional" influences, where different building forms and landscapes are integrated into new dwelling types that are read by different users as theirs.

We can also find useful lessons in terms of designing to support users in developing a sense of empowerment vis-à-vis their own particular imagined community. This is again evident at two levels. At the level of use, we can identify different cultural traditions of Kuala Lumpur's many neighbourhoods, old and new. This is also evident in Lim's houses designed for a variety of clients where high art of architectural design and popular art and craft traditions of various Malaysian cultural groups are united.

At the meaning level, this is particularly strong in Lim's "additive" approach to design where buildings are made up of many parts, inherited or rescued from other buildings, and brought back into life to connect symbolically with Malaysia's many cultural groups.

Notes

1 Lim Jee Yuan, 1987.
2 Ibid.
3 Ibid.
4 Ibid.
5 Ibid.
6 Ibid., 4.
7 Abel, 2000, 152.
8 Ibid.
9 Lim Jee Yuan, 1987, 20.
10 Ibid.
11 Ibid.
12 Ibid., 75.
13 Yeang, 1987.
14 Too, 1980, 50.
15 Ibid., 53.
16 Abel, Ibid.
17 Ibid.
18 Chay, 1989, 10.
19 Ibid.
20 Yeang, 1987, 15. In Yoong (ed.), *Post-Merdeka Architecture Malaysia 1957–1987*.
21 Ibid.
22 Chay, 1989, 23.
23 Ibid., 211.
24 Ibid.
25 For fuller discussion of these issues, see Dolbani, PhD Thesis, Oxford Brookes University (unpublished).
26 Yeang, 1986.
27 Abel, 2000, 217.
28 Lim, 2000.
29 Discussions between Georgia Butina Watson and Jimmy Lim in Kuala Lumpur in 1989, 1991, 1993, 1998 and 2001.
30 CSL Associates (undated, unpublished office document).
31 Ibid.
32 Ibid.
33 Lim, 2000, 188, in *Asian Architects*.
34 Ibid., 191, in *Asian Architects*.
35 Ibid., 192, in *Asian Architects*.
36 CSL Associates (undated, unpublished office document).
37 Abel, 1991, Introductory page, Associates' Extracts.

38 Ibid.
39 Lim, CSL Associates, Extracts I, undated.
40 Ibid.
41 Discussion between Georgia Butina Watson and Jimmy Lim, Kuala Lumpur, 1999.
42 Lim, undated article.
43 Discussion between Georgia Butina Watson and Jimmy Lim, Kuala Lumpur, March 1989.
44 CSL Associates, Extracts, 1989–1991.
45 Lim, undated, quoted in Extracts, CSL Associates.
46 Ibid.
47 Ibid.
48 Lim quoted in CSL Associates, undated.
49 CSL Associates, undated, projects catalogue.
50 Lim, 2000, 192.
51 Discussion between Georgia Butina Watson and Jimmy Lim, Kuala Lumpur, 1991, 1998.
52 Lim, 2000, 205.
53 Ibid.

8

Reinforcing Boston's Emerald Necklace

The last chapter focused on the modern cultural landscape of Kuala Lumpur, where issues of place-identity were difficult to address because of deep-rooted feelings amongst Malaysia's culturally diverse imagined communities. We saw how modern development trends played off against this rich socio-cultural milieu, with its strong links with nature and local building traditions, to produce a "dual city" with a very unusual cultural landscape.

Complex cultural landscapes are also evident in the recent restructuring of the North American city of Boston; where tensions between global investment and the needs of local neighbourhoods, which are competing for land, services and their own sense of identity, have been addressed by politicians, professionals and local groups. To support as many different interests as possible, an important project was launched during the 1980s with the intention of re-shaping and strengthening Boston's place-identity, whilst uniting imagined communities which had become geographically and socially dispersed. Before exploring these initiatives, however, it is important to explain the evolution of Boston's cultural landscape, and of the historical and political contexts within which place-identity developed.

From its foundation, Boston's place-identity was underpinned by its location, geomorphology and topography. The city lies in the north-east part of the United States, known today as New England, and is one of the area's oldest cities. Located in Massachusetts Bay, where the Charles River runs into the Atlantic Ocean, Boston is exposed to harsh north-Atlantic winds. Surrounded by small islands, the coastline is ragged and distinctive, which led to the nickname "Athens of America".[1]

The Charles River separates the city into various neighbourhoods, with Cambridge and Charleston forming its western parts. The original territory was known by the Indian name Shawmut.[2] Later it became Boston, in honour of the small Lincolnshire town from which most of the early English settlers had come, in 1630, under the leadership of John Winthrop. It was they who made the first conscious efforts to construct place-identity by design; shaping the topography, utilising natural resources and planning the first settlement of Boston in the image of their homeland.[3]

In 1632 the little peninsula of Shawmut became the capital of the Massachusetts Bay Colony. The settlement was given a charter by James I, and was designated as the property of the Massachusetts Bay Company, with a relative autonomy that lasted some 50 years. Due to its excellent location and its deep sheltered harbour, the settlement became a centre of fishing, trading and shipbuilding. The first settlement resembled English Lincolnshire towns in its layout and the character of its buildings; and these resemblances still survive in the deep-rooted structure of what is now the North End neighbourhood. In the words of Anne Pollard, age twelve, North End in 1630 was "very uneven, abounding in small hollows and swamps covered with blueberries and other small bushes".[4]

A large tidal inlet, later known as Mill Pond, was one of the more prominent features of this landscape, and is clearly marked in William Burgess's Map of the Colonial North End[5] (Figure 8.1a). The peninsula was laid out in an irregular grid pattern, with the longer streets running north–south. Burgess's Map also shows several open spaces such as Snow Hill, Bowling Green and Beacon Hill. Streets were curvilinear, following the contours of the topography. Low lying marshes were controlled by a dam which, according to Woods,[6] created an island effect; severing North End from the rest of Boston, and giving

North End the popular nickname "Island of North Boston". According to Paula Todisco:[7]

> The first houses (small, thatched-roof buildings surrounded by pasture and green areas) were pretty much scattered willy-nilly, clustering around the area of North Square and North Street. This haphazard arrangement helped create the narrow streets, winding alleys, and secluded places which still characterize the North End.

Figure 8.1
(a) William Burgess's Map of Colonial North End, Boston. (b) The old North Church in North Square, North End, Boston. (c) Paul Revere's House, North End, the oldest house in Boston, built in 1676 but altered and restored in 1680. (d) Faneuil Hall, built in 1742 as a market with a hall above, given to the town of Boston by Peter Faneuil. In 1805, Charles Bulfinch doubled the width of the building and added a third floor.

In addition to gardening and keeping livestock, the early settlers engaged in various craft activities which they carried out in their own homes. A strict moral code was enforced, and great importance was given to education: in 1636[8] the Puritans established Harvard College, which grew into one of the world's finest universities. In 1650 the Old North Church was built in North Square and many other churches followed, giving the place a very religious feel (Figure 8.1b).

Early Bostonians were god-fearing people who became notorious for witch-hunting, beautifully portrayed in the film *The Scarlet Letter* which tells a story of a strong-willed independent English woman seeking fortune on behalf of her husband. In a highly religious, puritan society, there was very little scope to depart from highly restrictive norms of behaviour; and women seeking fortune were not welcome in such a puritan society.

Bostonians showed great skill in co-dwelling with nature. We have already seen the skills in the shaping of the landscape to make the place inhabitable. During the seventeenth century many creative innovations took place and the local settlers made good use of wind and water by building wind- and water-mills and other water-powered plants.[9]

During the seventeenth century several fires spread across North End and many timber houses were destroyed. The only remaining original building is Paul Revere's house, which was restored in 1680 after the fire of 1676 (Figure 8.1c). In 1684 the colony's charter was revoked and the Bostonians came under tighter British control. Many troubled events followed, with the famous "tea party" on 16th December 1773, where the local "Sons of Liberty", disguised as Indians, boarded a ship and dumped 342 chests of tea into the sea.[10] The route they took has remained an important historic path, known as the "Freedom Trail", used in Boston's place-identity interpretative material. On the 17th March 1776 the Declaration of Independence was proclaimed, and the city led the way in the development of a new nation.

The next phase of growth was marked by a wave of new public buildings such as the Market and Town Hall, built by Peter Faneuil in 1742, that still remains a key landmark, and is still important for Boston's place-identity (Figure 8.1d). Many rich and influential families owned their own wharves, and what used to be a local trade expanded to become an international economic activity. The increase in trade generated a new demand for taverns, popularly named after London's pubs – the Green Dragon being the most famous.

From the last quarter of the eighteenth century to the first half of the nineteenth, the city underwent both a territorial expansion and a radical transformation of its cultural landscape through a wave of Irish immigrants. New houses built on Beacon Hill and in Back Bay resembled those built in London and Paris (Figure 8.2a). The cultural landscapes of Beacon Hill and Back Bay were drastically changed between 1824 and 1826 when Mayor Josiah Quincy commissioned a large landfill project to create more land for the expansion of the city. This was achieved by radically altering the topography of the hilly areas, such as Copp's and Beacon Hill, which were levelled off to provide soil for landfilling the coastline and the marshy areas. Boston Common, which had been held in trust since 1634,[11] and used for grazing cattle, was declared a public park in 1830; and this opened up opportunities for creating one of the most desirable residential areas of the city (Figure 8.2b). Between 1860 and 1870 Arthur Gilman designed a grid plan consisting of Parisian style avenues such as the Esplanade to accommodate new elegant houses built in a variety of architectural styles, from Colonial Georgian to French Art Nouveau (Figures 8.2c and 8.2d). This generated a distinct cultural landscape that gave the area a very European feel, which can be sensed even today (Figures 8.3a and 8.3b). Wealthy North End families moved into these new neighbourhoods, leaving behind older properties that were soon occupied by Irish, German and Italian families. Due to social tensions, Irish and Italian groups kept apart; creating distinct, mini cultural quarters. Soon after, Portuguese and Jewish settlers from southern and eastern Europe arrived in North End. By 1920 some 40,000 people lived in this oldest neighbourhood of the city: North End had become a collage of many imagined communities, each bringing its own little bit of culture from Europe.

Another area of the city that changed radically during the nineteenth century is the Bulfinch Triangle. In 1804 Charles Bulfinch, famous Boston architect,

Figure 8.2
(a) The Boston Common in winter. (b) Massachusetts State House, built between 1795 and 1798. (c) Park Street with the Brewer Fountain on the Boston Common. (d) Elegant houses of Beacon Hill.

designed this district in a form of a triangle filled with narrow blocks of east/west streets. The completion of the landfill coincided with the introduction of the rail network in the 1830s[12] and the area prospered as a centre for furniture manufacturing, sales and distribution, operating in the Victorian style warehouses. The growth of the area was particularly rapid after 1889, when the North Station was opened.

The remaining cultural landscape of the nineteenth century city was related to the maritime economy; with the long ocean wharves of the Downtown Waterfront serviced by a fast-developing downtown area with bankers, lawyers, doctors and other professional groups. In addition to banks and legal offices, many public buildings such as Symphony Hall, Public

Library and the Museum of Fine Arts were completed during the second half of the century.[13]

By the end of the nineteenth century, Boston had become a collection of distinct neighbourhoods, each with its own socio-economic and cultural landscape: what the city lacked was something to unite them. The answer came from the landscape designer Frederick Law Olmsted, who became a consultant for the city's Park Commission in 1878. Olmsted's cultural tradition was rooted in American transcendentalist philosophy and in the English utilitarian school influenced by Jeremy Bentham.[14] Supporters of this movement had a common interest in hygiene, healthy improvement of the urban structure and the environment in general. Olmsted was also a

Figure 8.3
(a) The Back Bay residential development, a view from the John Hancock Tower. (b) Elegant, European-style, houses in the leafy Back Bay area.

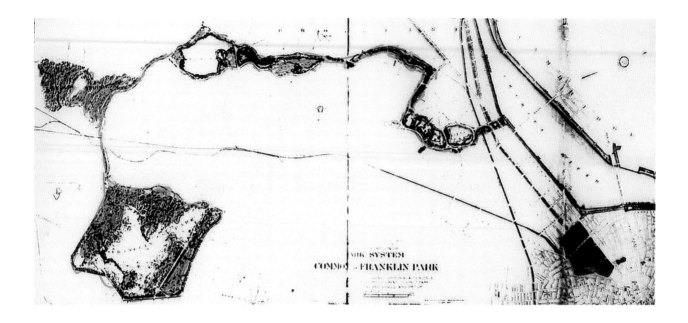

Figure 8.4
The Emerald Necklace, designed by Olmsted and Eliot in 1897.

member of the Fourierist movement, which led the campaign for parks. His designs for urban parks symbolised a sense of collective identity rediscovered through the social use of leisure, and his parks are integrated into the spatial system of streets. He was also highly influenced by G.P. Marsh's book *Man and Nature*, published in 1864, which was a polemical piece written for the defence of nature.[15] From the aesthetic point of view, Olmsted was a follower of the English picturesque school of landscape design and the *City Beautiful* movement. In 1896 Olmsted and Eliot proposed a system of parks and green open spaces to tie Boston's neighbourhoods into a unified system, popularly called *The Emerald Necklace* (Figure 8.4).

During the 1920s Boston began to experience an economic decline that lasted for several decades. The Bulfinch Triangle lost its manufacturing industry, and North End lost a third of its population. Many buildings fell into disrepair, and many of the city's inhabitants left in search of jobs and better living conditions elsewhere[16] (Figure 8.5a).

By the early 1950s, Boston's entrepreneurs began to reshape the city's economy around service industries such as legal and accounting businesses, insurance and banking. In order to attract the necessary

workforce back into the city, a number of improvement schemes were launched, some driven by new urban design and town planning ideas promoted by protagonists of modernist design. Based around the Boston Redevelopment Authority (BRA), formed in 1957, these modernists began a radical reshaping of Boston's urban structure and transport.

The city's tight historic streets could only cope with local traffic; and the modernist planners believed that an improved, fast-moving transport system would attract a new generation of business. The city therefore commissioned the construction of a new urban expressway. This two-level, six-lane elevated artery cut a deep wound through the city's historic morphological structure, as historic streets and neighbourhoods were destroyed to accommodate it. When it was opened, the artery was greeted with a great deal of business and professional support; but it was condemned by local people who lost their jobs and homes as a result of its construction (Figure 8.5b).

The implementation of this and other large-scale improvement and slum clearance programmes, such as those of West End and the new Government Centre area, changed Boston's historic feel and its

Figure 8.5
(a) Derelict edge of North End, 1997. (b) Boston's Downtown Artery under construction, 1954.

original place-identity. Instead of tightly grouped streets and buildings like those of North End, new modernist estates, public open spaces and government office buildings were introduced (Figures 8.6a and 8.6b). It is only due to influential professionals such as Jane Jacobs[17] and Herbert Gans,[18] supported by popular movements, that more damage was not done to the rest of the city.

Jane Jacobs's views are beautifully captured in her book *The Death and Life of Great American Cities* (1961) where she is particularly concerned with Boston's North End. North End, declared at the time by the city planners as a "civic shame", was seen positively by Jacobs as a neighbourhood full of little shops, work places, residences and children's play areas. It was a healthy community of social mix, diversity and variety, which seemed doomed to die and to be transformed into a monotonous and sterile place. Unlike its West End neighbour, North End managed to survive, though heavily marred; undergoing a drastic decline of its population from the 35,000 recorded in 1920 to a mere 9,000 accounted by the 1980s.[19]

Herbert Gans, a key figure from the Chicago School of urban sociology, was another influential Boston professional who defended traditional neighbourhoods, which he called "Urban Villages". Gans, like Jacobs, saw the importance of established local neighbourhood ties and cultural lifestyles, and he too condemned large-scale slum clearance programmes.

Modernist city planning ideas were also challenged at the time by a new breed of planners and urban designers such as Kevin Lynch and Donald Appleyard, who began explorations into perceptual and qualitative aspects of urban form. Particularly influential for the understanding of Boston's place-identity during the 1960s was Lynch's seminal book *The Image of the City*, published in 1960.[20] This work was based on information about users' perceptions of urban form in Boston, New Jersey and Los Angeles, to identify key elements that help users in grasping the legibility of places. The more legible a place is, Lynch claimed, the easier it is for users to orientate themselves; which is important in the construction of a sense of place and place-identity.

In order to understand how users conceptually structure places, Lynch pioneered the use of mental maps and other fieldwork techniques such as structured interviews, which can tell us how people recognise, recall and decode places. By comparing evidence from three structurally and culturally different places, Lynch came to the conclusion that users employ five key elements to navigate a place: the *paths* – comprised of streets, roads, lanes, and alleys – through which the users move, the *nodes* which represent crossroads where paths intersect, the *edges* – rivers, viaducts, waterways and the like – which divide the city into graspable and identifiable units, and the *landmarks* which stand out from the rest of the structure. The perceptual, recognisable units that remain form the characteristic "tissues" of *districts:* as we also saw in Rossi's work in Chapter 6, these provide a certain degree of homogeneity within such areas, whilst being different from other tissues within the settlement's overall structure (Figure 8.7).

Lynch's work began to influence the shaping of Boston, as both pedestrian and vehicular experiences became important sources of planning and design ideas. The BRA commissioned Lynch, with Donald Appleyard and Richard Myer to advise them on the townscape management of the city; and these newly appointed experts used their technical and aesthetic knowledge to produce the hugely influential book *A View from the Road*,[21] which guided Boston city planners in creating important vistas that would help city users in understanding and interpreting Boston's large scale structure and its sense of place-identity.

By the early 1980s, the negative consequences of an earlier style of thinking, embodied in the elevated artery, began to affect the business and residential communities of Boston. With a continuous increase of vehicles travelling daily on the artery its noise, pollution and other negative impacts became major threats to the city's liveability (Figure 8.8). The contrast between areas adjoining the artery and those of Beacon Hill could not be more different. The draft *Urban Issues Analysis Report* states that:

Boston is often described as a city of neighbourhoods, each with its own identity, history and culture, and all reflecting the social and architectural history of the City. For better and for worse, the Central Artery has played an important role in shaping and defining adjacent neighbourhoods.

Figure 8.6
(a) The Government Centre area, built during the 1960s. (b) City Hall, designed by Gerhard M. McKinnel and Edward F. Knowles, 1963.

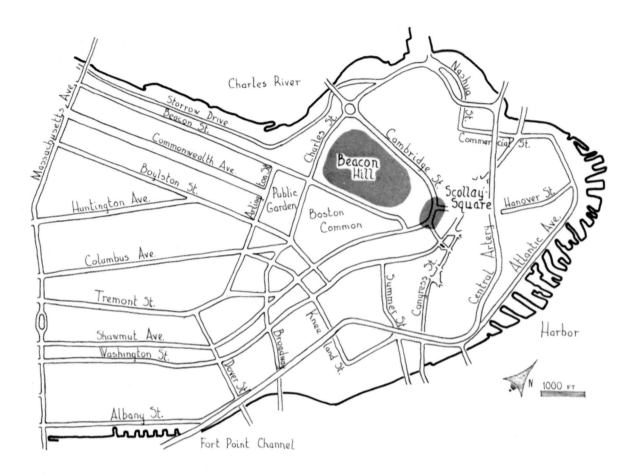

Figure 8.7
Lynch's study of Boston's legibility and imageability, 1961.

The Artery has been a homogenous linear wall through the City; it disrupted dense neighbourhood fabrics and histories such as the Bulfinch Triangle, the Hanover Street connection and the integral relationship between the waterfront and the city core.[22] (Figures 8.9a and 8.9b)

The ill fate of North End and other adjoining neighbourhoods started to change in 1984, under a new administration headed by Mayor Raymond L. Flynn. The dominant planning strategy became one of channelling the rapid economic growth of the 1980s into local neighbourhoods, through quality urban design and through the improvement of the areas negatively affected by the Downtown Artery. This urban intervention has become one of the biggest engineering, planning, urban design, management and above all financial tasks in Massachusetts's

history and some analysts rank it second only to the Channel Tunnel amongst the world's recent projects.

In order to direct Boston's economic growth, the *Plan to Manage Growth* was produced in 1985. According to Eric Schmidt,[23] former Director of Downtown Planning for Boston, the city's economic development had to benefit the people who lived there by providing job opportunities, housing and public facilities. In addition, Schmidt states, attention had to be paid to minimising the negative impacts of the restructuring process, and to respecting Boston's historic character. But above all, individual neighbourhoods affected by the improvement of the Downtown Artery area had to have strong voices in shaping the growth and spatial policies of the city as a whole.

Figure 8.8
Aerial view of Boston's Central Artery, 1990.

To achieve these objectives, Mayor Flynn's office set up an ambitious community participation process. Some 66 community groups provided invaluable ideas for forging a common, city-wide strategy, whilst redesigning their senses of their own particular "imagined" communities. Even school children had plenty to say in constructing their own visions: particularly keen to see improved educational and other community facilities, housing, shops, parks and play-fields,[24] they drew images of a future Boston, and gave titles to their creative solutions such as "Build a Better Boston" or "A Better Boston Community"[25] Some children's contributions made reference to saving the earth, and to the importance of creating green open spaces. Others emphasised the need for accommodating family activities, and for achieving community safety: as one young student eloquently said:

The open space [should be] next to the housing projects because when you're home alone after school you need a place to go with people.[26]

In addition to the ideas developed by school children, a number of community-based working groups were formed to express their views and their sense of imagined community. Whilst some groups focused their attention on city-wide issues such as the public space network and housing provision, others were engaged in developing local neighbourhood strategies. A number of business groups, environmental and historic societies, design experts and a variety of public agencies also contributed their ideas for the reshaping of Boston's identity.

To support this public consultation process, the BRA undertook extensive planning and urban design work. Their creative thinking was inspired by a wealth of practical and theoretical knowledge: Massachusetts Department of Public Works (MDPW)[27] carried out detailed technical studies and, jointly with the City Planning Department and Federal, State and local agencies, formulated a preliminary development process and a new vision for Boston. The new vision was to bury the artery in a tunnel, directly

Figure 8.9
(a) Boston's Central Artery, a view into the North End neighbourhood, 1997. (b) View of Central Artery from Rowes Wharf, 1990.

beneath the existing expressway system. By doing this, the city of Boston would create both a new supply of open space and the potential to remedy some of the mistakes made during the 1950s and 1960s.

In addition to addressing the artery's technical problems, the BRA experts – working with a range of local and international design consultants – began to study Boston's character and its morphological structure; focusing particularly on the Emerald Necklace, designed by Olmsted some 100 years earlier. Particularly influential was William H. Whyte, whose expertise helped articulate a proposal for Boston's new open space skeleton. This new space skeleton, the BRA experts stated,[28] should promote for Boston a city-wide identity that would tie together individual neighbourhoods, whilst also displaying the unique socio-spatial characteristics associated with each particular local community. In addition to rehabilitating old neighbourhoods, the conceptual plan also included new social and private housing, community and city-wide facilities and many new job opportunities; with more than 70% of land retained as public open space.

Various other experts also contributed to the conceptual shaping of Boston's new place-identity. The Boston Society of Architects, for example, proposed the development of most of the artery with commercial and residential buildings, in order to reintegrate the artery corridor completely into the existing downtown context.[29] They also proposed a series of small parks totalling 10% of the 5 million square feet of new building. Another idea, introduced by the eminent Spanish architect and urbanist Ricardo Bofill, defined a "vertebral spine" consisting of gateway towers at North Station, South Station and Central Wharf, with public spaces – totalling 40% of the land area – including an elliptical plaza in the North End neighbourhood, a formal downtown park, a winter garden, the extension of Waterfront Park, a public athletic and recreational facility, and a new Haymarket Pavilion.[30] Alex Kreiger, a well known Boston-based urban designer, proposed two parallel avenues, running along the edges of the Downtown Artery zone, with the mixture of open space and building complexes occupying the Artery's central core; using morphological elements typical of each district to produce locally distinctive character

zones, influenced by Lynch's concept of districts (Figure 8.10).

All these four proposals were interrogated by politicians, local enterprise firms, amenity groups and a variety of professional experts; whilst city planners and designers held over two dozen public briefings on the four scenarios.[31] Once responses from this process had been analysed, the BRA Team produced a final version, which is a synthesis of the best aspects of each proposal; again utilising the "inquiry by design" method, explained in Chapter 5, where different stages of the final design process were discussed with key actors and were then progressively refined. Alex Kreiger, William H. Whyte and Vanasse Hangen Brustlin were retained as key consultants, to provide further guidance on urban design, traffic and movement and on open space design issues.

This synthesis of ideas was adopted in 1990, and published in the same year as a progress report called *Boston 2000 A Plan for the Central Artery*[32] (Figure 8.11). The report brings together three main long-term goals: economic success as a place of work; ecological and sustainable city; and socially, politically and culturally bound local communities: now which aims had to be translated into consolidated urban design strategies.

According to Richard (Dick) Gavers, of the Boston Redevelopment Agency urban design team,[33] the Plan for the Central Artery is first of all based on the fundamental idea of the city as a community. The collective vision, developed jointly by urban professionals, local community groups and other key stakeholders, is formulated to connect different neighbourhoods whilst providing a strong underlying structure at the city-wide scale. Dick Gavers felt that it was very important to retain the original spine of the artery, once the motorway itself was completely buried under the ground, as it had become deeply embedded in the minds of local Bostonians, as revealed in the mental maps drawn by participants during the consultation process. The Downtown Artery, therefore, provides strong, deep-rooted legibility clues; important for Boston's legibility. Kevin Lynch's work from the 1960s and the BRA's findings from the 1980s and the 1990s provide an interesting set of interpretations that further reinforce the importance of legibility.

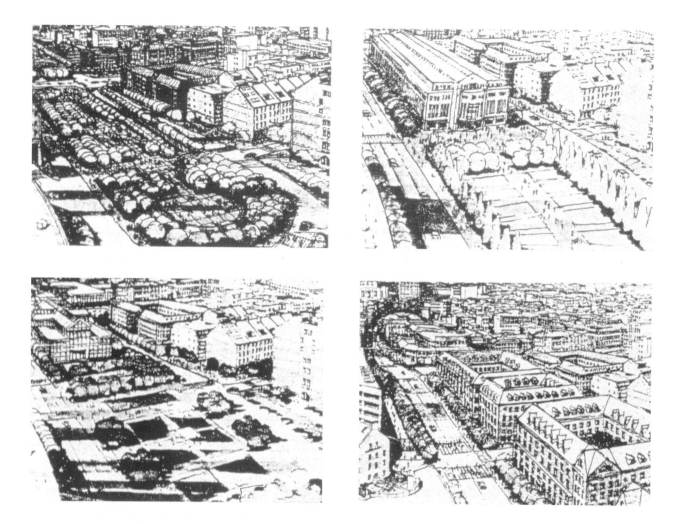

Figure 8.10
Four proposals for restructuring the Central Artery; (1) the City Redevelopment Authority scenario; (2) the Alex Kreiger scheme; (3) the Ricardo Boffil's concept; (4) the Boston Society of Architects' ideas.

The main new skeleton was designed as a tree-lined boulevard system that stretches from Bulfinch Triangle in the north, down to Chinatown and South Station in the south; East–West streets crossing the boulevard system, and connecting historic neighbourhoods that had been severed in 1959. New sidewalks and other traffic control measures were designed to give pedestrians priority over vehicular movement; opening up greater opportunities for different users to encounter each other. The Boston 2000 report states that:

Tree lined boulevards will be the ribbon which ties the neighbourhoods together. The trees will be in several varieties to emphasize the varying nature of the different spaces, weather shading and shielding benches and tot lots, or creating a leafy pattern of shadows on busy sidewalks.[34] (Figures 8.12a and 8.12b)

The new road network was also designed to connect downtown with the waterfront area; opening up possibilities to explore those parts of Boston that had been cut-off from the rest of the historic city for decades. Boulevard roadways were also proposed as normal city streets, rather than as sections of inter-state

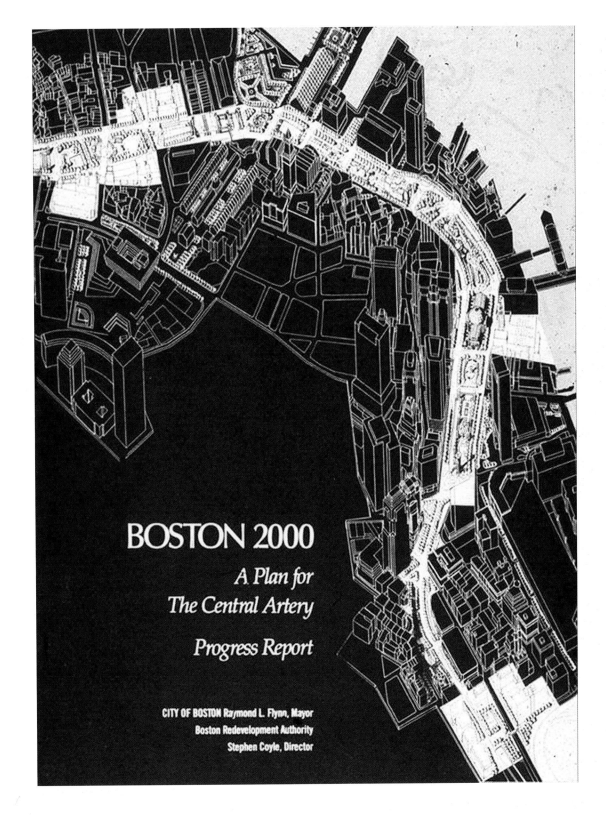

Figure 8.11
Boston 2000 – a plan for the Central Artery Progress Report, 1990.

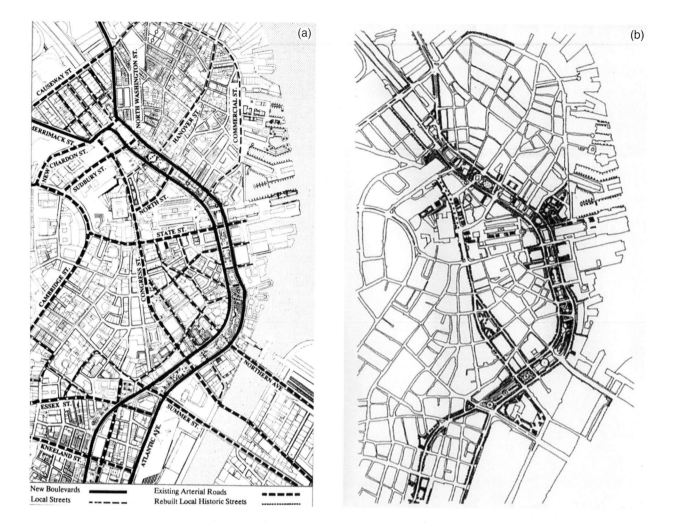

Figure 8.12
(a) Proposed street hierarchy map. (b) Proposed open space sequence.

roads. This new movement framework, experts claimed, would restore a deep-rooted historical structure that was lost when the elevated artery was constructed. Whilst the surface road and street system would accommodate local traffic, the underground tunnel would cater for through traffic.

The report also suggests that:

One of the major benefits of the depression of the Artery will be the removal of the barrier which cuts across so many of these pedestrian routes. In fact, the removal of the Artery will allow the city to rebuild fine historic streets, thus restoring the connections

between the pedestrian core of the City, the water-front and new Harbourpark.[35]

In order to strengthen the city's legibility at the local scale of movement, each road crossing is marked by distinct landmark buildings or other elements. The new boulevard street system, when fully completed, will be integrated into the larger morphological structure of the city: such an integrated system will allow different city users and travellers to encounter each other, and to explore once again the city's deep-rooted historic layers.

Once the surface and underground technical aspects had been solved, the next stage in the design process was to decide what to do with over 50 acres

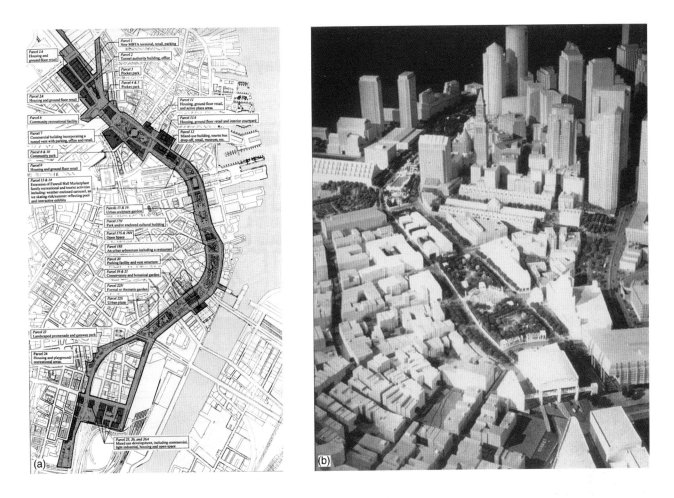

Figure 8.13
(a) Parcelisation and land use map. (b) Model of Haymarket and Faneuil Hall sites.

of land which had been freed up by relocating the artery and forming the new surface road network. We have already seen how different design teams had suggested addressing this issue in their individual proposals: we shall now discuss how these ideas were brought together into a consolidated urban design solution.

The overall design concept forms a sequence of distinct parks, linked by tree-lined boulevards, extending from Causeway Street in the north to Chinatown in the south (Figures 8.13a and 8.13b). According to William H. Whyte:

> ... it is a park system whose effect in the quality of life in the city will be as dramatic as that of the Esplanade of the Emerald Necklace. Because of its downtown location and its convenience to the

largest concentration of visitors to the city, the park system will become part of the identity of Boston in the 21st century.[36]

Although the completed park system would benefit all users, Whyte suggests that the highest percentage of park users will come from the local neighbourhoods within a three-block radius: parks should therefore be designed to reflect the character of local neighbourhoods, whilst providing support for a new overall city-scale place-identity. Five distinct park spaces are therefore planned, each linked to a particular neighbourhood: North End Neighbourhood Park; Downtown Markets and Waterfront Park; Fort Hill Square; Botanical Garden and Urban Arboretum, located in the Financial District; and Chinatown Community Park and Asian Garden. This new sequence of open spaces and city parks will form Boston's new Emerald Necklace, reflecting a common vision expressing ideas of co-dwelling with nature.

Once the overall conceptual plan had been finalised, a new document entitled *Toward Boston 2000-realizing the vision* was published in 1997.[37] This included a feasibility analysis and recommendations for project implementation. Dick Gavers explained[38] that it was important to form a Working Group and Task Forces, to link participatory groups and professional teams in charge of various projects. This was strongly supported by the new Mayor, Thomas M. Menino, who took his seat in 1995 and, like his predecessor, had a strong commitment to the city's restructuring process. The Boston 2000 Working Group organised itself into three main Task Forces: Disposition and Open Space Management, Development and Finance, and Land Use and Urban Design, all chaired by eminent experts. Given the size and the complexity of such a large project, it was important that the Working Group and its task forces keep a close eye on the process, so that the various decisions made in the overall plan and implementation documents could be adjusted to take account of new needs identified during the various charettes and consultation meetings.

Some hundreds of individuals and organisations – from voluntary, public and private sectors – helped formulate specific implementation strategies. Some of the challenges that faced these groups were of a financial or a management nature: it was therefore essential to form collaborative partnerships to fund such a large project, estimated to cost about $14.6 billion. It was also important to channel some of the potential private gains into social and community benefits, and a creative solution was found through a "parcel-by-parcel" development tool. This, Dick Gavers explained,[39] was introduced to channel $5 per square foot of commercial development into social housing. This financial mechanism also meant that specific projects, and their social partners, could be identified at the start of the development negotiations, not at the end. Similar deals were also introduced for new "job training" schemes, whereby $1 per square foot of new development was allocated for training and job creation opportunities. This meant that local

community groups could also learn new skills for participating in the creation and management of such projects. As one of the local community participants explained,[40] it was important for the residents to understand how development finance works, so that they could negotiate social or cultural benefits directly with developers. Eric Schmidt also suggested[41] that it was important to involve the business community of Boston in making financial contributions to public open spaces adjacent to their corporate offices; as such improvements would positively contribute to both the value of their real estate and to the success of their businesses. Here we can see how "place-marketing" tools were employed in creating a common vision for Boston's position in the global market.

The biggest expenditure to sort out was the construction of the new underground tunnel, demolition of the surface artery and the provision of the public open space network: the primary responsibility for the tunnel and the artery rested with federal and state sources, whilst the operating costs and the open space provision became the responsibility of the city and of a variety of private organisations.

Also important were land use and spatial design matters, where more detailed issues had to be addressed: it was important to integrate urban design guidelines with the artery development into existing land-use and neighbourhood regeneration strategies. The Task Force group responsible for this aspect of the project saw that the new corridor needed "a unifying theme which captures its essential character",[42] whilst at the same time design solutions "should respond to the social character of each district as well as the cross district connections".[43]

The best way to explore how the new road and public space network is intended to reinforce Boston's new place-identity is to take a journey, starting in the north with the Bulfinch area, and finishing in the south with Chinatown and South Station. We have already explained how the cultural landscapes of the historic neighbourhoods were originally formed, and we shall now focus on the ideas and the work in progress in this large restoration initiative.

The plan for Bulfinch Triangle was designed to ensure that old buildings would be rehabilitated, and new ones built, to accommodate a mix of different housing schemes, both private and for social gain (Figures 8.14a and 8.14b). Retail and other non-housing uses are introduced at the ground level, to encourage the "round-the-clock"[44] pedestrian activity that contributes to a sense of vitality. The area has already attracted service, media and newspaper firms as well as young professionals and their families. Nearly half the historic buildings have been listed, to protect the historic heritage and its associated sense of imagined community; whilst the restoration of historic streets emphasises wider links with the neighbouring West End and North End communities. With still wider scope, the new Zakim Bunker Hill Bridge, opened in 2002, together with the tree-lined boulevards and small city parks which form the Bulfinch Triangle's contribution to the new part of the Emerald Necklace, connect the area into the larger city proper.

Continuing our spatial sequence, we come to North End with its green open spaces. We have already discussed the area's complex, deep-rooted cultural landscape and its many imagined communities. Throughout the consultation process it was this neighbourhood that contributed most to the development of new ideas, and also in managing the implementation process of various specific projects through its Task Forces (Figures 8.14c and 18.14d).

Figure 8.14
(a) The Bulfinch Triangle, proposal. (b) The Bulfinch Triangle, proposal for the Boston Garden, looking down Canal Street. (c) A development proposal for North End. (d) The North End housing improvement area.

As Boston's oldest neighbourhood, and one of its most densely populated, North End needed initiatives for rejuvenating both its physical and its demographic structure. According to Dick Gavers,[45] North End must be strengthened with new housing and new residents in order to achieve a better mix of socio-cultural and age groups. Already supported by other broader regeneration programmes, the area already exhibits many positive signs of these interventions; with many buildings restored and given new leases of life (Figure 8.15a). With the demolition of the elevated artery in 2004, many historic streets have been reconnected into the rest of the city fabric, making important links once again. North End streets have become vibrant again, offering rich sensory experiences: strong coffee, freshly baked bread and other aromatic products blend with natural scents of flowers and trees. North End residents have also contributed a great deal to developing detailed design proposals for their neighbourhood parks and public open spaces, where visions proposed by children and other residents have been fed into the design process (Figure 8.15b).

When it comes to the detailed design of North End's neighbourhood parks, Richard Rabinowitz of the American History Workshop team, who advised Wallace Floyd Design group and Gustafson Partners on detailed design aspects of the North End parks, states that,[46] "this land is really a kind of a bridge" … "it is a low place between the hilly part of North End and what we now call downtown, which once was the South End".[47] The proposed design, when fully implemented, is intended to reflect the neighbourhood's different cultural landscapes: residential and business (Figure 8.15c).

Hanover Street, which bisects the site and therefore separates two parks, is detailed as a bridge: it has sidewalks abutting low walls and balustrade railings. One park presents the "city" side of the boundary and is designed to encourage group activities such as games and performances. A terrace, a gently sloping lawn, and a play fountain encourage games and performances. The other park, with a community orchard and bulb meadow, suggests a more intimate character; where neighbourly conversations and quieter activities can take place. A shallow pool, flowing underneath Hanover Street, connects the two parks.

Continuing South from North End is Downtown Waterfront, also rich in cultural heritage, housing historic landmark buildings such as Faneuil Hall, Quincy Markets and the Custom House. With restoration in progress since the 1970s, this area has already set the stage for new Boston: it has already become a magnet for tourists, for shoppers and other city dwellers.

Fourteen million people visit Faneuil Hall Marketplace every year. Daytime and evening pedestrian activity is spilling into adjacent State Street, with new restaurants and bars serving the growing number of visitors.[48] (Figures 8.16a–8.16d)

This part of the open space complex is designed to promote city-wide place-identity, providing facilities for all kinds of imagined communities. Nine parcels of land totalling over eight acres are allocated for the creation of new green open spaces in this area, forming the heart of the new Emerald Necklace, named in 2004 as the Rose Fitzgerald Kennedy Greenway. Experts claim that the construction of the Wharf District Parks and about five acres of parks and open space "will provide breathtaking views and recreational space not seen in Boston for more than 50 years"[49] (Figure 8.17a).

These new parks, designed by EDAW of Alexandria and Copley Design Group of Boston, will connect the historic downtown area back to its waterfront; and will form a sequence of open outdoor spaces "each unique in character, but unified by a common palette of planting, paving and lighting. The character of each square is strongly influenced by the adjacent land use, architecture and user groups."[50] The northern parks will be connected to the existing tourist area, offering new spaces for festivals and performances; whilst those to the south will be incorporated into quieter residential and office developments. Because this section of green open space needs to respond to high-rise buildings, the character of the city park here is radically different to the smaller-scale North End neighbourhood parks. Along the western edge is a 40-foot-wide paved promenade with retail kiosks: triangular, pointed glass-fronted structures, 60-feet tall, that

Figure 8.15
(a) A proposal for a reconnected Hanover Street as a gateway to the North End neighbourhood. (b) A view from North End towards the Downtown area. (c) A detailed design proposal for the North End parks, designed by Wallace Floyd Design Group and Gustafson Partners.

Figure 8.16
(a) Proposal for the Downtown Waterfront area. (b) The Faneuil Hall Marketplace area. (c) Restored Quincy Market buildings. (d) Quincy Market in winter.

also function as lanterns and mediate visually between the park and the tall buildings to the west.[51]

Some of the ground surfaces are designed to resemble waves, with beach grasses filling out the wave patterns; whilst two tall fountains have their heights synchronised with the ocean's tides. At the southern end of this section of the park system there will be another large fountain, placed off-axis; with a diagonal path aligned with the entrance to Rowe's Wharf and the city waterfront area. This attention to the detailed aspects of park design shows again a great deal of sensitivity to what we call co-dwelling with nature; as well as demonstrating how functional,

visual and other sensory aspects have been incorporated.

Next on our journey is the Financial District; a densely developed area housing the financial, legal and business services communities. Where tall buildings give this area a rather international look. During the consultation process, it was very important to involve the business community in creating a vision for this part of Boston, so that all imagined communities are represented in shaping Boston's future. Following the initial conceptual plan for the central open space area, more detailed design solutions were developed; including proposals for a

Figure 8.17
(a) The Central Artery in the Financial District. (b) A proposal for the Financial District open space system. (c) A proposal for the Financial District parks. (d) A view through the Rowes Wharf Rotunda.

major public conservatory and a botanical garden. When completed, this area will contain a large variety of trees, shrubs and other types of planting, and will be used for both leisure and educational purposes. According to BRA experts, these new parks and other open space provisions "would provide cultural and educational opportunities at a four-season green oasis in the heart of the downtown".[52] This area also establishes key links with the waterfront scene, enabling pedestrians to explore the city on foot and to enjoy its many exciting views (Figures 8.17b–8.17d).

Boston's Chinatown also benefits from the Downtown restructuring initiatives. Despite considerable

territorial losses over the past four decades, Chinatown is still a lively community; rich in small businesses, schools and cultural facilities. In the initial proposals, this area was designed to gain more public space provision, and to integrate this old neighbourhood into the rest of the city fabric. *The Plan for the Central Artery* was prepared in 1991 to complement the *Chinatown Community Plan* that was based on revitalising socio-economic and cultural aspects of the area. Major economic opportunities were identified around the Chinatown Gateway to act as a "front porch" into the Asian Community. The remaining open space was conceptualised as an Asian garden, with planting native to China and

Figure 8.18
(a) The Boston's Chinatown area. (b) A proposal for Boston's Chinatown Asian garden. (c) A detailed design proposal for the Chinatown open space solution, proposed by Carol K. Johnson Associates and Turenscape of Beijing. (d) A proposal for Boston's Chinatown Asian garden.

other Asian countries. The Boston 2000 report suggests that:

> As the largest public space in the historic retail core of Chinatown, this park will create a major entryway which invites people onto bustling Beach Street to experience the sights, sounds and smells of Chinatown.[53]

In January 2003 the Massachusetts Turnpike Authority chose a landscape design team, led by Carol R. Johnson Associates and Turenscape of Beijing, to develop these initial ideas into a more detailed design solution. The team suggested that:

> The long, skinny, slightly curving piece of land will feature a series of Chinese park/garden design elements, including a bridge over a dry stream, a light tower and a well.[54]

The inclusion of the well is symbolically important, claims the design team, "Because in China when you move from one community to another, you carry soil from your old home and put it into the well of your new community. In this park, the well becomes metaphor for landing in a new world and creating a sense of place and belonging in the Chinatown community[55] (Figures 8.18a and 8.18b).

Other design elements include a mixture of hard and soft surfaces, and "green elements include portals lined with bamboo as vertical screens, azaleas and ginkoes up and down the street"[56] (Figures 8.18c and 8.18d). In this space, residents will be able to enjoy Tai Chi and other Asian dance practices, as well as celebrate Chinese New year festivals with puppet theatre, dragon dancing and lantern decorations.

It is not only the physical design of Boston's new parks which matters: many local parks, playgrounds

Figure 8.19
Boston's historic buildings in the Downtown area.

and community centres have also benefited from a series of *Neighbourhood Life* initiatives. Arts programmes, for example, have become important aspects of Boston's place-making process: more than 300 artists' spaces have been created; theatres and performance centres have been restored; and historic buildings have been refurbished (Figure 8.19).

The implementation of the huge overall project has proven a major challenge for all key players, and particularly for mayor Thomas M. Menino. Constant digging, noise, vibration, technical and traffic problems have required an army of project managers, professional experts and publicity campaigns. Daily information on "What is going on in Boston" is regularly updated through newspapers, TV and other media, in order to come to terms with all the negative aspects of the city's restructuring processes, whilst reminding the city's residents and other users about the importance this grand vision has for all of them, and for generations to come.

In conclusion, what have we learned from the Boston experience? First, the positive aspects. At the most general level, Boston has always been home to many cultural groups that over centuries have shaped the city's distinct character, and through these processes have shaped their own identities, their many imagined communities. This has largely been achieved through creative partnerships between the city dwellers and the professionals. Of particular relevance today, are the most recent interventions in restructuring Boston's twenty-first century place-identity. The approach developed during the 1980s and 1990s is primarily focused on supporting user choice. However, as we have seen, supporting user choice has a long history in Boston; from its early "freedom fighters" during the seventeenth century, to the 1960s popular neighbourhood movements, to more recent political, professional and user partnerships in shaping the city's cultural landscape.

At a more physical level of design, what have we learned about designing to support a rooted sense of imagined community? First, on the negative side, must be counted the overall financial cost of this project and the negative impacts of the noise, pollution, vibrations and traffic congestion, experienced by the city dwellers and other users during the construction process. The design and planning ideas popular during the 1950s and 1960s have left deep scars, and require huge political and financial commitment to rectify the problems they created. Positive lessons can be learned across both the use and the meaning levels of experience. At the use level, the approach developed for restructuring Boston's Downtown Artery employs a number of theoretical approaches, from Lynch's study of imageability to Jacobs's ideas about mixed use and streets and Whyte's work on public open space design. A combination of these theories has contributed to the design of an integrated public open space network at both the city and the local neighbourhood scales. This new public open space system allows different users, vehicular and pedestrian, to travel at different speeds; enabling a variety of travellers to encounter each other in more positive ways, compared with the old Artery network, which separated them and gave priority to long-distance and fast moving travellers. The new public open space network also connects better into the finer grain of mixed uses, achieved through the integration of new open spaces and the old, deep-rooted historic neighbourhoods of Boston. The new, linear system of parks, when completed, will enable different groups of users to encounter each other in their daily journeys and life experiences. At the meaning level, we can see how users and professionals utilised Lynch's work on legibility, explored through mental mapping exercises, carried out both in the 1960s and in the 1980s to reveal deep-rooted landmarks, paths, nodes, districts and edges as important in the interpretation of Boston's place-identity.

We also find useful lessons for designing to support harmonious living between members of different communities. Important here is the inclusive, participatory process; where different interest groups, politicians and professionals contributed to the creation of a common vision, at both the city-wide and the local neighbourhood scales. At the use level, we can see how different cultural groups defined their own neighbourhood and city-wide open space connections and mixed use developments. At the level of meaning, we find a great degree of multi-cultural layering in the construction of modern Boston: united, progressive and modern at the city-scale of design, whilst keeping the deep-rooted, local cultural landscapes of different neighbourhoods.

The Boston approach to redefining the city's place-identity also demonstrates a huge commitment in designing to support the users' sense of empowerment; this is where we find, as we did in the case of Bologna, coherent and integrated participatory processes for engaging different actors to create a new vision for the city, a city loved and enjoyed by different groups. Here we find how the "inquiry by design" approach was utilised at different stages of the design process; involving children, elderly people, local business communities, politicians and professionals in creating Boston's new cultural landscape.

Particularly useful, in Boston, are lessons in designing to support a sense of harmonious co-dwelling with the wider ecosystem. This is evident at both the use and the meaning levels. At the use level, we have seen how different generations of Bostonians learnt to adjust to the harsh climate and topography; and how they created a sequence of open spaces such as the old Emerald Necklace to promote health whilst at the same time providing a natural support system for rich flora and fauna within historic neighbourhoods. This human/non-human symbiosis is also evident in the way different designers and community groups are re-instating natural systems, right in the heart of a very busy city. At the meaning level, we see how attitudes to nature, to its deep-rooted sense of what it means to be a Bostonian, are reinforced through the new Emerald Necklace, extended to tie different neighbourhoods into a united whole. This is also apparent in the detailed aspects of design where water, sea grasses and other types of plant life are used symbolically to tie the historic city together with and a more progressive, multi-cultural landscape.

Notes

1   Sammarco, 1995.
2   Brooke, 1996.
3   Morris, 1997, 6.
4   Woods, 1902, 11, cited in Todisco, 1976, 1.
5   Todisco, 1976.
6   Woods, 1902, cited in Todisco, 1976.
7   Todisco, 1976, 2.
8   Ibid.
9   Ibid.
10 Ibid.
11 Sammarco, 1995, 44.
12 Boston Redevelopment Authority (BRA), 1990.
13 BRA, 1990.
14 Tafuri & Dal Co, 1976.
15 Ibid.
16 Ibid.
17 Jacobs, 1961.
18 Gans, 1962.
19 BRA, 1990.
20 Lynch, 1960.
21 Appleyard, Lynch, Myer, 1966
22 SMWM, 2000, 20.
23 Schmidt, 1997, 2.
24 BRA, 1990.
25 Ibid., 37.
26 Ibid.
27 BRA, 1990.
28 Ibid.
29 Ibid., 35.
30 Ibid.
31 BRA, 1990.
32 Ibid.
33 Gavers, 1997, discussion between Georgia Butina Watson and Dick Gavers, Boston City Hall.
34 BRA, 1990, 9.
35 Ibid.
36 Ibid.
37 BRA, 1997.
38 Gavers, 1997, discussion between Georgia Butina Watson and Dick Gavers, Boston City Hall.
39 Ibid.
40 BRA, 1997.
41 Schmidt, 1997.
42 BRA, 1997, 10.
43 Ibid., 11.
44 BRA, 1990, 19.
45 Gavers, 1997, discussion between Georgia Butina Watson, Boston City.
46 Freeman, 2003, 65.
47 Ibid.
48 BRA, Ibid., 24.
49 http://www.masspike.com/bigdig/parks/wharfparks.html
50 Ibid.
51 Freeman, 2003.
52 BRA, 1990, 28.
53 Freeman, 2003, 66.
54 Ibid.
55 Ibid.
56 Ibid.

9

The beginnings of a synthesis: The responsive environments approach

Each chapter so far has yielded useful insights about how to design in ways which are positive from our place-identity perspective. Since we are designers as well as authors, we have naturally found ourselves drawing inspiration for our own design work from each of these case studies: indeed, that is why we carried them out. In this final chapter we shall explore how, with other colleagues, we have drawn together these various insights in the development of the Responsive Environments design approach with which we are both associated.

To explore the origins of the Responsive Environments approach, we have to go back to studio debates with our graduate students during the mid-1970s in the Joint Centre for Urban Design, which had then recently been set up as a bridge between the schools of architecture and town planning at Oxford Polytechnic, now Oxford Brookes University. Students came to the Joint Centre from diverse backgrounds. In terms of professional cultures, they came mostly from architecture, from planning and from landscape, with occasional mavericks from as far apart as property development and biology. These students were (and remain) equally diverse in their geographical origins, and consequently in the design traditions which they brought with them. In the period during which Responsive Environments developed, intense debate between two very different traditions was to prove particularly salient. On the one hand, students from the English-speaking world – primarily from the UK, Australia, Canada, New

Zealand and the US – brought with them the tradition of Anglo-Saxon empiricism. They saw knowledge as founded on experience, had relatively little interest in design theory, had a conception of design quality focused largely on perception, and often drew inspiration from Gordon Cullen's *Townscape* approach[1] and from Kevin Lynch's perception studies in *Image of the City*.[2] On the other hand, students from Continental Europe and from Latin America came largely from a rationalist tradition, in which knowledge was seen as stemming primarily from the intellect. They had a far greater interest in theory, which the Latin Americans in particular often linked to a Marxian understanding of politics; and they were deeply influenced by the "urban morphology" approach of Aldo Rossi and La Tendenza which we explored in Chapters 5 and 6.[3]

Studio design work at the Joint Centre was (and still is) carried out partly in cross-cultural groups. This way of working was developed precisely to foster cross-cultural debate, and has proved highly successful in this regard. During the late 1970s, these discussions – often intense and conflictual – succeeded in developing a politics of space linked directly to the making of practical design decisions: the foundation of the Responsive Environments approach. First articulated for a wider public in 1985 in the book *Responsive Environments*,[4] this approach sees built form as a political system which impacts on its users' lives in the most pervasive way. It takes the view that places should be designed so that these impacts open up as

237

many choices and opportunities as possible in their users' everyday lives. From this perspective, therefore, good design is a matter of promoting design qualities which support these benign impacts.

Since this quality-focused approach places its primary emphasis on the links between the physical design of a place and the development of its users' lives, through the promotion of choice and empowerment, we can with hindsight see its potential for engagement with place-identity issues. At the time, however, this potential was not conceptualised; though it became progressively clearer as the approach developed through a process which John Zeisel was to categorise as "Enquiry by Design".[5] Through this process, the approach was used in a variety of practical projects; progressively developing to capitalise on opportunities and to ward off threats which presented themselves in practice.

We shall start our account of this process with a competition-winning speculative housing scheme at Fobney Street, near the centre of Reading, in South-East England. Design work here was completed in 1986, but the project was initially developed as a test bed for the Responsive Environments approach itself, and it was written up – in early sketch form – as the basis for the book's final integrating chapter. This gives the Fobney Street scheme a particularly direct relevance for exploring the approach's place-identity implications; so we shall explore its genesis in some depth, with an insider's knowledge, because of personal involvement in the development team itself.[6]

Speculative housing is a particularly interesting type of development from the place-identity perspective. On the one hand, housing has a threefold importance in these terms: it constitutes over half of current development, most people spend about three quarters of their time in and around it, and their homes have a particular emotional importance in most people's lives. On the other hand, large speculative housing developments are often seen as particularly negative in their place-identity impacts, because of a tendency to replicate standard products, regardless of local situations. This is therefore a context which poses a tough test for any design approach.

The most fundamental of the qualities which the Responsive Environments approach sees as supporting user choice is termed *permeability*: the capacity of a place's public space network to offer a choice of routes to and through the place concerned. Its fundamental importance for user choice stems from the fact that no place can offer choice of any kind unless users can get to it and through it in the first place. Though the place-identity implications of permeability are not discussed in *Responsive Environments* itself, it seems clear that high levels of permeability are likely to be positive in place-identity terms. Designers seeking high levels of permeability in their work are necessarily trying to achieve the experience of continuity in public space which, so we have argued in our earlier chapters' case studies, offers pregnant raw material for constructing the sense of "us-ness" on which any social identity must be founded.

At Fobney Street, however, it proved difficult to achieve a high level of permeability relative to the city as a whole, because the site was separated from the rest of Reading by a river to the North, and by a motorway-standard road on an embankment to the South and West. To overcome these shortcomings as far as possible, the first step in the design process was to map all the links we could find to our site from outside, including *potential* links for the longer term, as well as ones which could be made immediately. We therefore included links which were *spatially* possible even though no right of access currently existed, as well as others which might be made in the future through adjoining sites with obvious development potential in the reasonably short run (Figure 9.1). As we mapped these current and potential links, we tried to gauge their respective "connecting power", both into the site's immediate surroundings, and into the city as a whole, according to the directness of their layout and their eventual destinations. At the time, this analysis could only be carried out with the aid of common sense, but nowadays it could call on the help of the "space syntax" software developed by Bill Hillier and his team at London University.[7]

Having established the respective "connecting powers" of the various actual and potential links, the next step was to develop a preliminary street layout to link them, and particularly those with the most connecting power, as directly as possible across the Fobney Street site (Figure 9.2). This

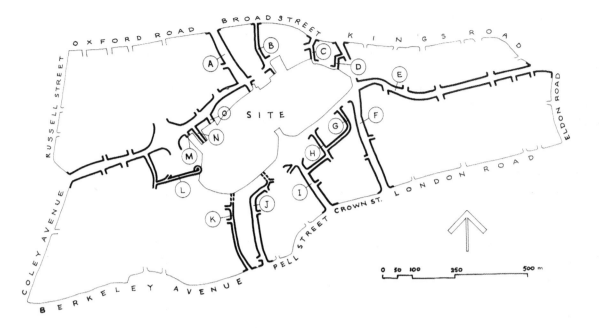

Figure 9.1
Fobney Street: identifying potential links.

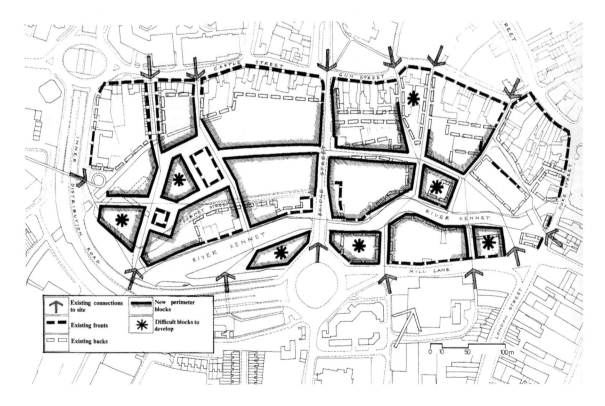

Figure 9.2
Fobney Street: preliminary street layout.

239

highly connected street layout would usually be anathema to transport planners, at least in the UK at the time, because they would see its desire to foster through communication and its frequent cross-roads as fraught with traffic dangers. Paradoxically, however, the site's history as a poorly connected enclave allowed us to make many local connections *within* the site, precisely because most of the new connections to the urban fabric beyond could only be pedestrian ones, at least in the short term, and did not immediately create many opportunities for through vehicular traffic.

This work on permeability generated a preliminary site layout which, however, was still only a tentative one: although permeability has a fundamental importance in the Responsive Environments approach, it is not *all* that matters. The point of permeability lies partly in *other* levels of choice it opens up for users, and in practice it has to be traded off against other key spatial qualities.

One of the most important of these other qualities is *variety*: variety of experiences from which users can choose. Designing to maximise the choice of experiences implies seeking out any special existing or potential experiences which any particular site might offer, and making sure that the new design brings out their impact rather than diminishing it. Like permeability, therefore, variety might be expected to support place-identity as well as offering user choice: the emphasis on building on any site's existing potential for special experiences supports both the distinctiveness and the historical continuity dimensions on which place-identity depends.

In the case of the Fobney Street site, a most important potential for such special experiences was offered by a network of culverted waterways inherited from the site's previous use as a brewery. An early design decision, therefore, was to open these up; and to adjust our initial ideas on street layout so that the resulting network of streams would be visible and audible from the public spaces of the scheme (Figure 9.3).

As well as building on the variety of experiences inherited from the past, however, it is clearly important, in terms of user choice, to develop as much *new* variety of experience as possible, to combat the homogenising pressures of today's speculative development process.[8] A key role in fostering variety of experience is played by the pattern of land uses which any project contains. A variety of land uses almost automatically brings with it a variety of sounds and smells, as well as a variety of visual experiences through the different forms of buildings and outdoor spaces which such a use-pattern implies. A variety of uses also brings with it a variety of different sorts of people: kids visiting sweet shops, trendies visiting boutiques, bikers visiting workshops and so forth. Given this variety of sensory experiences and human encounters, such a place is likely to take on a variety of meanings too.

At Fobney Street, the relatively poor potential for linkage to the wider surroundings meant that there was corresponding little potential for land-use variety within the site itself: primarily, this was a housing site. However, this meant that we would be introducing housing as a new addition to the town-centre land use mix, and therefore increasing variety at the more global scale. To maximise this potential, we wanted to include the maximum possible variety of dwelling types; but this was not initially an attractive idea so far as the developers were concerned. To achieve it in practice, we had to develop a convincing rationale for it. This had to be cast not in our own place-identity terms, but in terms which related to the developers' own interests in winning the competition, with a scheme which could generate the level of profit which they required. Given that the planners, like us, were concerned with place-identity issues, the developers could see that our proposal might increase their chances both of winning the competition, and thereby acquiring this desirable site, and also of gaining a rapid planning permission thereafter. From their perspective, however, there would be no point in all this unless the resulting development were to yield them a satisfactory level of profit. We therefore had to prove our proposals in these terms.

To do this, we first carried out careful consultations with local estate agents, as experts about the local market demand for different types of dwellings in this town-centre location. Drawing on this advice, we developed a set of 12 dwelling

Figure 9.3
(a) Fobney Street: opening up the streams. (b) Fobney Street: stream as green corridor.

types, ranging from apartments with one bedroom to houses with three; together with hard evidence about the likely sales prices which each type could achieve. In parallel, we worked with quantity surveyors to establish what each type would cost to build, so that we could construct a simple spreadsheet to work out the overall costs and values – and therefore levels of overall profit – of each evolving proposal as the design process developed. At each design team meeting, we tabled not only our drawings of the current scheme, but also – with the estate agent and QS also present – the spreadsheet which showed its outcome in financial terms.

This attempt to erode the barriers between the separate specialists who constitute the overall design team was far more unusual at the time than it would later become. To many architects and urban designers then – and to far too many even now – any serious concern with financial issues carries implications of a lack of focus on urban quality. It seemed to us that this was a silly view: a set of drawings, after all, is a more-or-less abstract *spatial* model of a design proposal, whilst a financial spreadsheet is merely another model of the *same* scheme from a different perspective. They are not, in the end, different things so much as views of the same thing from different angles. Without looking at our scheme from the developer's perspective as well as our own, the scheme itself could all-too-easily have been brushed aside by a claim that it was not financially viable: a claim which is heard over and over again by far too many designers who do not know how to marshal the resources to refute it.

The search for variety, then, led us to develop not only physical design ideas, but also ideas about how the design process itself should be designed. This was also the case as we considered a further key quality of the Responsive Environments approach: a concern for urban *legibility*.

A place is legible, in Responsive Environments terms, to the extent that it is more or less easy for its users to form accurate and stable "mental maps" of it.[9] This is important from the point of view of user choice, because the easier it is to find one's way around a place, the easier it is to use the place effectively for whatever purposes one has. It is also important from the wider place-identity perspective. First, legibility is closely linked to the "distinctiveness" dimension of identity; to the extent that places which are so confusing that they have no easily graspable patterns of form or use are often described, in everyday language, as "lacking identity". Second, legibility is in practice also closely linked to the "continuity" dimension of identity, because an extremely powerful approach to creating legible places is to build on whatever might *already* be noticed by users, as an initial springboard for design, rather than sweeping this aside or ignoring it to take a "clean sweep" approach. Once again, we find that the underlying structure of qualities for supporting choice, as articulated in the Responsive Environments approach, also seems positive in wider place-identity terms.

It seemed to us that the most helpful approach we could draw on for supporting legibility at Fobney Street would be the work of Kevin Lynch, as explored in *The Image of the City* many years before.[10] Lynch pioneered the use of mental maps – maps of what people remember about an area – as a way of grasping the factors which affect urban legibility. From the study of these maps, Lynch suggests that there is a skeleton of key features which people use to navigate the city: the *paths* – roads, streets, lanes, alleys – through which they move, the *nodes* at which these paths intersect and which therefore represent decision-points for users, the *edges* – motorways, viaducts, rivers and the like – which divide the overall settlement into graspable "bite-sized chunks", and the *landmarks* which stand out from the general background as particularly memorable features. The perceptual "flesh" on this structural skeleton is then formed with a "tissue" of *districts*: areas which have some degree of perceptual homogeneity within them, and some degree of perceptual contrast with other areas around them. This analogy of a skeleton fleshed out with districts of more generalised tissue is useful at a range of different scales; so that each district in turn can be seen as having its own *internal* skeleton, as indeed can each building within it. To offer the maximum support for legibility, then, the designers of any urban area have to consider how it might strengthen the larger perceptual structure of which it forms a part, as well as designing a strong perceptual skeleton within it. At any scale the paths, nodes, edges and landmarks form the basic raw material from which the perceptual skeleton is constructed, but it is not enough for an urban area merely to *contain* such elements. Legibility depends to a large extent on the relationship *between* elements too: the path which focuses attention on a recognisable landmark, for example.

Starting at the broadest district scale, we had first to decide whether our particular site ought to be perceived as a new district in its own right, as a new part of some existing adjoining district, or even perhaps as some kind of link *between* existing districts. For reasons already explained, we wanted to avoid any perception of our scheme as an isolated enclave, so we quickly decided against the "separate district" idea; attractive though that was to our developer client, who was strongly drawn towards the "exclusivity" implications inherent in the enclave concept. In terms of its potential relationship to existing districts, the Fobney Street site lay between two districts formed by the town centre and a housing area called Katesgrove. It was hard to see how we could make our scheme perceptually part of the town centre, because the financial constraints already discussed meant that the patterns of uses and of building types, both highly significant for district character, had to be very different from those long established in the town centre itself. On the other hand, it was equally hard to see how our scheme could ever be perceived as an integral part of Katesgrove. Though Fobney Street was also a housing area, it was separated from Katesgrove by the powerful twin edges of the Inner Distribution Road motorway and the River Kennet, and it seemed to us that this was too powerful a perceptual separation to overcome. We therefore decided that as far as possible we ought to form our design as a link between the districts of Katesgrove and the Town Centre.

If we could achieve it, this "transition" character would reduce the likelihood of the Fobney Street scheme being perceived as a separate enclave within the town as a whole. We therefore felt that the area could *also* have a particular internal place-identity of its own, without creating negative enclave implications at the larger scale. Because of the historical importance of its waterway system, and the way we had integrated this into our layout in search of variety, it seemed appropriate to use this as the foundation for creating the internal perceptual skeleton; an idea which was reinforced by naming the new development *Waterside*.

Following Lynch's ideas, we began by constructing our own mental map of the Fobney Street area, and then enriching this with insights about more local perceptions by asking people who worked in the area, or lived nearby, to draw us maps of what they themselves remembered (Figure 9.4). This exercise was very limited in scope – we only got maps from 12 people besides ourselves – because our design resources were limited by the fact that we knew that we would only get paid for our work if we won the competition. Nonetheless, when we came to review the results of the mapping exercise we found that these insiders' perceptions drew our attention to aspects of the place whose significance had not been noted from our own outsiders' perspective.

We began analysing the set of maps by making a list of all the features which had been noticed in any of them, and then arranging this list as a table in the order of the frequency with which the maps' various authors had noted them. We then used this table as the basis for a graphic which mapped all these significant features in their real positions on the ground; each shown at a size which reflected the frequency with which they had been noticed, to remind us at a glance of the features which had most stood out in people's minds (Figure 9.5). Comparing this composite mental map with our own evolving site layout, we could see how the new scheme might be adjusted to increase both its own legibility, and that of the larger town centre of which it formed a part, by building on and enhancing the features which people already remembered; for example by slightly re-aligning one of our new public spaces, both to create a focal space round an ancient

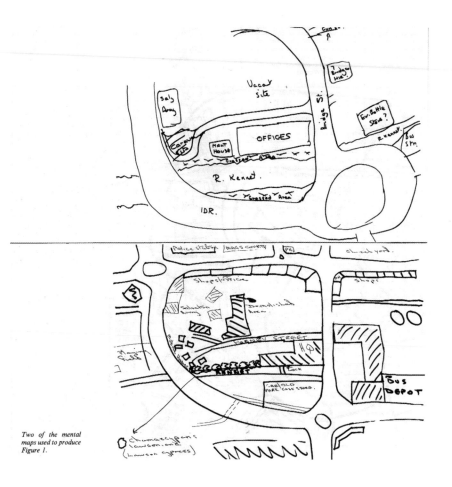

Two of the mental maps used to produce Figure 1.

Figure 9.4
Fobney Street: mental maps.

yew tree, and to focus on the existing memorable landmark of a church tower (Figure 9.6a).

Working in this way, we arrived at an overall site layout which seemed to us to make the best perceptual use of the paths, nodes, edges and landmarks which figured most strongly in our own and others' mental maps, so as to reinforce the legibility of the perceptual skeleton of the area as a whole. Following through at a more local scale, the next step was to apply the same logic to designing for legibility *within* our own site; for example by proposing landmark forms for buildings at the ends of street vistas (Figure 9.6b).

To summarise, then, our design decisions had been made primarily to maximise the potential for offering choice, and therefore "open futures", to the place's everyday users. As we have seen, this is important in itself in place-identity terms; but in the course of our review of the project so far we have also teased out ways in which the responsive environments qualities can help to foster a rooted sense of imagined community, and to some extent – for example through opening up the culverted waterways – to promote a sense of co-dwelling with nature too.

Some indications of how various groups of users and producers responded to our work on the ground, at least in terms of the "roots" dimension, is offered by research carried out on the implemented scheme by the architect Lucia Vasak, one of our graduate students,[11] as part of a comparison with Aldo Rossi's Perugia scheme which we explored in Chapter 6. Lucia's findings showed that by and large the residents and users she interviewed felt that our

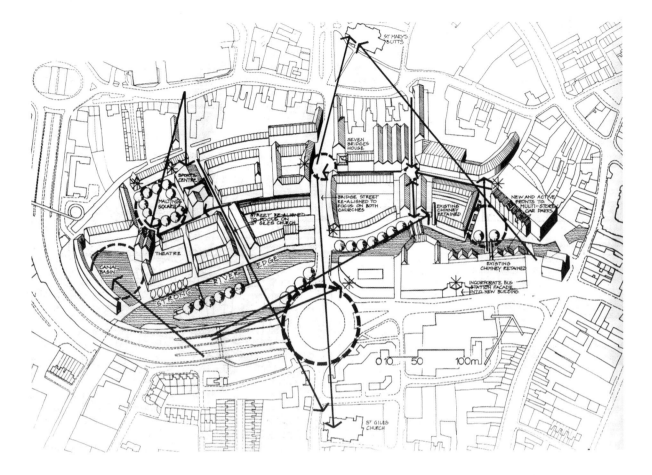

Figure 9.5
Fobney Street: composite mental maps.

most detailed, small-scale decisions reinforced the local Reading character, whilst our larger-scale decisions about the street pattern, block structure and overall massing did not: roughly the opposite to what she found in her analysis of Rossi's Perugia work. Probably this otherwise negative finding is a reasonable trade-off for the permeability we achieved through the street and block layout, but we were keen to achieve more positive results at a wider range of morphological levels in future work. The opportunity came with both authors' involvement, from 1989, in the regeneration of Brixton's Angell Town Estate.

Angell Town, initially designed by Lambeth Borough architects' department, was developed during the 1970s. In its morphology, it represents an intermediate stage in the shift from 1960s modernist blocks towards the more traditional street-orientated layouts of the 1980s; for it has something of the plan geometry of the traditional perimeter block, but modified to form a rigid pedestrian/vehicular segregation because high levels of car ownership were predicted. To this end, the ground level was largely given over to car use (Figure 9.7a), whilst pedestrian access was concentrated on pedestrian decks or "pedways" at first- or second-floor levels (Figure 9.7b). These pedways were linked from block to block by bridges; and originally these were intended to link across the busy Brixton Road to the neighbouring Stockwell Park estate, which houses all the social facilities such as shops and a doctor's surgery. Sadly, the bridge was never built, so Angell Town for years had no communal facilities at all for its 4,000 people.

Figure 9.6
(a) Fobney Street: opening landmark views. (b) Fobney Street: landmark bay window.

Despite this disadvantage, Angell Town's first residents were happy to move in. The estate is conveniently situated in relation to Brixton as a whole, and expectations were high. In the words of one early tenant, who moved to Angell Town from bedsit accommodation, "we saw it as a luxury pad". Though the morphology was unfamiliar, the first residents were not suspicious of it: "we knew it had been designed by experts, and we trusted them to know what they were doing".[12]

Soon, however, the lived experience of the estate began to overwhelm these favourable first impressions. First, residents began to notice that there were few chances to meet people in casual ways, because there were no windows opening onto the pedways: "In ordinary houses, you can see people in the street through the kitchen window, so there's a chance to see what's going on, and maybe say 'hi' if you want to – but we soon found out you can't do that here".[13]

The blindness towards the public realm also made it difficult to control children, who wanted to play there with their peers. The ground-floor garages were hidden from view, so the residents never used them from the start: they soon became vandalised, and this quickly contributed to a depressing image for the estate as a whole. Soon people gave up requesting to live in Angell Town, and the only new arrivals were those whose problems meant they had no other choice. Angell Town, with its problems exacerbated by the management problems of a well meaning but bureaucratic local authority, had become a sink estate; widely seen as a disaster even before its construction was complete. "Angell Town becomes Hell Town" said the South London Press.

Partly as a reaction to experiencing the negative results of being excluded from decisions about their own living environment, a group of concerned residents began to push for a greater degree of tenant participation in the much-needed process of improving the estate. Beginning with voluntary youth work, then taking over the tenants' association and eventually forming the Angell Town

Figure 9.7
(a) Angell Town: a pedway. (b) Angell Town: ground floor given over to the car.

Community Project (ATCP), residents began to take ever greater initiatives; first on their own, but eventually recognising the practical need to work with consultants of various sorts. As part of these initiatives, Oxford Brookes Urban Regeneration Consultancy was asked by ATCP to set up and manage a tenant consultation process, to help them articulate first what was wrong with the estate in design terms, and second what could be done to improve it.

In taking this initiative ATCP saw the need for urban design expertise, but was also aware of the potential danger of the professionals taking over. The process was therefore set up on the model of "two sets of experts", where the tenants took the role of experts about life on the estate and its problems and opportunities, whilst URC provided expertise about what was possible in terms of design, rather than pushing a particular line about what ought to be done.

This philosophy of keeping ATCP firmly in the driving seat was attractive to URC as well as to ATCP, both on grounds of political conviction and also because it clarified whose side we were on in a situation fraught with potential conflicts. It was reinforced in the practical arrangement of the consultation process at four levels. First, our consultancy contract was directly with ATCP. Though our funding came ultimately from Lambeth Council, it was paid first to ATCP; and it was the ATCP management committee who decided whether to pay us or not. Second, a group of residents was trained to take an important role in running the process themselves. Third, the consultation process was to be designed as far as possible to involve *all* the people on the estate; as far as possible the process would have to be taken to *them*, rather than just involving those who could be persuaded to come to *us* by taking part in public meetings. And fourth, the process was to begin with a clean sheet of paper, rather than with URC making proposals to be discussed.

The clean sheets of paper – long rolls of lining paper – were put up on the walls of a community room which ATCP had already managed to carve out of redundant garage space, and an initial series of agenda-setting public meetings began.

ATCP made strenuous efforts to get as many people from different age groups, genders and ethnic backgrounds as possible. This represented a considerable organisational effort, including the provision of an impromptu crèche (where the children were encouraged to draw their ideal homes) and escorts to see the older participants safely home.

The "clean sheet of paper" policy meant that there was no structured agenda of design issues to discuss: rather, residents were asked to talk first about their experience of problems on the estate. Not surprisingly these were not issues whose links with urban design were immediately obvious, so our role was to help uncover whether such links existed, and if so what they were. An example may help to make this clear. At the first meeting, we were disconcerted to discover that dog shit was the topic which people were most anxious to discuss. The links between this prevalent nuisance and urban design were initially unclear, but were uncovered as the meeting progressed, through a process of give and take between the two sets of experts. "Why is there so much dog shit, anyway?" we asked. "Because there are so many dogs" came the reply, delivered in a tone of voice which made it clear that the speaker found this a pathetically stupid question. "But why are there so many dogs then?" At this point, the answers began to uncover a dog culture which was utterly new to us middle-class urban design consultants, to whom "dog" had hitherto been equivalent to "family pet". It became clear that to many dog owners at Angell Town, the dog was at least partly a cost-effective, high tooth-powered security device; and someone recited what was later to become a familiar *bon mot* about neighbouring Stockwell Park: "The estate where even the Rottweilers patrol in pairs"

— "But why do people feel so threatened anyway?"
— "Because the place is always deserted"
— "Most of the time nobody can see what's going on when you're outdoors …"

By now, we were clearly into urban design issues, which we as consultants felt able to grasp. And the point is that these were issues about community safety, the perception of threat in public space and so forth, which our previous urban thinking had only engaged in the most peripheral way. These are issues, after all, which are almost entirely ignored by the initial *Responsive Environments* frame of reference and in our Fobney Street work, and yet they were massively top of the residents' own agenda. The frame of reference itself was thereby subjected to a powerful critique and was subsequently enriched, much to the benefit of URC's design approach as a whole. It is hard to see how that could have happened without engaging with this previously unfamiliar culture in a process of action research, and without the residents driving the design process, according to *their* agenda, from the outset.

This is not to say, of course, that we did not bring our *own* agenda into the process: merely that we tried hard not to introduce our own pet concerns until a basic framework of issues had been articulated by the residents; and we did our best to avoid manipulating the situation to make it come out how we wanted. In the nature of things, we probably failed in this to some extent – it is difficult to become a "neutral instrument" after all – but the fact that we are still around, still with a positive relationship with ATCP, 16 years later at the time of writing, suggests that the residents feel they are getting enough of what they want.

Armed with the information from the meetings and feedback from a subsequent exhibition, the next step was to prepare a questionnaire to be administered to all the households on the estate. This was produced through discussions with a paid group of residents who had taken active roles in the process so far, drawn from different interest groups, with URC producing drafts on the basis of these discussions. These drafts went through a lengthy and sometimes hilarious process of revision, largely devoted to changing them from what the residents called "Oxford Polyspeak" into language which they felt would be understood by the prospective respondents. Together we had to arrive at a trade-off between precision and comprehensibility; and this was no easy task.

To the professionals of Lambeth Council, who were monitoring the consultation process as a whole, the final form of the questionnaire represented

something of a threat, because it was designed to elicit residents' reactions to specific design proposals as well as to general design principles. The Council's own architects and landscape architects felt that this would remove the potential for them to use their creative ability to do the best job for the residents, and wanted to be told about problems rather than guided towards solutions. The residents, on the other hand, were worried that this would allow the Council's professionals to import their own agenda into the design process: the very problem which the consultancy process had been designed to avoid. As the residents saw it, the purpose of the questionnaire was to generate a design brief which would (inevitably) call for a great deal of detailed design interpretation, but would be as prescriptive as possible about key issues of site layout, relationships between buildings and public space, access to dwellings, locations of uses and so forth. This conflict ran deep, and was never amicably resolved: in the end the residents, with our help, just did it their way; but at the cost of worsened relationships between ATCP and the Council officers concerned.

Once agreed by ATCP, the questionnaire was administered by the members of the working party who had been involved in its design and who were therefore in the best position to help respondents fill it in. Despite shrinking Council funding, which meant we could not approach all households, the level of interest in the project as a whole can be gauged from the fact that return rates of these complex questionnaires, which took about an hour to complete, were as high as 70% in one block.

When analysed, the results showed a very clear pattern of preference for street-orientated housing laid out in perimeter blocks, clearly linked into the surrounding areas of Brixton to reduce the "ghetto" effect of the current layout: a factor also in the "character brief" (which we would now call an identity brief) which we have already reviewed in our overall Introduction. To recap, the identity brief called not only for more spatial and perceptual integration with Brixton as a whole, to break down "ghetto" perceptions, but also for a non-institutional "homely" image, and a "modern" character to encourage perceptions of Angell Town as home to forward-looking people. Again, the

Figure 9.8
(a) Angell Town: a "big block" turns into a series of dwellings. (b) Ground floors reactivated.

benefits of working closely with the residents is manifested here: this is the experience which enabled us to see the links between place-identity and social identity which had previously been opaque to us, and would have remained so had we continued to think about architectural imagery solely from within our own design-culture ghetto.

The first physical result of this process was a pilot project for 43 dwellings, designed by the London architects Burrell Foley Fischer with us as "expert clients" helping to articulate and support the views of the Community Project. This pilot project demonstrated once again the advantages of removing "dead" spaces such as the pedways. These were replaced by ground-level front doors from public spaces defined by active building fronts (Figure 9.8a); thus re-rooting the buildings in well-loved local precedent and enabling them to define the public space – as arena for constructing a sense of "us" – at the level of use as well as cultural meaning.

The animation of the public space and the fostering of community empowerment, both at the level of use, were further supported by replacing previous dead garage walls with a new shop,

hairdresser, launderette and workshops. Despite careful thinking about financial viability, not all these ventures proved financially successful. Enough of them have survived, transformed and prospered, however, to generate sufficient income to enable ATCP to survive in the face of local government grant cuts; providing a degree of independence which is itself vital in terms of ATCP continuing to act as a focus for developing the sense of empowered community solidarity on which a progressive (rather than nostalgic) sense of "us" must ultimately depend.

At the level of meaning, quite minor physical changes were used to reinforce a "small things matter" message. In particular, the residents were eventually surprised to find themselves agreeing that the expression of rainwater downpipes, hidden in the estate's original architecture, made a radical impact in changing "one big block" into "a series of dwellings" (Figure 9.8b); whilst the replacement of unusable municipal grass banks by individual front gardens gave great scope for personalisation, with considerable public impact (Figure 9.9).

Overall, then, the pilot project was highly successful as a test bed for the ideas we had worked

Figure 9.9
Angell Town: personalised front gardens.

with ATCP to develop, but it proved more much expensive than new build would have been. To cut short a very long story, a master plan was drawn up by Calford Seaden Trimmer, embodying ATCP's version of the *Responsive Environments* principles of well-linked streets bordered by active building fronts; to be implemented by a varied range of architects to avoid any danger of drifting into a "total art work" approach. Funding for implementation too was broken down to the smallest possible scale, with the involvement of three different housing associations; again to reduce the dangers of monolithic character which, it was feared, might have resulted from any single funding institution.

New housing by Burrell Foley Fischer, designed within this overall master plan, shows one creative way in which the "identity brief" has been addressed in practice. At the largest scale of design, the overall street/block layout and overhead "bridges" make perceptual links with central Brixton, helping to break down any enclave, "ghetto" sense of separation (Figures 9.10a and 9.10b); whilst the ability to read the new public spaces as positive "figures" enables their significance to be further reinforced through names, chosen by the residents to celebrate events in the Angell Town story, and thereby to further support a sense of "us". At a smaller scale, the massing in yellow-brick "villa" blocks resonates with well-loved earlier high-status housing nearby (Figures 9.11a and 9.11b); whilst the panelled abstraction of the facades makes links with the modernist vocabulary of mainstream design culture's "proper architecture", albeit with timber's more "homely" connotations. The results have the degree of transculturality needed to bridge gracefully between the professional cultures of the architects and the cultures of the residents themselves.

Figure 9.10
(a) Overhead bridges characteristic of Central Brixton. (b) Overhead bridges in the new housing.

Figure 9.11
(a) Well-loved nearby villas. (b) Villa format in the new housing.

Place-identity issues are also engaged through the detailed design of outdoor space, particularly in a public garden designed by the landscape architects Planet Earth. Created as a memorial to the life of a much-loved community leader, the Dora Boatemah memorial garden addresses all the issues on our place-identity agenda.

Through her own life and work, Dora Boatemah embodied both transculturality and empowerment to an extraordinary degree. Born in Ghana, Dora was raised largely in Brixton, and worked hard and successfully for many years to help build a transcultural sense of empowerment in a common cause, amongst residents from a hugely diverse range of cultures. By encouraging people to remember Dora, the very existence of the memorial garden reinforces the concern for transcultural empowerment which her own life

embodied; reinforcing and broadening this concern through many elements of its physical design.

Key amongst these elements are a series of low walls, constructed from crushed material salvaged from the estate's demolished 1970s buildings, bound together in cages of steel rods to form blocks known as gabions (Figure 9.12). The meanings which these walls suggest are complex ones. On the one hand, they celebrate the community's triumph over the demise of the hated original buildings, now crushed and caged in the new design. But the overall pattern of connotations here is more subtle: the creative use of this old material in the form of gabions – an up-to-the-minute, even "forward looking" material in its early third millennium context – also suggests the optimistic, empowering message that even the most negative experiences can not only be overcome, but even turned to positive, future-orientated advantage.

Figure 9.12
Angell Town: the memorial garden.

These messages of empowerment are linked to an amplified concern for transculturality through the garden's key memorial focus. This takes the form of a tree: a memorial whose own living character itself suggests that the concern for transcultural empowerment, for which Dora is remembered, is relevant not only in the human sphere, but also in relation to a wider biotic community. The particular type of tree chosen for the memorial suggests further transcultural meanings. On the one hand it is a type of palm, suggestive of Dora's African roots; but on the other hand it is also a species chosen to flourish in a British climate, and it is firmly rooted in Brixton soil.

The Responsive Environments approach itself began consciously to seek ways of designing to foster a sense of forming part of a wider biotic community from the early 1990s onwards, first at a theoretical level,[14] and then in practice too. We found design implications at the levels both of use and meaning. At the use level, the concern is to make design decisions which support not only human choice – which remains crucially important – but also the overall positive development of the wider ecosystem of which humans form part. At the level of meaning, we need to design so as to showcase how this harmonious co-dwelling works.

To our initial surprise, widening our focus seemed to require very little conceptual reworking of the basic Responsive Environments approach. We found, for example, that our core qualities of permeability, variety, resilience and legibility still offered a valid conceptual framework: we simply had to consider their implications more widely, in relation to the wider ecosystem rather than in relation to human life alone; with the overall aim of making design decisions to benefit both as far as we could. For example, we had to consider permeability in terms of supporting not only the movement of people, but also of wildlife, water, and flows of air and solar energy. Only in one area did we need to expand our conceptual framework. In order to focus specifically on negative interactions *between* human activity and wider ecological systems, for example as manifested through global warming or pollution, we articulated the additional quality of *resource-efficiency.*

Work carried out by our graduate student Mariana Castaños,[15] in the small Oxfordshire town of Witney, shows how this widened approach can work in practice. The first step here was to consider permeability beyond the human sphere, by forming a system of green corridors to link the particular project site into the wider biotic system of the Witney area. Just as for human linkage, work has to begin by considering the existing potential for green linkage offered by the wider context of the particular site itself. This involved using maps and aerial photographs to identify patches of land around the site which had particular local or regional significance for biotic support (Figure 9.13). In the UK, information of this kind is readily available, but this can be supplemented through the study of old maps to identify areas which, for example, might have been heavily planted for long enough to have acquired major ecological significance.

Once these significant contextual patches had been identified, Mariana's next step was to indicate conceptual desire lines between them which might help to link them into the overall green linkage system (Figure 9.14). The closer study of aerial photographs of the site and its context then revealed existing green patches on or near these lines, for example along the bottoms of existing back gardens or along watercourses. In turn, this analysis suggested the best locations for green corridors through the project site itself, so as to link it as closely as possible into these wider potentials (Figure 9.15).

The eventual aim here would be to link and extend the planting areas and waterbodies into a "green grid", to increase permeability for non-human life. Unlike permeability for humans, however, this "natural" permeability is less affected by the grid's geometry. The intensification of the green grid, therefore, can be postponed until later in the design process, and located in relation to the geometrical demands of the public space network. The next step, therefore, was to lay down the public space network itself; integrated as well as possible into the existing connections to the site.

These more local connections were laid out to mediate between three key aims. First, it was important from the harmonious co-dwelling perspective that the human links should disturb the "green grid" as little as possible. Second, to support resource efficiency, it was important for the overall

Designated Wildlife Sites in and around Witney

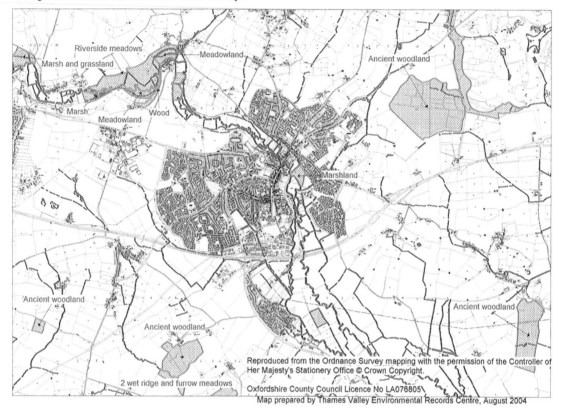

Figure 9.13
Witney: potential for biotic support.

"grain" of the network to run as far as possible within about 30 degrees of east–west, so that as many as possible of the street-orientated buildings would get good solar orientation. Third, it was important for human permeability that connections within our site, and into the adjoining public space system were as well integrated as possible. The overall public space structure mediating between these three considerations is shown in Figure 9.16.

In the next stage of design, attention turned back to water, and its ecological role. Drainage of the public space network and the buildings was conceived as a Sustainable Urban Drainage System. This was designed so that grey water was recycled, brown water was purified in reed beds and surface water was allowed to permeate into the ground as gradually as possible, through means such as swales

and ponds. Finally, the whole drainage system was tied back to support and enrich the site's initial biotic support system, with which our design process had begun (Figure 9.16).

All the design decisions so far had been intended to support harmonious co-dwelling between humans and the wider ecosystem at the level of use. It was important, however, to foster harmonious co-dwelling at the cultural level of meaning too. As far as possible, therefore, we tried to "showcase" the design decisions we had made so that users were helped to understand the co-dwelling process as they went about their everyday lives. The structure of paths, roads, edges, landmarks and districts which impacts on the place's overall legibility, for example, was clarified and strengthened through planting, and through the water system, as much as through

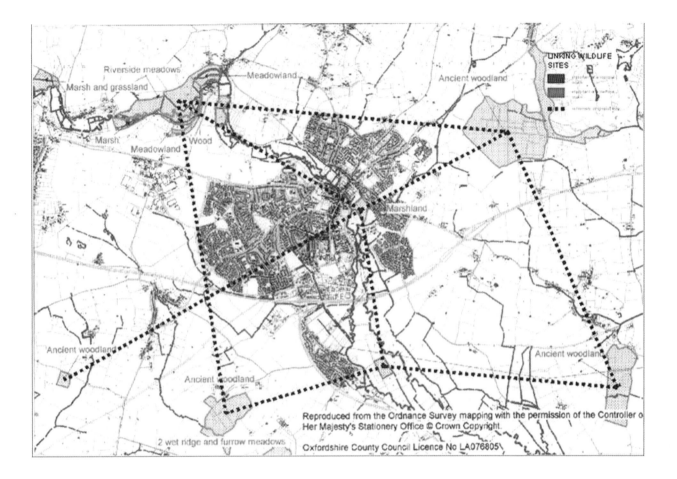

Figure 9.14
Witney: green desire lines.

building forms. At the smaller scale, the swales and ponds of the drainage system too were located in clearly visible positions, so that users could see and understand the system's workings.

By this stage, we had an overall urban design structure which took account of both human and wider ecological concerns together. In place-identity terms, both the everyday experience of habitation and the meanings of the place, we hoped, would help people identify themselves in co-dwelling terms. In the course of designing, we found all sorts of conflicts and made all sorts of trade-offs between the design qualities we sought. There can never be any single "right" way of deciding whether any particular set of trade-offs is valid or not. We see the attempts to make design decisions transparent, as explained through the very different

Fobney Street, Angell Town and Witney projects, as powerful aids to enabling this debate to happen.

In conclusion, what have we learned from investigating the development of the Responsive Environments approach? At the most general level, two key points stand out. First, Responsive Environments seems broadly positive in terms of place-identity issues, despite the fact that it does not address these directly. This is heartening, but not ultimately surprising. The approach, after all, is focused on supporting user choice; and choice, at the most fundamental level, clearly includes choosing the kind of person one wants to become. Second, the Responsive Environments approach is systematic, at least to some extent. To that extent, therefore, it can also be made transparent; and can therefore open up to debate and to the involvement of

Figure 9.15
Witney: green linkage through the project site.

"unofficial" designers, such as users, in creating cultural landscapes. In addition, our case studies have yielded useful lessons at more detailed, concrete levels of design. Let us now explore these, in relation to our four key place-identity issues.

First, what useful lessons have we learned about designing to support a rooted sense of imagined community? Insights here span across both use and meaning levels of experience. At the use level, Responsive Environments pulls threads together from the case studies of several earlier chapters, to offer a practical technique for designing an integrated public space network able, particularly with the aid of Space Syntax, to predict likely levels of human encounter in the various spaces of the overall system. Further, it offers a structured approach to enriching the grain of mixed uses, thereby further

encouraging a richer range of human encounters; and it shows how the chance of achieving this in practice can be increased through understanding how to check financial feasibility. At the meaning level, the approach shows how the legibility of an area can be explored through mental mapping, and how the results of mapping exercises of various kinds can be used in design: for example, using "rooted" landmarks as at Fobney Street, or drawing on the best-loved aspects of existing district character in new buildings at Angell Town.

The Responsive Environments approach has also developed over time to offer useful lessons in designing to support harmonious living with members of other communities. At the level of use, harmonious transcultural living requires at least a minimally acceptable sense of safety vis-a-vis "others". Here the

Figure 9.16
Witney: the integrated access network.

approach is positive in demonstrating how the links between a sense of safety and "signs of life" in public space are fostered through highly integrated public space networks, defined by the active interfaces of adjoining buildings. At the level of meaning, Responsive Environments articulates a way of working towards a "common ground" transcultural imagery, through systematic consideration of how significant elements of building form can be designed to support different actors' interests. Burrell Foley Fischer's work at Angell Town, for example, shows how this issue can be addressed, to generate imagery which resonates across the professional/lay divide.

Responsive Environments has a particular advantage over the other case studies we have explored so far, in designing to support the user's sense of empowerment, since this is where the approach specifically focuses through its qualities to support user choice. At the level of use the qualities

of permeability and variety, offering choice of routes and activities, are central; and once again space syntax techniques and financial feasibility studies are valuable design aids.

Finally, what can Responsive Environments offer in terms of designing to support the development of a sense of harmonious dwelling with the wider ecosystem? Early projects such as Fobney Street, like the case studies in previous chapters, largely focus on the meaning level here: for example, Fobney Street's opening up of the city's water systems merely suggests that "water systems matter". At the deeper level of use, however, the developing approach does have more to offer. Tentative directions can be drawn from the Witney project, with its emphasis on designing to support *both* user choice *and* the viability of the area's ecological structure, and to demonstrate the ecological workings of the resulting cultural landscape as clearly as possible to its human users. Though it currently opens up as many questions as it answers, this latest phase of the approach does seem pregnant with possibilities.

Overall, then, Responsive Environments has much to offer in place-identity terms; not so much because it generates startling new insights in itself, as because it helps us to synthesise a great many of the insights we have gleaned from earlier chapters into a comprehensive overall structure. It is clear, however, that the use we have ourselves made of the earlier chapters by no means exhausts their potentials for inspiring new approaches. Differing users and designers, from differing cultural backgrounds, in differing places with differing situations will make differing uses of the cultural raw material which the earlier chapters contain. We do feel, however, that there are some more general lessons to be drawn out. It is these that we shall address in the final conclusions which follow.

Notes

1   Cullen, G., 1971.
2   Lynch, 1960.
3   Rossi, 1982.
4   Bentley, I. et al., 1985.
5   Zeisel, 1981.

6   Ian Bentley was, at the time, a partner in the urban design practice Bentley Hayward Murrain Samuels which won the competition to develop this site in 1986.

7   For an exploration of Hillier's work, see Hillier and Hanson, 1984.

8   For a detailed exploration of these pressures, see Bentley, 1999, Part 2.

9   For discussion, see Downs, 1977.

10   Lynch, 1960.

11   Vasak, 1989.

12   Cited in Bentley, 1993.

13   Ibid.

14   See, for example, Bentley, 1999, Part 3.

15   Castaños, 2005.

Conclusions: Pulling the threads together

In this concluding chapter, our aim is to bring out useful lessons from our case studies, to help designers address place-identity issues through their work. To recap, we see five key questions which call for the designer's attention. First, how can built form best support an open range of choices in our everyday lives, and how can it help us develop the sense of empowerment we need if we are to take advantage of these opportunities in practice? Second, how can design support the construction of a rooted sense of imagined community, needed to dispel the feelings of lonely rootlessness which so easily arise when choice becomes the supreme quality in so many of our lives? Third, how can this support for imagined community be achieved without drifting into a nostalgic culture of low expectations, which renders us fearful of living with *others'* imagined communities? Fourth, how can this capacity for living together be actively promoted through transcultural, inclusive design? Fifth, and finally, how can built form help us contribute positively to the wider ecosystem of which humans form a part?

From our various case studies, we have developed a complex tangle of insights in relation to all these issues. As we have encountered these through the case studies themselves, however, they do not automatically offer any clear overall pattern for designers to use in their work. In these conclusions we shall pull together ideas across all the case studies, to build up such a pattern. How should we best get started?

Throughout our case studies, we have seen the importance of part/whole relationships in place-identity terms. In Prague, for example, we saw the dangers inherent in the "total art work" approach, in which each individual detail is subordinate to an overall, dominating whole; promoting a sense that

the individual is submerged within the collective in Stalinist design. Conversely, in Plečnik's Ljubljana work, we saw the symbolic potential of wholes built up from fairly autonomous parts, in promoting a potentially liberating sense that "individuals matter". Whatever the decisions one might make in any particular design situation, it seems clear that part/whole relationships *matter* for empowerment; so design decisions, at all physical scales, ought to be made at least partly in relation to the next largest "whole" of which they form a part. Any useful design process, therefore, will have to be constructed so as to help designers keep part/whole relationships in focus throughout.

We found a very well-established, powerful way of conceptualising parts and wholes in the "urban morphology" approach which we explored in Chapters 5 and 6. In its original Italian form, however, this engages only with the human contribution to cultural landscapes; but we saw, through our study of the Responsive Environments approach, how urban morphology might be broadened to link together both human and non-human spheres. Between them, then, the Urban Morphology and Responsive Environments studies identify a range of "morphological levels", at different physical scales, which each have a degree of relative autonomy; typically changing at different rates over time.

At the most fundamental level, changing most slowly, is the *underlying topography* of geological and hydrological structures. This topography is then occupied for human and non-human use, to form the *overall cultural landscape*; which in turn can be considered at a range of different morphological levels, typically subject to more rapid change.

At the largest scale, and with the slowest rate of change, are the networks of linkage spaces without which no human or non-human system can operate or reproduce. In human terms, we are here concerned with *public space networks* of streets, squares and the like, which are paralleled by *wildlife corridors* in the non-human sphere. These linkage networks generate spaces in their interstices, changing at the same rate as the networks themselves. In the human sphere, these interstitial spaces form *blocks*, whose non-human counterparts are *patches*.

Blocks are typically subdivided into smaller areas of land over which particular individuals or groups have occupation rights, either legal or customary. These smaller spaces are the *plots* whose importance we saw in Bologna. They tend to change more rapidly than the overall blocks of which they form parts. In part or whole, the plots and patches are further modified as human or non-human users occupy them for their own particular use; in the process forming still smaller and usually less permanent morphological elements. For the non-human sphere, this occupation takes place primarily through the construction of *non-human shelters* such as nests, burrows and the like. The search for shelter greater than that afforded by the bare plot itself also motivates much human occupation; generating *buildings* and their associated private outdoor spaces.

It is these morphological elements – topography and hydrology, linkage networks, blocks/patches, plots and buildings/shelters – which form the basic raw material of parts and wholes from which cultural landscapes are formed through design. In place-identity terms, the designer's task is to organise these elements and the relationships and interfaces between them, so as to foster positive support for our place-identity agenda: maximising choice, constructing the rootedness of imagined community, overcoming nostalgia, supporting a sense of transcultural inclusiveness and co-dwelling with the wider ecosphere, for as many users as possible. Using these ideas, we can range across our case studies to bring out a pattern of useful design principles, across all the morphological scales, which can help designers create the potential for positive place-identities; both at the practical level of how places are used, and at the symbolic level of their meanings.

In addition to lessons about the physical product of design at each level, however, our case studies also offer valuable insights into techniques of design, related to different morphological scales, which can help make positive place-identity outcomes more likely. In drawing out principles at each scale, therefore, we shall review these design processes as well as physical design ideas themselves. To start with, though, a couple of cautionary words about how these lessons might be used.

First, the importance of the part/whole issue means that we should never focus our design attention myopically on any single morphological level. Rather, we should try to keep the emerging form of the whole morphological ensemble in mind as decisions at each particular level are made. Second, no set of design principles can ever form a foolproof recipe for "good design". It should already be obvious, from the case studies themselves, that design from the place-identity perspective is shot through with internal complexities and contradictions: there *is* no single "right answer", though there may be many inappropriate ones. The lessons we can learn, therefore, are merely useful aids for making better-informed design decisions, and for evaluating the pros and cons of alternative design ideas. We need to see principles as forming a springboard for creative design, rather than a rigid straitjacket of "how to do it" rules.

Despite the need to think broadly across the morphological levels as we design, there is also a pragmatic need to decide where best to *start* this complete process. To avoid drifting into a superficial "image-making" approach to place-identity, there is a strong presumption in favour of starting at the "deepest" morphological level, by first considering the underlying structure of topography and hydrology which forms the (literal) bedrock of any cultural landscape.

Even these underlying structures do not necessarily form a totally fixed, immutable "given" for the designer: as we saw in Boston, for example, they can be altered in radical ways to fit with particular imagined communities' ideas about what "their place" should be like; whilst the London Underground explored the creation of an altogether new, parallel topography. Nonetheless, the underlying topography is always the "deepest" morphological element, most resistant to change; and most attempts to appropriate it for place-identity construction involve moulding its *meanings*, through the arts and other media representations, rather than materially altering its physical characteristics to any radical extent. In many of our case studies, we have seen such appropriations and interpretations carried out to help construct imagined communities of various kinds. At the most obvious level, we have seen the strengths and dangers of naming and renaming places, from Prague to Boston; but many of our examples are more complex. In their very different ways, for example, Bedrich Smetana's musical appropriation of "My Country" in support of Czech nationhood and Edvard Ravnikar's graphic representation of Mount Triglav – first as a symbol of anti-fascist struggle, and then appropriated to give symbolic support to communist and then post-communist administrations – both show the potential range and power of this way of articulating and appropriating the distinctiveness of particular topographies through the arts.

At the level of built form itself, however, we have to begin with ways in which the underlying topography can be modified through the design of the linkage spaces which form the next smaller scale of our morphological elements. Since these are the spaces which most directly affect how people encounter strangers, both human and non-human, they are crucial for transcultural inclusiveness, and for the construction both of human imagined communities and of a sense of wider ecological community too. Until recently, most designers have concentrated almost exclusively on human concerns when designing linkage spaces. The ecological outcomes of this myopic focus are patently negative: to redress the balance here, we shall start by considering spaces for non-human linkage.

The key place-identity issue here is concerned with co-dwelling between humans and the wider biosphere: how can we design wildlife corridors to optimise this? As we saw in Mariana Castaños's work on Witney, in the Responsive Environments chapter (Chapter 9), we can lay down a solid foundation by identifying the key elements of the surrounding non-human linkage system in relation to our own design site. For small schemes, this may be a straightforward, commonsense matter of identifying the potential for wildlife corridors in the immediate vicinity – perhaps formed by existing hedgerows or ditches, or by the relatively non-manicured areas at the bottoms of adjacent private gardens – and then making sure that the layout of the new scheme extends these as far as possible. For larger schemes, which will inevitably make a wider impact on biotic linkage systems, the designer's net may have to be cast more widely; perhaps reaching out to major wildlife patches at some distance from the designer's particular site, as we saw both in Witney and in the overall planning of Boston and Bologna.

At this larger scale, it is no easy matter to decide how wide to cast the net. In some situations, as in the Witney example, helpful local, regional or central government information about the relative biotic significance of different patches may be available. In other situations, the study of old local maps may help to identify the relative ages of current patches, giving a steer as to their likely ecological value; and the involvement of naturalists or landscape architects in direct site survey work may also offer valuable guidance. In any case, remembering to think about biotic linkage rather than remaining blind to the issue, as most designers have traditionally been, is the first prerequisite for making better decisions about this key place-identity issue. At all scales, the design objective remains the same: to make the new scheme contribute as much as possible to the overall non-human linkage system.

Once we have made tentative decisions about locating wildlife corridors, attention can be turned to public space networks for humans. A *leitmotif* of all our case studies has been the manifold advantages, in place-identity terms, of forming public space into highly connected networks, rather than designing a system of relatively isolated enclave spaces. The more highly connected the spatial system, the greater the choice of routes through it; and therefore the greater the chance of meeting people from other imagined communities in the normal run of everyday life, with consequent advantages for transcultural inclusiveness.

This is not to say, however, that the mere *quantity* of links is all that matters. As we saw in Boston and Kuala Lumpur, high-speed regional links can form fearsome barriers to more local linkage; and all

263

scales of human linkage can obstruct non-human connections. Bearing these caveats in mind, however, there is from our perspective a general presumption in favour of highly connected networks, rather than more enclave-like public space structures.

In terms of how linkage spaces are used in everyday life, there is an urgent need to foster the availability and appeal of public transport; both to increase choice for those people without guaranteed access to private cars, and also to reduce carbon emissions in the cause of co-dwelling with nature. To reduce reliance on private cars, therefore, there is a need to support the construction of new imagined communities of public transport users. Here the design of the relevant linkage spaces will have an important role to play: London Underground's spatial handling of linkage spaces from street to platform, to help overcome earlier resistance to underground travel, has much to teach us.

On any site which slopes, the relationship between the public space network and the landform itself is also probably important in place-identity terms. At the level of use, this relationship affects street gradients, and therefore the everyday bodily experience of moving around the place: once established, this typical pattern of experience becomes part of the "roots" from which imagined community grows. Aldo Rossi's work at Perugia gave a striking example of how such patterns can be used in new designs.

As well as considering the overall public space system, it is also important – particularly in large schemes which are embedded within existing settlements – to investigate whether there is any thematic patterning of "special" spaces, which can be used in new schemes to reinforce local distinctiveness. Brixton's spaces between bridges, reused to help link perceptions of Angell Town into the wider Brixton scene, and Plecnik's "habitable bridges" which have become such a strong feature of Ljubljana's character are both pertinent here.

At the level of use, most non-human species benefit from being separated from public space; so it is best to keep the human and non-human linkage network apart as far as possible. First thoughts on linkage layouts, therefore, may stem from the idea of locating the public space network in the interstices between the green links, to form the "tartan grid" we saw at Witney; making the largest possible proportion of the public space network run within about 20 degrees of the east–west axis, to achieve ecologically benign energy conservation advantages.

Many of our case studies also show the importance of the detailed design of public space. In terms of user choice, these details of public space affect both the uses to which the space can be put, and the meaning it has for its users. At the level of use, detailed design can affect the potential for different uses to take place; making it more or less easy, for example, for people to play, socialise or drive their cars. At the level of meaning, public space detail can also support user choice by making the place more legible. Jože Plečnik's use of street furniture – changing in character from rustic to formal as the city centre is approached – is a case in point.

In terms of helping public space support a rooted sense of imagined community, detailed design can help to develop the historical depth of local distinctiveness by using materials and planting which are locally well established – many of our case studies demonstrate examples here – or through public art works which celebrate people or events which have significance for the imagined community concerned; either through literal representation, as in Jan Hus's statue in Prague's Old Town Square, or through more conceptual allusion, as in the Chinese Garden of Boston's Emerald Necklace, or Dora Boatemah's memorial palm tree at Angell Town.

The details of public space can also be used to help break down structures of meaning which impact negatively on particular imagined communities. The principle which we can draw from our case studies here is to take some symbol of the negative forces concerned, and somehow encourage people to see it as harmless. One important strategy here involves the use of humour: making people laugh at what previously frightened them into submission. For a big, dramatic example in the realm of public art, recall the substitution of the inflatable Michael Jackson in place of Prague's monumental Stalin; or at a smaller, gentler scale, the Pink Tank, repainted from military khaki to charming "feminine" pink to subvert its symbolism of violence and domination. Or, at a still smaller scale, the gabion walls in Angell

Town's Memorial Garden; their cages imprisoning the crushed remains of the hated earlier buildings.

Given that public space is the natural meeting place for people from different imagined communities, it is extremely important that its details also play their part in developing a sense of inclusive transculturality. At the level of use, inclusive detailed design has to develop the capacity of public space to support a choice of culture-specific activity patterns. Drawing together threads from our case studies, we can see the outlines of a useful design process here. The first step is to map out the range of imagined communities which are likely to use the space concerned: local public involvement will be helpful here; but taken together, our case studies suggest that age, class, gender and ethnicity will probably be involved. Having established *who* will likely use the space, the next step is to investigate the typical patterns of public space use by members of these communities: again, public involvement will help, as we saw in Boston. Having established *which* patterns of use the design should support, the final step is to decide how best to cater for these patterns, as well as minimising the likelihood of negative interactions between them.

As at larger scales, the principle of designing public space details to support inclusive transculturality at the level of meaning is to link together forms which have cultural significance across a range of different communities. Examples from our case studies include Prague's statue of Saint Wenceslas, uniting Christian and nationalist communities (but dangerously leaving out Jewish people). Or at a less grand scale, but with far wider resonance, consider Edvard Ravnikar's Slovene graffiti which linked the form of Mount Triglav, with its "Slovene Nation" resonance, to the Communist morning star: a symbol which has survived in the iconography of Slovenia through successive governments of radically different politically persuasion, for more than 60 years so far. Although it was developed for more commercial reasons, there is also much to learn from the London Underground's campaign of posters and other graphics; pointing out the system's potential with subject matter and graphic styles chosen to communicate with different travelling publics, and developed with user involvement through test marketing.

Finally, the detailed design of public space can also be used to help develop a sense of positive co-dwelling with nature. Ideas from our case studies show how this aspect of identity might be promoted through design at the levels of both use and meaning.

At the level of use, some degree of additional support for non-human linkage can be developed through public space planting. As we saw from the Responsive Environments chapter, however, public spaces and wildlife corridors are probably best kept apart, as far as possible, from the practical point of view; so an important aspect of detailed design concerns the points where, nonetheless, they inevitably intersect. The key idea here is to design the public space so that its human use at such points is least likely to interfere with wildlife crossing; for example through traffic calming to reduce traffic speeds and therefore cut down roadkill.

At the level of meaning, the key point is to make humans *aware* of the way the overall design promotes co-dwelling in practice. Here, we have seen how detailed design can help in a number of ways. The café terrace on Plečnik's Shoemaker's Bridge in Ljubljana, for example, encourages people to linger and experience the natural systems of the river without negative interference, since the human and non-human spaces are grade separated. At a deeper level of meaning, co-dwelling is further supported by the symbolic link between religion and nature which is forged by the detailed design of the bridge outside the church at Trnovo. At a more prosaic level, interpretation through signage can also help public awareness at such points.

The choice of tree species for use in such situations is in itself important in place-identity terms. Trees and other plant species which are long established in a particular locality might be used to maximise the rootedness of new developments, as at Zicatella in the Mexican chapter (Chapter 3), and in Jimmy Lim's Malaysian work. Alternatively, completely "alien" ones may well be appropriate in particular situations; as in Boston's Chinese garden, or the palm tree used for its particular cultural resonance in the Dora Boatemah memorial at Angell Town.

Once the layouts of the key linkage systems have been decided, at least tentatively, then design attention can move on to the next subordinate morphological level: the development blocks which are formed in the interstices of the public space network. These blocks are important for place-identity in a range of complementary ways.

First, the patterning of the sizes and shapes of blocks may itself have a thematic character in any particular place. If so, this too may be an important aspect of local distinctiveness; whose maintenance in new development may therefore contribute to a sense of rootedness through historical continuity around which, as in the Bologna study, established imagined community might be confirmed.

The sizes of blocks also have a crucial importance beyond issues of historical continuity, for these dimensions affect the ways in which private/public relationships can be spatially mediated: a crucial issue in place-identity terms. In several of our case studies, ranging from the regeneration of Bologna's historic core through Prague's modernist Baba development to the Responsive Environments work at Reading and Angell Town, we have seen the importance of designing blocks which are large enough to allow development fronting onto all the surrounding public spaces, together with the potential for private space at the back.

Privacy at the back can only be achieved by allowing a certain distance – which will vary from one culture to another – between the backs of buildings on opposite sides of the block. Blocks which make this distance too small will have a number of disadvantages in place-identity terms. First, some of the buildings will have to back onto public space. When this happens, the need to maintain privacy means that in practice they will be able to provide only a relatively "dead" edge to the space itself, with a consequent lack of surveillance. As we saw at Angell Town, this decreases the sense of safety and security for people using the public space. Particularly in communities under stress, this increases the chance that negative cultures of fear will develop; with growing mistrust of "others", and a reduced potential for transculturality.

The scope for non-human use is also greatly affected by the widths and lengths of blocks. Wider blocks allow longer plots, which increase the potential for areas of less-manicured outdoor space at the

ends of the plots furthest from the backs of the buildings. In turn, these less-manicured areas have increased potential for the formation of wildlife corridors, separated from public space and therefore with relatively little human interference. It is clear that longer blocks also allow this potential for backland wildlife corridors to extend further before being interrupted by cross-streets. All in all, then, larger blocks have clear advantages from both the human and the non-human perspectives, enhancing both transculturality and co-dwelling potentials; though this has to be traded off against possible reductions in permeability.

Within the blocks themselves, the sizes and shapes of plots also have important place-identity impacts. Considered in their own right, plots have implications for locally rooted distinctiveness, for co-dwelling within the wider biosphere, for transculturality and – because of the constraints they place on the selection of building types – for choice as well.

As we saw in the Bologna study, the particular patterning of the plot widths which border any specific public space is one of the most important factors affecting the visual character of the public space itself. This is so for two key reasons. First, the importance arises because the interaction between plot widths and building types affects the proportion of public space frontage which is built or unbuilt. This in turn affects the degree of plan enclosure – and hence the potential for "figural" quality – of the public space itself. Second, the pattern of plot widths affects the underlying visual organisation of the walls which define the public space, and which are so important in local distinctiveness terms. In the Prague chapter (Chapter 1), for example, we saw how the established, rooted district character of Vyśehrad was reinforced by continuing the deeper structure of plot subdivision as a counterweight to the radically new, unfamiliar architecture of Czech Cubism: a sophisticated example of a place rooted in its plot structure, but not stuck in its architectural expression. This seems a far more promising balance than could ever be achieved by the reverse strategy which is so often seen in recent years: the Disneyesque attempts to achieve rooted continuity with surface detail, but contradicting this with an alien plot structure at a deeper level.

Patterns of plot frontage also have important impacts on transculturality, because they affect the number of building entrances along a given length of public space. As we saw at Angell Town, this in turn affects perceptions of community safety in relation to the public space itself, and therefore supports the sense of confidence which reduces fear of "others", and therefore fosters transculturality.

In relation to harmony with the wider biosphere, the orientation and frontages of plots affect the capacity for the ecologically positive use of solar energy. This gives the potential for developing different plot structures on streets of differing orientation: wider frontages on east–west streets, with narrower ones elsewhere; creating the new type of recognisably "co-dwelling" pattern which we saw in the Responsive Environment chapter (Chapter 9).

Finally, the pattern of plot subdivision is also important for place-identity because it constrains the types of buildings which a place can accommodate. Our case studies offer many lessons, at the levels of both use and meaning, about how these buildings impact across the place-identity spectrum of choice, rootedness, transculturality and co-dwelling within the wider ecosphere.

Starting with choice through the *use* of buildings, it is clear that choice in people's everyday lives is greatly affected by the grain of mixed use which is accessible without reliance on private motorised transport. In turn, this grain is affected by two key aspects of building design. First, it depends in the short run on having a sufficiently wide range of building types to accommodate the full spectrum of building use which is financially viable at the particular time and place concerned: as many of our case studies showed, this is no easy matter in practice. In the longer run, it depends on having buildings which are resilient enough to be able to adapt to *new* uses over time, as we saw in Bologna, Boston and Kuala Lumpur's shop-houses, as demand and financial feasibility change; so that the area as a whole can – at least potentially – increase its capacity to widen users' choices, rather than shrinking them.

Such resilience is also very positive in transculturality terms. Adaptable room sizes and shapes, linked by adaptable circulation and servicing systems, allow for patterns of uses which could never have been foreseen by the original designers; and thereby open the building to users with many different cultural mores.

The interface between buildings and adjoining public spaces is also crucial in transculturality terms. As we saw at Angell Town, the level of "nosey neighbour" surveillance, so important for the sense of community safety on which outgoing transculturality depends, is strongly affected by the percentage of the public space edge which is offered "signs of life" through the presence of buildings' doors and windows. In turn, this proportion depends on the internal arrangements of the buildings themselves. As Angell Town showed, lively interfaces with public space can only be created by locating those internal activities which require least privacy on the ground floor at the front; living spaces or offices, for example, rather than lavatories or the car stores with which Angell Town was originally so richly endowed.

The advantages of active interfaces between buildings and public spaces suggest the potential for designing new composite building types; "sleeving" those types which in themselves have little capacity to create active interfaces by adding more active programme elements, at least on the ground floor front. The design ideas explored in London Underground stations, with commercial facilities sleeving the otherwise inactive exterior walls, have much to offer here.

In considering design at the building level, it is important also to focus more directly on issues of meaning. Here, our case studies amply show how building design can contribute to the rootedness of imagined communities of various kinds. Most obvious, perhaps, was the regeneration of Bologna's city centre, where old buildings were restored *en masse* with a great deal of direct community involvement. As a counter example, we saw at Angell Town how existing buildings, which had acquired overtones of alienation and despair, were demolished or radically converted, again with active community consultation, to help local people reimagine their community in new, forward-looking ways.

From these examples, we can again distil some useful design principles. The first step is to identify as clearly as possible which imagined communities are relevant to the project in question. This requires as much community participation as resources allow: the Bologna, Boston and Angell Town studies all offer insights here, at very different scales. As part of this process – indeed, a major aid to uncovering communities which are relevant in place-identity terms – we have to identify any existing buildings in the project which are important to each community, in either positive or negative terms. Those buildings which are highly valued should then be kept, and as far as possible given showcase future roles in relation to the community concerned; whilst those which have negative connotations are prime candidates for demolition, if that is financially possible, or at least for radical image change.

Our case studies also showed how new *types* of buildings have been developed and sited to foster a sense of roots. From Prague to Mexico City, for example, we saw how museums were developed to showcase and interpret communities' past achievements, and to bring out their relevance to present situations. And, in the case of London's Underground Railway, we saw how the new building types required by new practical issues were designed so as to foster the sense of belonging to a new, forward-looking travelling community.

London Transport's buildings, as we saw, were also designed to promote a sense of *transcultural* inclusiveness, if only for commercial reasons. Between them, many other case studies also demonstrated a range of design approaches which are supportive in this regard.

One important design strategy, as we saw, involves being rooted in the past but not stuck in the past. One powerful version of this strategy achieves "roots" through using "deep" building types – types of massing and key spatial structures – which are rooted in local traditions, but then using whatever counts as a "forward-looking" designing vocabulary in the particular time and place concerned, at a more detailed level of design. The Czech cubist buildings we explored in Prague, the works of Barragán and Legorreta in Mexico, Rossi in Perugia and Jimmy Lim in Malaysia are powerful examples.

Prague's cubist architecture also achieves a further level of "rooted but not stuck" design *within* its detailed language of form. Here, the cubist vocabulary itself acts as a transcultural bridge between "the latest art ideas" on the one hand, and the uniquely local "roots" of the Bohemian Baroque Gothic on the other. Elsewhere in Prague, the Baba housing scheme achieves a similar "rooted but not stuck" status, through an identical strategy; this time using the well-rooted "villa in a garden" morphology with a *later* generation's forward-looking design language – this time avant-garde Modernism – for its detailed design vocabulary. Far away in London, Charles Holden's work for the London Underground pursues a similar strategy, fusing the latest Modernist imagery with traditional English materials; whilst Jože Plečnik's Križanke cultural centre in Ljubljana shows a similar "rooted but not stuck" approach, this time by using an ancient form type – The Roman velarium roof – but reinterpreting it with the latest tensile technology of its time.

From all these different examples, we can draw out a single unifying design principle. The buildings are conceived as embodying different subsystems which co-exist at different "depths" of overall form – mass, spatial structure, technological systems or surface vocabulary. In practice, these subsystems always have some limited autonomy in relation to each other, which enables them to play different roles in this "rooted but not stuck" approach to design. One level (usually the "deepest" in cultural terms: the underlying spatial type rather than, say, technology or surface design vocabulary) is used to achieve a sense of rootedness; whilst other, more "surface" levels are given the "forward-looking" role.

Plečnik's Ljubljana work, and our examples from Mexico and Malaysia, take this complex-design approach a stage further in supporting transcultural inclusiveness, by synthesising the form vocabularies associated with different social groups – peasants, middle class and intelligentsia – into a single formal language which, precisely because it is held in affectionate regard across social boundaries, eventually comes to form a major part of the distinctiveness of these places.

Given the recent two-generation period during which few designers focused on issues such as these in their work, it is hardly surprising that much of the "post modern classicism" of the 1980s, some of which was exploring these transcultural themes, met with little initial success in this difficult area, and was quickly rejected by the mainstream design community. It is heartening, therefore, to see designers from within that mainstream community, such as Burrell Foley Fischer at Angell Town, finding ways of integrating creative work around a transcultural identity brief into their own modernist design culture, with apparently positive reactions from the multicultural end users.

Buildings also affect place-identity at the level of co-dwelling with nature. Here, a major contribution can be made by energy-efficient building design, reducing energy consumption and therefore carbon emissions, as we saw in our Malaysian examples and at Zicatella. In addition, buildings have the potential to provide habitats for urban wildlife, for example through green roofs or Jimmy Lim's houses on stilts which allow wildlife access underneath. Though not itself strictly a building, Jože Plecnik's tree-planted bridge at Trnovo, which we explored in the Ljubljana chapter (Chapter 2), might be used as a springboard for creative design ideas at the building level too.

The empowering idea that "small things matter" can also be fostered (or contradicted) through building design. Here, for example, Plecnik's Ljubljana "Houses Under a Common Roof" dramatise the capacity for relationships between individual buildings to foster the feeling that individuals and families *matter* in relation to wider social collectives. The principle here involves finding an architectural expression for the smaller scales of social organisation on which the workings of any large building – or complex of buildings – must in fact depend.

We have also seen many examples in which the idea that small things matter is promoted at more detailed levels of design. Plečnik's National and University library in Ljubljana, for instance, is shot through with such examples; as when the individual stones which make up the monumental external walls are each strongly expressed as design elements in their own right. The design principle here seems to be that whatever is perceived as a "part" at each larger scale, becomes a "whole" in smaller, more close-up terms. For example, a building might be perceived at long range as a whole mass with windows as subordinate parts, whilst at closer

range each window might be seen as a whole with glazing bars as parts. In turn, at a still closer range, each glazing bar might be perceived as a whole; with patterns of light and shade, formed by the contours of its moulded cross-section, perceived as *its* component parts.

As we saw, Plečnik's work in particular takes this "wholes and parts" approach still further in empowerment potential, by occasionally setting up "riddles" in the form of minor but clearly intentional inconsistencies between the part and the whole within which it is set. Because it is part of the human condition to try to make sense of inconsistencies, and because there is ultimately no "correct" sense to be made in these cases, each user has the empowering feeling of making sense of the place in their *own* way, rather than passively "reading" something which the designer has decided in advance.

At a more detailed level, similar aims can be addressed through buildings designed to foster personalisation by their users. Jimmy Lim's Precima House is a clear example here, but perhaps the most thorough-going version in our case studies is seen in London Underground's stations; where the permanent walls of the platform spaces form a kind of "adjustable architecture", using tiled frames to incorporate ever-changing graphics into the architecture itself, rather than treating them merely as stuck-on appendages. Though this particular example was designed primarily for commercial rather than wider social reasons, the design strategy of building-in "frames" for personalisation has itself a far wider potential in place-identity terms.

To summarise, our overall case study review has brought out a wide range of lessons which can inform the design debate, from the largest to the smallest scales. Like everyone else, however, designers also need to feel *themselves* part of some larger imagined community and, for many mainstream designers this depends on their conceptions of themselves as Modernists, as innovators, as experts and/or as artists. There are problems here: as currently conceived in the mainstream, such conceptions create powerful inhibitions at all levels of the place-identity debate.

At the level of detailed design, for example, debate is frustrated by the established conception of Modernism as implying a particular vocabulary of form. At a deeper level of form, debate is stifled by a conception of innovation which makes many designers suspicious of patterns of form which cannot be seen as "new". And at the deepest level of design process, debate is cut short by old-established conceptions of the artist and the expert which encourage all-too-many designers to rubbish the idea of user-participation in design.

To move the debate forward, then, these mainstream conceptions have somehow to be developed to more sophisticated levels. This cannot be done by attacking them from outside: given their importance for imagined community, such attacks will merely lead to a closing of ranks, and a further ossification of the concepts themselves. The only way forward here, it seems, is by making these conceptions confront themselves. We have, in other words, to modernise our conception of Modernism. We have to develop more innovative conceptions of innovation. We have to use rebellious artistic creativity to break free from the straightjacket of established conceptions of art. And we have to use our expertise to understand more deeply the nature of expertise itself.

In terms of modernising Modernism, we have to clarify what "Modernism" *means* in design: the use of the best available, most up-to-date knowledge to construct a better world, without being held back by outworn conventions. The test for whether new forms are better than old ones, from the truly modernist perspective, is the extent to which they help produce a better world, rather than how "new" they are. To forget this simple but radical test, as many designers do when they foreclose debate by equating design quality with the conventions of a particular modernist *style*, is merely an example of an imagined community getting "stuck": in this case in a "nostalgia for the new" which leads just as surely to a fearful design culture of low expectations as any other form of nostalgia must do. True modernism, in contrast, requires that we use the best knowledge we have to face up to current design challenges – today certainly including problems of place-identity – and have the courage to move in whichever direction that may lead, no matter how negative that might seem to other members of one's own modernist community.

In relation to innovation, too, we have to remember the *point* of valuing it in design; which is to address current problems in the best ways we can without *having* to rely on direct precedents or traditional ways of doing things. If innovation begins to *get in the way* of addressing current problems, by *prohibiting* the use of precedents such as highly connected public space networks or active building interfaces despite the advantages our case studies have shown, merely because they *are* precedents with long historical pedigrees, then this is not true innovation at all. It has merely become a rigid, formalistic and ultimately *anti*-innovative tradition – a nostalgic "tradition of the new" – whose never-ending search for novelty, for its own sake, straightjackets designers rather than setting them free. The innovative conception of innovation which we need to free us from this arid tradition, by contrast, would rule out *nothing* which could help us build a better world.

At the deepest process level of design, current conceptions of professional expertise also need a thorough overhaul, because they make it difficult for "expert" designers to take seriously the involvement of "lay" users in the process through which design decisions are made. Here again, we have to remember that the *point* of acquiring professional expertise is to help designers build a better world. Now it is perfectly clear that in today's increasingly multi-cultural world – a world whose multiculturality is ever on the increase through every current force from the global economy to climate change – no professional designer can ever hope to understand, or be in a position to empathise with, more than a fraction of the imagined communities to which a given place's users might belong. In such a situation, unimaginable when current mainstream conceptions of professional expertise were developed during the nineteenth century, it is hopelessly inefficient not to call on the local expertise of ordinary people across as wide a range of imagined communities as we can manage, no matter how difficult an undertaking that might seem. The search for efficiency, which is the *point* of expertise, demands that we develop the expertise to do it.

Many designers, particularly architects, also feel that they belong to an imagined community of *artists.* This sense of being an artist has a great deal of positive potential for facing up to new problems in radical ways. As many of our case studies showed, art has a capacity for tearing holes, so to speak, in established conventions; opening a space for new ideas to address new place-identity issues. As with expertise, however, current ideas of art within the mainstream design professions have tended to dissipate this potential so far as place-identity is concerned. The problem is that much late second-millennium art, at least in Western cultures, became extremely individualistic; so that artistic quality is even now often seen as arising almost entirely from individual genius. This makes designers, if they identify with such an art community, either unwilling or unable to take seriously the idea of collaborating with users in their work: such collaboration, almost by definition, is seen as some sort of craven sell-out in terms of artistic quality. In practice, this feeling has the same negative implications as those we have already sketched out in relation to professional expertise. This means that mainstream conceptions of art, in relation to built form, have begun to betray modernist art's radical concern for ripping aside the veil of convention which prevents us from seeing and understanding our current condition, and therefore prevents us from taking radical action to improve it. Indeed, all too much "artistic" built form has shrunk its focus to a concern for producing places which are merely "beautiful", "interesting" or perhaps "sublime", to taste. Art like this has become a styling exercise; literally superficial in place-identity terms.

If issues of place-identity are indeed central to our time, then it is crucial for art to reconnect with them. The logic of our argument suggests rather strongly that this can only happen through a conception of the artist which invites users, as performers, into a positive, co-creative working relationship. This is, of course, commonplace in other fields of artistic work such as music and dance. If a third-millennium art of cultural landscapes is to face up creatively to place-identity issues, it will have to learn much from these fields. Architecture will have to become frozen music in a radical new sense.

In conclusion, then, the case studies we have explored in this book have opened up a storehouse of ideas to help drive design thinking forwards. Between them, they help to map out the boundaries of a new imagined community within design culture itself, able to offer us the support and sense of direction we need if we are to produce places which can help us face up to the third-millennium's ultimate design challenge: designing cultural landscapes to help us redesign ourselves.

Bibliography

http://www.masspike.com/bigdig/parks/wharfparks.
html (accessed December 2005). Anon.

Abel, C. (1991). *Foreword*. In CSL Associates, 1991.

Abel, C. (2000). *Architecture and Identity – Responses to Cultural and Technological Change*. Oxford: Architectural Press.

Accame, G. H. (1974). *Conoscenza e coscienza della città*. Bologna: Galleria d' Arte Moderna.

Adjami, M. (ed.) (1994). *Aldo Rossi – Architecture 1981–1991*. London: Academy Group Ltd.

Alić, D. and Gusheh, M. (1999). Reconciling national narratives in socialist Bosnia and Herzegovina: The Baščaršija Project, 1948–1953. *Journal of the Society of Architectural Historians*, 58(1), March 1999, 6–25.

Åman, A. (1992). *Architecture and Ideology in Eastern Europe During the Stalinist Era: An Aspect of Cold War History*. Cambridge, MA: MIT Press.

Anderson, B. (1983). *Imagined Community, Reflections on the Origin and Spread of Nationalism*. London: Verso.

Anderson, S. (1999). Memory without monuments. *Traditional Dwellings and Settlements Review*, XI(1), Fall 1999.

Anon (1940). Without comment. In De Profundis, *Organ of the Air Raid Shelterers at Swiss Cottage Station*, September 1940.

Anon (2001). *New Connections: New Architecture, New Urban Environments and the London Jubilee Line Extension*. London: Royal Academy of Arts.

Antliff, M. (1992). Cubism, celtism and the body politic. *Art Bulletin*, 74, December 1992, 655–668.

Antliff, M. and Leighten, P. (2001). *Cubism and Culture*. London: Thames and Hudson.

Appleyard, D., Lynch, K. and Myer, J. R. (1966). *The View from the Road*. Cambridge, MA: MIT Press.

Aristides, M. and Karaletsou, C. (eds) (1992). *Proceedings of IAPS 12 Conference*, Thessalonika, Commission of the European Communities.

Ayala, E. (1996). *La Casa de la ciudad de Mexico. Evoluciones y transformaciones*. Mexico, D.F.: Consejo Nacional para la Cultura y las Artes.

Bain, J. S. (1940). *A Bookseller Looks Back*, cited in Meade and Wolff (1996).

Bakhtin, M. (1981). *Epic and Novel*, in Holoquist (ed.) (1990).

Ballantyne, A. (ed.) (2002). *What is Architecture?* London: Routledge.

Bandarin, F. (1978). The Bologna experience: planning and historic renovation in a Communist city. In Appleyard, D. (1979), pp. 178–202.

Bandolini, S. (1996). Introduction. *Rassegna*, XVIII(66), 5.

Barman, C. (1979). *The Man who Built London Transport*. Newton Abbot, David and Charles.

Barnes, J. (1981). *Metroland*. London: Jonathan Cape.

Barton, H. and Guise, R. (2003). *Shaping Neighbourhoods: A Guide for Health, Sustainability and Vitality*. London: Spon.

Baudrillard, J. (1990). *Cool Memories*. London: Verso.

Bauman, Z. (1992). *Intimations of Postmodernity*. London: Routledge.

Bauman, Z. (1995). *Life in Fragments: Essays in Postmodern Morality*. Oxford: Blackwells.

Bauman, Z. (2000). *Liquid Modernity*. Cambridge: Polity Press.

Beck, U. (1998). *Democracy without Enemies*. Cambridge: Polity Press.

Bell, V. (ed.) (1999). *Performativity and Belonging*. London: Sage.

Belletini, P. (1995). *Bologna – the Oldest University in Europe – "Bologna the learned"*. Paris: Gallimard Guides.

Belletini, P. (1995). *Bologna – The University District*. Paris: Gallimard Guides.

Belodi, N. (1999). *Bologna and the Rehabilitation Programme*. Unpublished Conference Paper, Lisbon.

Benedikt, M. (2002). Environmental stoicism and place Machismo. *Harvard Design Magazine*, Winter/Spring 2002.

Bentley, I. (1981a). *The Owner Makes His Mark*. In Oliver, Davis and Bentley (1981), pp. 136–154.

Bentley, I. (1981b). *Individualism or Community*. In Oliver, Davis and Bentley (1981), pp. 104–121.

Bentley, I. (1993). *Community Development and Urban Design*. In Hayward and McGlynn (eds) (1993), pp. 72–82.

Bentley, I. (1999). *Urban Transformations: Power, People and Urban Design*. London: Routledge.

Bentley, I. and Gržan-Butina, D. (eds) (1983). *Jože Plecnik*. Oxford: Joint Centre for Urban Design.

Bentley, I. et al. (1985). *Responsive Environments: A Manual for Designers*. London: Architectural Press.

Bernik, S. (1990). Slovene architecture from secession to expressionism and functionalism. *Journal of Decorative and Propaganda Arts*, 17, Fall 1990, 43–53.

Bideleux, R. and Jeffries, I. (1998). *A History of Eastern Europe: Crisis and Change*. London: Routledge.

Birnbaum, H. and Vryonis, S. J. (eds) (1972). *Aspects of the Balkans, Continuity and Change*. The Hague & Paris: Moutan.

Blakstad, L. (2002). *Bridge: The Architecture of Connection*. London: August Media.

Blau, E. and Troy, N. J. (1997). *Architecture and Cubism*. Cambridge, MA: MIT Press.

Blokland, T. (2003). Trans. Mitzman, L. K., *Urban Bonds*. Cambridge: Polity Press.

Blumenfeld, R. D. B. (1930). *RDB's Diary 1887–1914*. In Meade and Wolff (1996).

Boston Redevelopment Authority (1990). *Boston: A Plan for the Central Artery*. Progress Report. Boston: BRA.

Boston Redevelopment Authority (1997). *Toward Boston 2000 – Realizing the Vision*. Boston: BRA.

Bourne, L. S. (1972). *The Internal Structure of the City*.

Bown, M. C. (1991). *Art Under Stalin*. Oxford: Phaidon.

Breveglieri, W. (2000). *Bologna 1950–2000*. San Giorgio di Piano: Minerva Edizioni.

Brooke, M. (1996). *Boston*. Singapore: APA Publications.

Brubaker, R. and Cooper, F. (2000). Beyond "Identity". *Theory and Society*, 29, 1–47.

Büchler, P. (1997). *Stalin's Shoes (Smashed to Pieces)*. In Harding (ed.) (1997).

Burckhardt, F. (1992). *Czech Cubism Today*. In von Vegesack, A. (ed.) (1992).

Burckhardt, F., Evens, C. and Podrecca, B. (eds) (1989). *Jože Plečnik Architect: 1872–1957*. Cambridge, MA: MIT Press.

Burks, R. V. (1972). *Nationalism and Communism in Yugoslavia: An Attempt at Synthesis*. In Birnbaum and Vryonis (1972).

Butina Watson, G. (1999). *Shaping Places: The Politics of Urbanism*. Ljubljana: UPIRS.

Caniggia, G. (1983). Discussions with Georgia Butina Watson, Oxford.

Castaños, M. (2005). *Wildlife Corridors in Urban Design*, unpublished MA thesis, Joint Centre for Urban Design, Oxford Brookes University.

Castillo, F. F. (1987). *Apuntes Para la Historia de San Angel y sus Alrededores: Tradiciones, Historia, Leyendas*. Mexico: anon.

Cataloli, G. (2003). From Muratori to Caniggia: the origins and development of the Italian school of design typology. *Urban Morphology*, 7(1), 19–34. Birmingham: ISUF.

Cervellati, P. L. (2001). Interview with Georgia Butina Watson, Bologna.

Charvat, P. and Prosecky, J. (eds) (1996). *Ibrahim ibn Yaqub at-Turtushi: Christianity, Islam and Judaism Meet in East-Central Europe, C. 860–1300 AD*. Prague: Academy of Sciences of the Czech Republic.

Chay, P. (1989). *Kuala Lumpur – Minarets of Old, Visions of New*. Kuala Lumpur: Foto Technik Sdn. Bhd.

Cherry, D. (2000). *Beyond the Frame: Feminism and Visual Culture, Britain 1850–1900*. London: Routledge.

Church, R. (1928). *Mood without Measure*. London: Faber and Faber.

Cohen, S. (2001). *States of Denial: Knowing About Atrocities and Suffering*. Cambridge: Polity Press.

Corcuera, M. P. C. (1994). *Mexico: Casas del Pacifico*. La Jolla, CA: Alti Publishing.

Cottington, D. (1997). *The Maison Cubiste and the Meaning of Modernism in pre-1914 France*. In Blau and Troy (1997).

Courmont, V. (2001). Poverty, a few definitions. *Villes en Developpement*, 53, September 2001, 4.

Craven, D. (2001). Post colonial modernism in the work of Diego Rivera and José Carlos Maviátegni – or new light on a neglected relationship. *Third Text*, Spring 2001.

CSL Associates (undated). *Projects Catalogue*. Kuala Lumpur.

CSL Associates (undated, unpublished). *Extracts – 1989–1991. The Works of Jimmy Lim and CSL Associates*, Kuala Lumpur.

Cullen, G. (1971). *The Concise Townscape*. London: Architectural Press.

Danto, A. (1981). *The Transfiguration of the Commonplace: A Philosophy of Art*. Cambridge, MA: Harvard University Press.

Davis, M. (1990). *City of Quartz*. London: Verso.

De Anda Alanis, E. (1989). *Luis Barragán-Clasico del Silencio*. Bogota: Escala.

De Angelis, C. (1995). *Bologna – Architecture*. Paris: Gallimard Guides.

De Bruyn, G. (2000). *Luis Barragán – The Quiet Revolution*, Barragán Foundation, Vitra Design Museum.

Delanty, G. (1995). *Inventing Europe: Idea, Identity, Reality*. London: Macmillan.

Djilas, M. (1985). *Rise and Fall*. New York: Harcourt Brace Jovanovich.

DoE (1996). Analysis of responses to the discussion document. In *Quality in Town and Country*. London: HMSO.

Dolbani, M. (1997). *Responsive Public Open Spaces in Kuala Lumpur*, unpublished PhD thesis. Oxford: JCUD.

Donald, J. (1996). *The Citizens and the Man About Town*. In Hall and de Gay (eds), 1997.

Douglas, H. (1963). *The Underground Story*. Newton Abbot: David and Charles.

Dovey, K. (1992). *The Bond and Bondage of Place Attachment*. In Aristedes, M. and Karaletsou, C. (eds) (1992).

Downs, R. M. (1977). *Maps in Minds: Reflections on Cognitive Mapping*. London: Harper and Row.

Du Gay, P., Evans, J. and Redman, P. (eds) (2000). *Identity: A Reader*. London: Sage.

Dyos, H. J. and Wolff, M. (1973). *The Victorian City*. London: Routledge and Kegan Paul.

Edwards, D. and Pigram, R. (1986). *London's Underground Suburbs*. In Meade and Wolff (1996), p. 7.

Efimova, A. (1992). Review of the Total Art of Stalinism. *Art Bulletin*, 74(4), December 1992.

Efimova, A. and Manovich, L. (eds) (1993). *Russian Essays on Visual Culture*. Chicago: Chicago University Press.

Eggener, K. (1999). Postwar Modernism in Mexico – Luis Barragán's Jardines del Pedregal and the International Discourse on Architecture and place. *JSAH*, 58(2), June 1999.

Eisenman, P. (1986). *Preface*. In Rossi, 1986.

Facaros, D. and Pauls, M. (2000). *Bologna and Emilia Romagna*. Cambridge: Cadogan.

Facaros, D. and Pauls, M. (2002). *Umbria*. London: Cadogan Guides.

Fanti, M. and Susini, G. (1995). *Bologna – History*. Paris: Gallimard Guides.

Felshin, N. (1995). *But is It Art? The Spirit of Art as Activism*. Seattle: Bay Press.

Flores, S. (2001). Interview with Georgia Butina Watson, Mexico City.

Fortier, A.-M. (1999). *Re-membering Places and the Performance of Belonging(s)*. In Bell, V. (ed.) (1999).

Forty, A. (1986). *Objects of Desire: Design and Society 1750–1980*. London: Thames and Hudson.

Frampton, K. (1985). *Modern Architecture – A Critical History*. London: Thames and Hudson.

Franklin, A. (2002). *Nature and Social Theory*. London: Sage.

Fraser, V. (2000). *Building the New World – Studies in the Modern Architecture of Latin America 1930–1960*. London: Verso.

Freeman, A. (2003). Above the cut. In *Landscape Architecture* (3).

Freshman, P. (ed.) (1993). *Public Address: Krzysztof Wodiczko*. Minneapolis: Walker Art Center.

Furedi, F. (2002). *Culture of Fear: Risk-taking and the Morality of Low Expectation*. London: Continuum, Revised edition.

Gans, H. (1962). *The Urban Villagers*. Glencoe: Free Press.

Garland, K. (1996). Henry C Beck and the London underground diagram. *Rassegna*, XVIII(66), 16–23.

Gartman, D. (2000). Why modern architecture emerged in Europe, not America: the new class and the aesthetics of technocracy. *Theory Culture and Society*, 17(5), October 2000, 75–76.

Gavers, R. (1997). *Discussion with Georgia Butina Watson*. Boston City Hall.

Gellner, E. (1998). *Culture, Identity and Polities*. Cambridge: CUP.

Giddens, A. (1984). *The Constitution of Society: Outline of a Theory of Structuration*. Cambridge: Polity Press.

Giles, R. (1999). Letter from Kuala Lumpur. *Architectural Review*, 1232, October 1999, 41.

Gillcott, J. and Kumar, M. (1995). *Science and the Retreat from Reason*. London: Merlin.

Gilroy, P. (1997). Diaspora and the detours of identity. In Woodward (1997), pp. 299–346.

Goldblatt, D. (2002). The dislocation of the architectural self. In Ballantyne (2002), pp. 153–172.

Goldstein, R. J. (1989). *Political Censorship of the Arts and the Press in Nineteenth-Century Europe*. New York: Palgrave.

Gonzalez de Leon, T. (2000). Interview with Georgia Butina Watson, Mexico City.

Grabrijan, D. (1957). Lik Plečnikove Ljubljane. In *Naši Razgledi*, No. 4.

Grabrijan, D. (1968). *Plečnik in njegova šola*, Maribor.

Grabrijan, D. and Neidhardt, J. (1957). *Arhitektura Bosne i Put u Suvremeno*. Ljubljana: Anon.

Gray, R. (1978). *A History of London*. London: Hutchinson.

Griffin, W. (2002). Laibach: The Instrumentality of the State Machine, http://www.artmargins.com/content/feature/griffin1.html

Groys, B. (1992). *The Total Art of Stalinism*. Princeton: Princeton University Press.

Groys, B. (1993). Stalinism as aesthetic phenomenon. In Efimova and Manovich (1993).

Hall, R. (1994). On values and role models: the making of a planner. In *Regenerating Cities*, No. 7.

Hall, S. (1997). The question of cultural identity. In Hall, S., Held, D. and McGrew, T. (eds), *Modernity and Its Futures*. Cambridge: Polity Press.

Harding, D. (ed.) (1997). *Decadent: Public Art: Contentious Term and Contested Practice*. Glasgow: Foulis.

Hassan, A. K. M. et al. (1990). *1890–1990 – 100 Years of Kuala Lumpur Architecture*. Kuala Lumpur: PAM.

Haufe, H. (1991). *The Modern University City*. In Schütz, 1991.

Havel, V. (1989). *Untitled Speech in Acceptance of a German Peace Prize*. London: The Independent, Weekend Section, 9 December 1989.

Hayward, R. and McGlynn, S. (eds) (1993). *Making Better Places: Urban Design Now*. Oxford: Butterworth Architecture.

Hetherington, K. (1996). Identity formation, space and social centrality. *Theory, Culture and Society*, 13(4), 1996.

Hillier, B. and Hanson, J. (1984). *The Social Logic of Space*. Cambridge: Cambridge University Press.

Hillier, J. and Rooksby, E. (eds) (2002). *Habitus: A Sense of Place*. Aldershot: Ashgate.

Hinrichs, N. (1995). *Bologna*. Paris: Gallimard Guides.

Holquist, M. (ed.), 1990 (1981). *The Dialogic Imagination*. Austin: University of Texas Press.

Hough, M. (1990). *Out of Place: Restoring Identity to the Regional Landscape*. New Haven, London: Yale University Press.

Howard, E. (1898). *To-morrow: A Peaceful Path to Real Reform*. London: Swan Sonnenschein.

Hueffer, F. M. (1907). *England and the English: An Interpretation*. In Meade and Wolff (1996).

Inglis, F. (1993). *Cultural Studies*. Oxford: Blackwells.

Institute of Contemporary Arts (1983). Exhibition *Aldo Rossi, Architecture Projects and Drawings*. London: Institute of Contemporary Arts.

Ivanšek, F. (1995). *Edvard Ravnikar – Publicist*. In Ivanšek (ed.) (1995).

Ivanšek, M. (1995). *Youth in the Shadow of St. Joseph's Bell Tower*. In Ivanšek (ed.) (1995).

Ivanšek, F. (ed.) (1995). *Hommage à Edvard Ravnikar, 1907–1993*. Ljubljana: Ivanšek.

Jacobs, J. (1961). *The Death and Life of Great American Cities*. New York: Penguin Books.

Kettenmann, A. (1997). *Diego Rivera – A Revolutionary Spirit in Modern Art*. London: Taschen.

Kim, K. K. (1996). *Kuala Lumpur – The Formative Years*. Kuala Lumpur: Verita Publishing SDN, BHD.

Ko, A.K.P. (1999). *Feng Shui and Urban Design*, unpublished MA thesis, Joint Centre for Urban Design, Oxford Brookes University.

Kotera, J. (1900). O Novem Umeni. In *Volny Smeri*, Vol. 4, p. 92.

Krečič, P., Murko, M. and Zavašnik, M. (1975). *Ljubljana*. Ljubljana: ČGP Delo.

Krečič, P. (1990). Jože Plečnik and Art Deco. *The Journal of Decorative and Propaganda Arts*, 17, Fall 1990, 27–35.

Krečič, P. (1993). *Plečnik: The Complete Works.* London: Academy Editions.

Kristeva, J. (1991). *Strangers to Ourselves.* Trans. Roudiez, L. S. New York: Columbia University Press.

Kubová, A. and Ballangé, G. (1986). *Plečnik et la ModernitéTcheque.* In Burckhardt, F., Evens, C. and Podrecca, B. (eds) (1989).

Kundera, M. (1984). *The Unbearable Lightness of Being.* Trans. Heim, M. N. New York: Harper and Row.

Kundera, M. (1992). *The Joke.* London: Faber and Faber.

Kundera, M. (1996). *The Book of Laughter and Forgetting.* London: Faber and Faber.

Lanzarini, V., Piombini, G. and Renzi, R. (1995). *Bologna.* Paris: Gallimard Guides.

Lash, S. (1999). *Another Modernity, A Different Rationality.* Oxford: Blackwell.

Latour, B. (1993). *We Have Never Been Modern.* New York: Harvester.

Lawrence, D. (1994). *Underground Architecture.* Harrow: Capital Transport.

Leach, N. (2002a). *The Dark Side of the Domus.* In Ballantyne (2002).

Leach, N. (2002b). *Belonging: Towards a Theory of Identification with Space.* In Hillier and Rooksby (2002).

Leboff, D. (1994). *London Underground Stations.* Shepperton: Ian Allan.

Legorreta, R. (2001). Interview with Georgia Butina Watson, Mexico City.

Leśnikowski, W. (ed.) (1996). *East European Modernism: Architecture in Czechoslovakia, Hungary and Poland Between the Wars.* London: Thames and Hudson.

Leśnikowski, W. (1996). *Functionalism in Czechoslovakian, Hungarian and Polish Architecture from the European Perspective.* In Leśnikowski (ed.) (1996).

Lim, C. S. (1989). Interview with Georgia Butina Watson, Kuala Lumpur.

Lim, C. S. (1991, 1993, 1998, 2001). Interviews with Georgia Butina Watson, Kuala Lumpur.

Lim, J. C. S. (2000). The Rites of the Tropics. In Leng, T. K. (ed.), *Asian Architects.* Singapore: Selected Books.

Lim, J. Y. (1987). *The Malay House – Rediscovering Malaysia's Indigenous Shelter System.* Pulan Pinang: Institut Masyarakat.

Lippard, L. R. (1997). *The Lure of the Local: Senses of Place in a Multicentred Society.* New York: New Press.

Lobo, C.G. (1992). Luis Barragán. In *MIMAR, Architecture and Development,* Vol. 12, June 1992. London: Concept Media.

Loos, A. (1900). *The Story of a Poor Rich Man.* Trans. Meek, H. In Münz and Künstler.

Lunghi, E. (1991). *Umbria.* Florence: SCALA.

Lynch, K. (1960). *The Image of the City.* Cambridge, MA: MIT Press.

MacCormac, R. and Stevens, M. (2002). *New Connections: New Architecture, New Urban Environments and the London Jubilee Line.* London: Royal Academy of Arts.

Mancini, F. and Casagrande, G. (1982). *Perugia.* Milan: Pellegrini.

Margolius, I. (1979). *Cubism in Architecture and the Applied Arts.* Newton Abbot: David and Charles.

Martinez, A. R. (1996). *Luis Barragán – Mexico's Modern Master, 1902–1988.* New York: The Monticelli Press.

Martinez, C. and Juarez, L. G. (1994). *Mexico City.* UNAM.

Marx, K. and Engels, F. (1848). *Manifesto of the Communist Party.* In Marx and Engels (1975), Vol. 6.

Marx, K. and Engels, F. (1975). *Collected Works.* London: Lawrence and Wishart.

McLeod, M. (1986). *Book Review.* In Rossi, 1986.

Meade, D. and Wolff, T. (eds) (1996). *Lines on the Underground: An Anthology for Circle Line Travellers.* London: Cassell.

Miller, E. (1986). *The Art of Mesoamerica.* London: Thames and Hudson.

Monroe, A. (2000). Twenty years of Laibach, twenty years of ...? *Central Europe Review,* 2(31).

Morris, M. (1997). *Boston.* New York: MacMillan.

Moscovici, S. (1990). Questions for the Twenty-first Century. *Theory, Culture and Society,* 7(4), 1990, 1–20.

Moudon, A. V. (1997). Urban morphology as an emerging interdisciplinary field. *Urban Morphology,* 1, 3–10.

Münz, L. and Künstler, G. (1966). *Adolf Loos: Pioneer of Modern Architecture.* New York: Praeger.

Mušić, M. (1981). *Jože Plečnik.* Ljubljana: Partizanska Knjiga.

Mutlow, J. V. (1997). *Legorreta Arquitectos*. Rizzoli International Publications, Inc., Mexico, Naucalpan.

Nedushivin, G. (1938). Monumentalnoe Iskusstvo v Strane Sotsializma. In *Tvorchestvo*, 11/38, 28.

Nietszche, F. (1974). *The Gay Science*. Trans. Walter Kaufmann. New York: Vintage Books.

Novitz, D. (2001). Participatory art and appreciative Practice. *The Journal of Aesthetics and Art Criticism*, 59(2), Spring 2001, 153–166.

Oliver, G. (1996). An underground memoir. *Rassegna*, XVIII(66), 34–39.

Oliver, P., Davis, I. and Bentley, I. (1981). *Dunroamin: The Suburban Semi and Its Enemies*. London: Barrie and Jenkins.

Park, R. (1967). *On Social Control and Collective Behaviour*. Chicago: University of Chicago Press.

Parker, S. F. (2001). Power and identity in the urban community. *City*, 5(3), 281–309.

Pevsner, N. (1942). Patient progress: The life work of Frank Pick. *Architectural Review*, XCII, 31–48.

Plečnik, J. (1908). Letter to the editor. In *Styl*, Prague, Vol. 1, 1908–9.

Plečnik, J. (1929). *Regulacija Ljubljane in njene okolice*. Arhiv Slovenije MAPA VI.

Pozzetto, M. (1979). *La Scuola di Wagner 1894–1912*. Trieste: Commune di Trieste.

Prelovšek, D. (1997). *Jože Plečnik 1872–1957: Architectura Perennis*. New Haven: Yale University Press.

Radford, E. (1906). *A Collection of Poems*, cited in Dyos and Wolff, 1973.

Rasmussen, S. E. 1990 (1928). First impressions of London. *A A Files*, 20, Autumn, 15–21.

Renzi, R. (1995). *The Bologna Dialect*. In Fanti and Susini, 1995.

Riedel, J. (ed.) (1999). *The Plastic People of the Universe*. Prague: Matla.

Roberts, T. (2002). The seven lamps of planning. *Town Planning Review*, 73(1), 24–26.

Rossi, A. (1982). Trans. Ghirardo, D. and Ockmen, J. *The Architecture of the City*. Cambridge, MA: Graham Foundation.

Rossi, A. (1986). *The Architecture of the City*. Cambridge: MIT Press, Oppositions Books.

Rossi, A. et al. (1990). *Aldo Rossi Architect – Works and Projects*. Barcelona: Gustavo Gilli.

Rowe, P. G. (1997). *Civic Realism*. Cambridge, MA: MIT Press.

Rubbi, P., Tassinari Clò, O. and Renzi, R. (1996). *Bologna la Bella*. Bologna: L'inchiostrobeu.

Sabloff, J. (1989). *The Cities of Ancient Mexico – Reconstructing a Lost World*. New York: Thames and Hudson.

Saint, A. (1996). What the Underground Means for London. *Rassegna*, XVIII(66), 24–33.

Sammarco, A. M. (1995). *Boston – A Century in Progress*. Dover, New Hampshire: Arcadia.

Sanchez Lacy, A. R. (1999). *En El Mundo de Luis Barragán*. Mexico, D.F.: Artes de Mexico.

Sandercock, L. (2002). *Difference, fear and habitus: a political economy of urban fears*. In Hillier and Rooksby (2002).

Sayer, D. (1991). *Capitalism and Modernity: Excursus on Marx and Weber*. London: Routledge.

Scannavini, R. (1995). *Bologna – Urban Development*. Paris: Gallimard Guides.

Schmidt, E. (1997). *Building a New Boston*. Unpublished Conference Paper.

Schütz, J. (ed.) (1991). *Mexico City*. Hong Kong: APA Publications.

Sells, M. A. (1998). *The Bridge Betrayed: Religion and Genocide in Bosnia*. Berkeley: University of California Press.

Short, J. R. (2001). Civic engagement and urban America. *City*, 5(3), 25–36.

Sidorov, A. (1991). *Stalin's art through Soviet eyes*. In Bown (1991).

Sitte, C., 1964 (1889). *The Art of Building Cities*. Ann Arbor: University Microfilms.

Šlapeta, V. (1986). *Jože Plečnik et Prague*. In Kubova and Ballange (1986).

Šlapeta, V. (1992). *Cubism in architecture*. In von Vegesack (ed.) (1992).

Šlapeta, V. (1996). *Competing Ideas in Czechoslovakian Architecture*. In Leśnikowski (ed.) (1996).

Šmejkal, F. (1990). *Devětsil: an Introduction*. In Švachá, R. (ed.) (1990).

SMWM (2000). *Boston Central Artery Corridor Master Plan*. Boston, MA: Boston Redevelopment Authority.

Steeve, J. (1992). Ricardo Legorreta. In *MIMAR, Architecture and Development*, Vol. 12, June 1992. London: Concept Media.

Stelè, F. (1967). *Arh. Jože Plečnik v Italiji 1898–1899.* Ljubljana: Slovenska Matica.

Stone, A. R. (1996). *The War of Desire and Technology at the Close of the Mechanical Age.* Cambridge, MA: MIT Press.

Street Porter, T. (1989). *Casa Mexicana.* New York: Stewart, Tabori and Chang, Inc.

Štursa, J. (Dec 1990). Interview with Ian Bentley and Georgia Butina Watson, Prague.

Šumi, N. (1983). *Plečnik and absolute architecture.* In Bentley and Gržan-Butina (eds) (1983).

Švácha, R. (ed.) (1990). *Devětsil: Czech Avant-Garde Art Architecture and Design of the 1920s and 30s.* Oxford: Museum of Modern Art.

Švácha, R. (1995). *The Architecture of the New Prague.* Cambridge, MA: MIT Press.

Sylvester, D. (ed.), 1969 (1944). *Henry Moore: Sculpture and Drawings,* Vol. 1, 1921–48. London: Lund Humphries.

Taffuri, M. and Dal Co, F. (1976). *Modern Architecture/I.* Milan: Electa.

Teige, K. (1932). *Nejmenši byt.* Prague.

Templ, S. (1999). *Baba: The Werkbund Housing Estate Prague.* Basel: Birkhauser.

The Times, June 14, 1879. Cited in Jackson, A.A. (1986), *London's Metropolitan Railway.* Didcot: Wild Swan.

Tisdall, C. and Bozzolla, A. (1977). *Futurism.* London: Thames and Hudson.

Todisco, P. J. (1976). *Boston's First Neighborhood; the North End.* Boston: Public Library.

Too, A. (1980). Didactic street-fronts and backlanes – The shophouse typology. In *Malajah Arkitek,* May. Kuala Lumpur.

Touraine, A. (2000). *Can We Live Together?* Cambridge: Polity Press.

Vanderwarker, P. (1982). *Boston Then and Now.* New York: Dover Publications.

Vasak, L. (1989). *Achieving Reinforcement of City Image.* Unpublished MA. Oxford: Joint Centre for Urban Design.

Villaseñor, D. (1994). Interview with Georgia Butina Watson, Punta Zicatella, Mexico.

Villaseñor, D. (1995). Interview with Georgia Butina Watson, Mexico City.

Villaseñor, D. (2000). Interview with Georgia Butina Watson, Mexico City.

Villaseñor, D. (2002). Interview with Georgia Butina Watson, Oxford.

Villaseñor, D. (2005). Interview with Georgia Butina Watson, Oxford.

Vine, B. (1991). *King Solomon's Carpet.* Harmondsworth: Penguin.

von Vegesack, A. (ed.) (1992). *Czech Cubism: Architecture, Furniture and Decorative Arts 1910–1925.* Montreal: King.

Vuga, B. (1995). Edvard Ravnikar: *Maybe You Are Too Young for This . . .* In Ivanšek (ed.) (1995).

Wagner, O., Trans. Mallgrave, H. F., 1988 (1896). *Modern Architecture.* Santa Monica: Getty Center.

Wales, Charles Prince of 1989. *A Vision of Britain: A Personal View of Architecture.* London, New York: Doubleday.

Welsch, W. (1997). *Undoing Aesthetics.* London: Sage.

West Dorset District Council (2002). *Visions for West Bay: Ideas for Consultation.* Dorchester: West Dorset District Council, Bridport Town Council and Bridport Town Assembly.

Westley, F. (1991). The affective side of global social innovation. *Human Relations,* 44, 1011–1036.

Woods, R. A. (1902). *Americans in Process.* Boston: Houghton Miffin.

Woodward, K. (ed.) (1997). *Identity and Difference.* London: Sage.

Yampolsky, M. (1993). *The Traditional Architecture of Mexico.* London: Thames and Hudson.

Yanosik, J. (1996). *The Plastic People of the Universe.* http://www.furious.com/perfect/pulnoc.html

Yeang, K. (1986). *The Tropical Verandah City.* Ampang: Asia Publications.

Yeang, K. (1987). *Tropical Urban Regionalism – Building in a South-East Asia City.* Singapore: Concept Media.

Yoong, C. C. (ed.) (1988). *Post-Merdeka Architecture.* Kuala Lumpur: PAM.

Ypma, H. (1997). *Mexican Contemporary.* London: Thames and Hudson.

Zeisel, J. (1981). *Inquiry by Design – Tools for Environment Behaviour Research.* Cambridge: Cambridge University Press.

Index